Recovering Bookchin
Social Ecology and the Crises of Our Time

More praise for *Recovering Bookchin*:

"For too long Murray Bookchin's contributions to political theory have remained ignored and marginalized in academic circles. Andy Price's book provides a much-needed corrective to this most unfortunate tendency. Price provides a very sophisticated account of the many strengths, as well as weaknesses, of Bookchin's body of work. Indeed, Price's critical perspective on Bookchin will undoubtedly help introduce the important debates within and around the paradigm of social ecology to a broader audience. To this extent, Price's account could hardly be more timely. For if Bookchin's diagnosis that the alternatives we face today are social ecology or catastrophe seems increasingly probable to more and more people, Price's close and sharp analysis of the theoretical bases of social ecology is bound to help us navigate this perilous terrain."

—Dr Thomas Jeffrey Miley, Lecturer of Political Sociology, Fellow of Darwin College, The University of Cambridge

Recovering Bookchin

Social Ecology and the Crises of Our Time

Andy Price

Recovering Bookchin: Social Ecology and the Crises of Our Time
Second Edition (first published in 2012 by New Compass Press)
© 2023 Andy Price
This edition 2023 © AK Press (Chico / Edinburgh)

ISBN: 978-1-84935-494-3
E-ISBN: 978-1-84935-495-0
Library of Congress Control Number: 2022948751

AK Press
370 Ryan Ave. #100
Chico, CA 95973
www.akpress.org
akpress@akpress.org

AK Press
33 Tower St.
Edinburgh EH6 7BN
Scotland
www.akuk.com
akuk@akpress.org

The above addresses would be delighted to provide you with the latest AK Press distribution catalog, which features books, pamphlets, zines, and stylish apparel published and/or distributed by AK Press. Alternatively, visit our websites for the complete catalog, latest news, and secure ordering.

Cover Design by Casandra Johns
Printed in the USA on acid-free paper

For Louise

Contents

Preface to the 2023 Edition

It's been eleven years since *Recovering Bookchin* was first published. So much has changed since then. I think back to the time of its publication and the field in which I worked. Every day I would head into the classes of various universities to teach not just Bookchin's ideas, but about the impending threat of the very things against which he railed: the irrationalities of capitalist society and the ecological catastrophe it was reaping. However, day-in, day-out, I would be met with the blankest of stares, with dwindling class attendance, with disquiet from colleagues about the "alarmist" ideas I was teaching, and, of course, with the eventual threat of whatever "green politics" module I was teaching being cut for lack of class uptake and interest.

Equally, outside of the classroom, friends or family members who read the book, or asked me about its focus, would recoil, telling me it was a bit "extreme," at any mention of impending ecological crisis. I was going too far, I was told. Exaggerating. The funny thing was, we had all the data back then, just as we do now. Sure, much mainstream research put the date of serious climatic change somewhere between mid- and end-of-century, which rendered the whole subject unworthy of discussion for many. However, the concept of key ecological tipping points was entering mainstream discourse even then, led by pioneers like James Lovelock and James Hansen, amongst others.

We academics can pick holes in our jobs very easily. It is our job to deconstruct and critique in our research. However, one thing that seldom gets mentioned is just how difficult teaching is. How emotionally draining it is; how trying to share ideas you are passionate about, in a way that respects both the ideas and the students—and then watching those ideas received in real time, for better or worse—takes a big chunk out of you, every time you do it, no matter the discipline. To do this in a field where the default response is scepticism, an unwillingness to receive or entertain the ideas, usually by the whole class is doubly draining. It is to toil in a space where you are a permanent outsider, and you are so because you are reflecting on the obvious destructiveness of the world around you, and no one else seems to see it. This weird, existential double-bind can eventually destroy you. It did me: after several years of this, I burnt out.

Reflecting on all of this the for the new, AK Press edition of *Recovering Bookchin,* makes me realise two key things: first, how much more respect and admiration I have for Bookchin, and writers like him everywhere. Bookchin spent his entire life working in the conditions I describe above in an attempt to share his vision for a project of saving ourselves. Indeed, his entire life was one big teach in—he wrote endlessly, day and night; when he wasn't writing and he was well enough, he taught wherever he could. And not just over a handful of years like me, but for *over six decades*. He was always an outsider, on the periphery, but with a fortitude and stamina, he kept doing it, day-in, day-out, for all those years.

Moreover, Bookchin had a double mission, that would render him a double outsider: he wasn't just bringing us news of the severity of the ecological and social crises that lay ahead of us, and how we may respond to them; he was also warning us, right from the outset, of the importance of getting our responses to these crises correct, of making sure our ideas were in the right area, up-to-date, focused on the means just as importantly as the ends; that essentially, we should remain mindful of the danger of our ideas losing focus in the bewildering information age of advanced capitalism. As early as the mid 1960s he was doing this, in articles such as "Ecology and Revolutionary Thought" (1964), and "Listen, Marxist!" (1969). I marvel how he set himself against not just the system as a whole, but against other anti-system-ers too, when he felt it necessary.

Such a difficult plough to furrow, for such a long time. And of course, there would be much blowback. Indeed, the whole reason to "recover" Bookchin was to address what had become by the 1990s a "Bookchin caricature"—this image of an elderly activist, bitterly shouting from the sidelines at his own movement in some attempt to remain relevant. It was never true: it always was a crude caricature, and I wrote this book to try and dispel it. But I can much more easily see where it came from now: in that tension between outsider and mainstream and even outsider in your own movement, things break. In my case it was me; in Bookchin's case, made of much sterner stuff, it was his reputation, and sometimes admittedly his temper too. But he still carried on, writing his teachings on the state we were in, and trying to move past his own mistakes too. I remain amazed at the lifelong fortitude.

The second realization is perhaps even more awe-inspiring: if we can marvel at Bookchin's strength to carry on in the fields of writer and academic, then I marvel even more so at the fact that the most prominent movement to have emerged expressly influenced by his work fights for those same ideas at the risk of their own lives. The revolution and ongoing struggle in North and east Syria (NES), also known as Rojava, to build a society based on radical democratic confederacy, partially influenced by Bookchin's ideas but taken much further by the participants themselves, led as equally by women as by men, shows not just the bravery of the people there, but also of the continuing strength of these ideas, that they are still rightly being fought for by people who somehow find the strength to do so.

It is my hope that readers will find in *Recovering Bookchin* both an introduction to the work of this important philosopher-activist, and an incisive dispelling of the Bookchin caricature. This latter aim is not just a matter of settling an old score. Rather, it handily allows perhaps the most accessible entry into a discussion of Bookchin's foundational philosophy, which I believe remains the central contribution of this book.

Andy Price, 2023

Preface

At an academic conference several years ago, I attended a workshop directed to an examination of Murray Bookchin and his place in the anarchist tradition. There, after giving a paper I had rather hastily cobbled together (I was a young, and not very adept researcher) from the opening years of my research on Bookchin's philosophical and political programme, I was confronted—collegially, and in good spirit, it should be noted—by a colleague who proceeded to tell me all about Bookchin's personal and political motivations. Agitated and animated, my erstwhile colleague told me that throughout the 1990s, Bookchin had "bestrode the anarchist world, looking to pick a fight with anyone and everyone," desperate for a conflagration, desperate for attention. I watched, bemused, as my colleague raised his arms in the vein of a muscle man, bending both arms to show his strength, seemingly a likeness of Bookchin's position down the years. Although I cannot be sure of the precise memory, I think he may have even "shadow-boxed" to illustrate Bookchin's pugilistic intentions.

The rhetorical and visual fireworks aside, this description of Bookchin jarred on a more fundamental level. I was struck by two immediate questions. First, was my colleague speaking of the same Bookchin whose philosophy I had been immersed in for what seemed like a lifetime, a philosophy I found creative, cooperative, inspiring, and, above all, humanistic? Was this the same Bookchin who had spent years refining a political programme that was explicitly directed towards the creation of a society of genuine equality, freedom, and, above all, non-conflictual forms of relations and forms of organisations? Second, how did my friend *know* of Bookchin's motivations? How did he know that Bookchin wanted to fight the rest of the anarchist world, know that he was desperately seeking people to argue with? Was there any evidence for such a position?

Of course, I had been aware of Bookchin's polemical works before the exchange with my colleague, and I had been aware of the many disagreements Bookchin had had with former friends and comrades, but I originally intended to ignore these polemics, to put them down to the usual political manoeuvre and disagreement that quite naturally emerges in the exchange of ideas. Mine was to be a project directed solely to an examination of Bookchin's *content*, to the fundamentals of his philosophical and political project. However, it soon became apparent that I could not avoid this problematic picture of Bookchin: I would meet many more people who would describe Bookchin in exactly the same way (gesticulation included); I would read *many* more texts that claimed identical things. Moreover, it became apparent that this was many people's experience of Bookchin: that is, the newcomer to Bookchin cannot help but be confronted in the first instance (and quite possibly overwhelmed) by the critical literature on Bookchin.

Yet the more I read of Bookchin, the more the evidence of a genuine attempt to remake society in the name of humanity and the natural world would pour from the pages of his work. I thus concluded early on that the initial and immediate picture of Bookchin was a *caricature*: it underplayed and undervalued a rich and detailed philosophy of nature and a practical political programme, worked out in great detail over the previous five decades by focusing on the relatively short period within which he had become embroiled in fierce disagreements. Originally, I argued that this vast body of work, when fully appreciated, would easily make-up for whatever Bookchin had done wrong in the 1980s and 1990s, that whatever mistakes he had made, this important contribution was still intact.

However, as I turned, with trepidation, to examine Bookchin's "wrongdoings," the problems that led to an extraordinary body of literature that casts his motives into doubt, it soon became clear that Bookchin had in fact done very little wrong. There was, in short, no evidence of Bookchin becoming dogmatic, controlling, or aggressive in his later years, as the critical literature claimed: quite to the contrary, there *was* evidence that the works and moments in Bookchin's biography that the critics would point to for their evidence of his ill-found motivations were in fact coherent expressions of his wider philosophy, and, by-and-large, informed critiques and challenges to the movements with which he was involved. Moreover, the most problematic of the criticisms of Bookchin *never* addressed his philosophical and theoretical fundamentals or even the criticisms he raised that were held up as evidence of his desire to attack.

It is from these early developments that the analytical framework of the current work stemmed. In the first instance, its aim is to recover the vital contribution to radical social thought that Bookchin provides in his work, a contribution that has been partially lost to the more problematic picture discussed above, by examining and exposing the foundations of the Bookchin caricature. In the second instance, this recovery also extends to the more robust critical pieces on Bookchin. It is argued here that there have been serious and reasoned critiques made of Bookchin, but that these too suffer from the existence of such a skewed caricature. They have often been mired by the more problematic literature, themselves not fully appreciated. They too will be recovered here from the rancour that surrounds Bookchin and his opponents and will be used to put Bookchin's foundations to the test. Finally, this recovery and reassessment, in keeping with Bookchin's own approach, is carried out not solely as a theoretical exercise, but as an examination of a theory that may suggest practical political possibilities to reverse the social and ecological crises of our time.

In terms of acknowledgements, thanks must go first to Professor Jules Townshend for years of mentoring and support. Thanks also to Eirik Eiglad and his colleagues at New Compass for their commitment and drive. To Chris Haworth for an unwavering interest in my work—and for proof reading. To my great friend, John Gregory for a constant supply of real discussion and for the steady stream of insights that only the artist can supply. But finally, most of all, this book would not have been possible without Louise, whose support in every conceivable sense is beyond anything I could ever put into words.

Introduction

In 1982, at the age of sixty-one, Murray Bookchin published the first of his two major works, *The Ecology of Freedom*, consolidating a career as one of the most innovative thinkers of the Left of the latter half of the twentieth century: a thinker who had formulated a body of work that brought together the radical strands of both anarchism and the ecology movement.[1] Exactly thirty years earlier he had announced himself to the world of critical social theory with something completely new: in the radical German publication, *Dinge der Zeit* and its English sister publication, *Contemporary Issues* he wrote the ecological critique "The Problem of Chemicals in Food," one of the earliest attempts to draw attention to the effect industrial-scale agribusiness was having on food production in the first instance and on the environment more widely.[2]

In the intervening period, Bookchin had carved out a distinct role in critical social theory: as a former Communist Party member and adherent of the Marxist thematic of history, he had, as early as the 1930s, begun to see the problems with Marxism, and by the 1950s had begun to make a vocal and critical split. However, unlike the many thinkers that fled Marxism in the 1950s and 1960s, Bookchin resolved to keep one central aspect of Marx's modernist approach: the notion of the dialectic unfolding of history, of the ability to examine and understand this unfolding, and the ability to understand the organisation of society as a whole. Like many other thinkers who moved into various forms of post-structuralism or post-Marxism that denied the existence of this type of "grand narrative" (many moving over to more relativist understandings of the social

1

and political), Bookchin did indeed dispense with the *Marxist* grand narrative, but his move was premised not on the basis that the Marxian approach had overreached, or that the meta-historical approach *in general* was unworkable, but rather, that the Marxian theoretical project *had not gone far enough*.[3]

Everything that had been missed by Marx—and for Bookchin, this included the widely different subjectivities of the proletariat, an understanding of pre-class hierarchies, the true extent of capitalism's effect on society, and most importantly, a clearer understanding of humanity's relationship to the natural world—should, for Bookchin, form the basis of a new approach, a new theory of society *and* ecology: a *social ecology*. This body of work, then, this grandest of narratives—"a narrative of epic proportions"—Bookchin would flesh out during the 1960s and 1970s.[4] He constructed his narrative via the two key strands of his work: through a critique of the failings of Marxism itself—in articles and essays, such as "Listen, Marxist!" and "Marxism as Bourgeois Sociology"—and through a concurrent working out of his alternative political and philosophical programme—rooted in ecology—in articles such as "Post-Scarcity Anarchism," "Ecology and Revolutionary Thought," and "Spontaneity and Organization."[5]

These articles, representing these two distinct strands of Bookchin's approach, were in the 1970s collected into two anthologies, *Post-Scarcity Anarchism* and *Toward an Ecological Society*, and their dual impact catapulted Bookchin into the position of a must-read radical thinker of the period.[6] In *The Ecology of Freedom*, Bookchin attempted to pull together both these strands into a coherent exposition of his life's work thus far, an ambitious attempt at transcending the failures of the radical Left through a full exposition of social hierarchy and domination and their effects on the natural world, and the suggestion of a possible solution to these failures in the form of social ecology.

The success of this project, on an initial reading of the literature that surrounds Bookchin, seems uncontroversial: it appears widely held that Bookchin had provided a valuable contribution to critical social theory in both transcending Marx and Marxism and creating a new approach based on anarchism and ecology. Indeed, the contemporaneous response to *The Ecology of Freedom* was unequivocal: the *Ecologist* argued in 1983 that Bookchin had produced "the most complete statement of the anarchist vision yet produced," that in fact he "*has* produced an alternative to Marxism," in the form of "the most coherent expression of an ecological philosophy yet formulated."[7]

Elsewhere, the acknowledgement of Bookchin's important reworking of Marx was noted, as was its far-reaching implications: "Bookchin's relationship to Marx," wrote Robin Clark in the *New Scientist* in 1982, "can be paralleled with that of Albert Einstein's relationship to Isaac Newton," in the sense that Bookchin had extended the analysis of social problems enabling the Marxist thematic to be now viewed as "a special example of the more general case" of social hierarchy and domination through his widening of the analysis of domination away from a strictly class-based approach.[8]

Bookchin was to further consolidate his position as a leading theorist of the Left with his 1986 collection of essays, *The Modern Crisis*, and through a thorough exposition of his political programme in his second major work, *The Rise of Urbanization and the Decline of Citizenship*, in the process creating a body of work that had assumed by now "an importance to the ecology movement that it would be difficult to over-estimate."[9] Indeed, by the end of the decade, Bookchin's position as *the* pre-eminent theorist of social ecology in the first instance, and one of the main theorists of anarchism and ecology in the second was recognised in the publication of an anthology of essays on social ecology dedicated to Bookchin: *Renewing the Earth: The Promise of Social Ecology*.[10] Subtitled "*A Celebration of the work of Murray Bookchin*," the individual contributors—leading academics and writers in the field of social theory and ecology—all "dedicate[d] their work to Murray Bookchin," "in view of [his] magnificent contribution to ecological thought and practice."[11]

Furthermore, during the late 1990s and early 2000s when theorists would again turn to Bookchin's work, the same sentiments were everywhere to be found. According to Damian F. White, Bookchin, as opposed to other post-Marxists and post-structuralist thinkers, "has maintained a focus on the emergence of and consolidation of social hierarchy and social domination that gives rise to a far more profound explanation of humanity's estrangement from itself and from the natural world than that offered by historical materialism," resulting in an "impressive example of historically informed grand social theorising."[12]

Elsewhere, Stuart Best argues that Bookchin's social ecology "is perhaps the most comprehensive and powerful ecological philosophy yet developed," the "originality and importance" of which is only now beginning to be appreciated.[13] Peter Marshall also confirms Bookchin's contribution in his extensive anthology of anarchism, describing Bookchin as "the thinker who has most renewed anarchist thought and action since the Second World War."[14] Colin Ward too would comment on the sheer scope of Bookchin's impact: there was Bookchin the ecological thinker, Bookchin the theorist of urban self-management, and Bookchin the revolutionary historian, Ward noted, concluding that "I cannot think of any other anarchist author who could, or would even aspire to, fill all these roles."[15]

It might reasonably be asked at this point: what, therefore, is the problem? What exactly is it that needs "recovering" in Bookchin? Does it not appear that Bookchin's reputation is intact, his theoretical contribution uncontroversial? In answering these questions, it is incumbent upon us to turn to a separate body of literature—a negative literature, as it were—that surrounds Bookchin and forms as strong a part of Bookchin's reputation as does the positive literature discussed thus far. Here, in direct contradiction to the comments above, we find Bookchin described not as a key figure in critical social theory for his development of the Marxist thematic but, variously: as a thinker who in truth wants to "displace" Marx, who wants to "wrestle with Marx and defeat him" so that "his own messianic ambitions are to be fulfilled," a thinker who is in possession of a "vindictiveness of Old Testament proportions"; as a thinker who has "regressed into ideological sclerosis," his work having "fossilized into dogma"; a thinker whose work centres on a "dogmatic and non-dialectical" outlook.[16]

Elsewhere in this literature, the critique becomes increasingly vitriolic, and we find descriptions of Bookchin's work as being made up of "hasty generalizations, ad hominem fallacies, flimsy slippery slope arguments, and outright nonsense," alongside claims of Bookchin's "ineptitude in philosophical analysis."[17] At the furthest extremes of this critical literature, we get assumptive reasoning concerning Bookchin's personal motivations. "I get the distinct impression," wrote Bob Black in 1997, "that Bookchin, an elderly man said to be in ill-health is cashing in his chips as a prominent anarchist theorist" by "demolishing all possible alternatives to his own creed."[18]

The literature here could not be more diametrically opposed to the praise Bookchin had been accorded earlier. The only similarity these two literatures share is in terms of their volume: at the time of writing, two book-length critiques, a collection of critical essays equal in length to the "celebration" discussed and a substantial number of articles make up the bulk of the critical literature, ensuring that the Bookchin legacy is mired in controversy.[19] It should also be noted that the contrast between these two bodies of literature is further highlighted by the fact that some of the harshest critiques come from the very same writers who a decade earlier had extolled the virtues of Bookchin in the anthology noted above (most notably, John Clark and Joel Kovel). Further, these critical and often acerbic contributions to the critical literature continue until this day.[20]

From this, it is argued that the newcomer to Bookchin is confronted with an almost schizophrenic portrait of Bookchin: the once-lauded theorist, who, however, is also riddled with problems. One gets an impression here of Bookchin as "the fallen angel," the once revolutionary thinker who had since lost his way and slipped into dogma.[21] Because of the volume of both critique and praise, one is left with a *caricature* of Bookchin as a writer who was constantly extolling the virtues of freedom and cooperation, yet one who at the same time was seemingly abrasive, intolerant, and even a hierarchical authoritarian. How else could a thinker generate such a contrary response across the spectrum? The answer, on first reading, appears to lie in an intrinsic failing in Bookchin himself—and, perhaps fatally in terms of his body of work, not just a personal failing, but a theoretical failing, a terminal theoretical contradiction.

It is the primary contention of the present work that nothing could be further from the truth. There is no such intrinsic failing in Bookchin, no such terminal contradiction. Of course, there *are* contradictions in Bookchin's work, and there *are* failings, as there are in all bodies of work (and as Bookchin himself would openly acknowledge throughout his career). There are also, no doubt, certain personal failings of Bookchin, as many of his critics were ever-eager to point out. But again, Bookchin would not be alone in this: to err is to be human. However, the contention here is that the individual cases of error and the problems of personal demeanour or argumentative style are not enough to substantiate the caricature of Bookchin as the flawed theorist that the critical literature has generated. That is to say, that the schizophrenic portrait of Bookchin that surrounds him and his work to this day finds no roots in his theoretical corpus taken as a whole. The caricature engendered through the negative literature is therefore misleading, and obscures the important contribution to social thought that Bookchin provided.

What, then, *is* the generative cause of this critical literature? And if they are so misguided in their focus, why? That is to ask: if the claim is that there is no fundamental flaw in the Bookchin theoretic, then what else explains the volume of the critique? It is argued here that they can be explained as a *political* phenomenon, rather than a matter of theory or philosophy. To explain, we need to try and pinpoint either a piece of work from Bookchin or a piece of politics, as it were, from where the opposition started to emerge. Here, two distinct bodies of criticism can be identified that mirror the two strands of Bookchin's work noted at the outset. That is, the critiques can be separated into criticisms of Bookchin's ecology, and criticisms of his anarchism. Both can be further separated temporally. Though we turn to examine each area of critique in full in the main text, a little background is required at the outset.

In terms of the critique of Bookchin's ecology, we can trace their emergence to a debate within the Green movement that had been emerging throughout the 1970s. Originally, a split had emerged—fostered in no small measure by Bookchin himself—between environmentalism, which was a reformist, state-centred approach to ecological concerns and a more radical ecology, that viewed the state-centred system of nation states as beyond reform, requiring far more wide-ranging social policies in achieving ecological redress based on the principles of the science of ecology itself.[22]

By the mid-1980s, this split had been given a more definitive form, in large part because of the work of the Norwegian philosopher Arne Naess who, in 1973, differentiated between a "shallow" environmentalism, and a more radical, "deep" ecology.[23] Later, Naess "would summarise fifteen years of thinking on the principles of deep ecology," drawing up eight basic, or "platform," principles that were included in the anthology *Deep Ecology*, coauthored by two U.S. academics, Bill Devall and George Sessions, an anthology that had become one of the main texts of this strand of the movement.[24]

One of the central tenets of deep ecology, underpinning the whole of the platform principles, was the notion of ecological redress being achieved through a move away from the modern, "anthropocentric" outlook of society—which viewed the natural world as a resource to be used (and exploited) by humanity—in favour of a "biocentric" outlook, a view that called for a commitment (of varying degree, from thinker to thinker) to a "biological egalitarianism." Here, the argument held, humanity should, as a general rule, have no right to interfere with other species unless absolutely vital. More fundamentally, human beings should not rank different species hierarchically, with humanity sat at the apex, and value accorded to the rest of the natural world in line with humanity's needs.[25]

Indeed, and as will be shown, there was much within the developing realm of deep ecology that Bookchin would initially agree with, and even that which he did not agree with, he was engaged in dialogue about with key thinkers within deep ecology (notably, with Bill Devall). Further, Bookchin even contributed an essay to a separate collection entitled *Deep Ecology*, further evidence that Bookchin originally had no problem with the idea of a deeper ecology being drawn out in contrast to a shallow environmentalism.[26]

However, this was about to change, and for a very specific reason. In June 1987, Amherst College, Massachusetts, held the inaugural National Gathering of American Greens, to which Bookchin was invited as a keynote speaker. Janet Biehl, a leading thinker in social ecology and Bookchin's partner and collaborator for the last twenty years of his life, takes up the story here:

> In January 1987, Murray was at the apogee of his acclaim, the Grand Old Man of ecology and anarchism. He had published *The Ecology of Freedom* five years earlier, and more recently his (in my view even more important) *Urbanization . . .* the previous year. He was invited to be the keynote speaker at the first gathering of the U.S. Greens in Amherst, in June 1987. I'm sure those who invited him expected him to give a nice talk about democracy and cooperative societies and the importance of eco-technics and what not. Between January and June the remarks of David Foreman were published in *Simply Living*—the interview by Bill Devall. Foreman said famine in Ethiopia was "nature taking its course," and Devall did not protest. So Murray wrote "Social Ecology vs. Deep Ecology" and brought copies to Amherst. He put a copy on each seat.[27]

Dave Foreman was at the time a prominent figure in the radical ecology group Earth First!, an activist group influenced by Edward Abbey and his notion of "monkeywrenching"—ecological direct action that included "spiking" trees (inserting steel rods to "stop" the chainsaws) that were scheduled for deforesting.[28] In the Australian journal *Simply Living*, Foreman was interviewed by Bill Devall, the prominent professor in the emerging field of deep ecology who had coauthored one of the movement's leading texts, as noted above.[29] Both Foreman and Devall were adherents to Naess's platform principles of deep ecology. To stress again, these principles were formed around the notion of *biocentrism*, an outlook that places humanity on an equal footing with all other life forms. Accordingly, humanity should not—apart from when absolutely necessary—interfere in the processes of nature. In the interview Biehl notes above, Foreman takes the principle of ecocentrism to its extreme: "the worst thing we could do in Ethiopia," he told Devall, "is to give aid—*the best thing would be to just let nature seek its own balance, to let people there just starve.*"[30]

As Bookchin was to constantly stress, it was to these *specific* comments that he addressed his presentation at Amherst.[31] But he also went further: Bookchin stridently criticised not only the comments of Foreman, but moreover, the lack of a critique from Foreman's interviewer, one of deep ecology's leading intellectuals, Professor Devall. This was more worrying for Bookchin than the outwardly racist comments of Foreman, as it reflected what he saw as an emerging consensus in the *theory* of deep ecology, stemming directly from its platform principles and its commitment to biocentrism, a commitment that could not help but result in the kind of positions outlined by Foreman. In "Social Ecology vs. Deep Ecology"—the article Bookchin took to Amherst and placed on every seat—Bookchin would stridently decry "the barely disguised racists" and "outright social reactionaries" that had carved out a role for themselves in the discipline of deep ecology.[32]

Moreover, he continued, deep ecology as a whole was premised on a form of "eco-brutalism" that finds parallels with the "ecofascism" of German Nazism, resulting in a philosophy that was "a black hole of half-digested, ill-formed, and half-baked ideas" wherein it is possible for its adherents to announce the "utterly vicious" notions proffered by Foreman.[33] This outlook now threatened to de-stabilise the ecology movement as a whole, to undo many of the insights ecology had provided into humanity's place in the world since it emerged in the 1960s. Thus the ecology movement had a choice, Bookchin argued, between "a vague, formless, often self-contradictory, and invertebrate thing called deep ecology," or a more "socially oriented" approach to ecological problems.[34]

Apart from the incontestable misanthropy and racism of Foreman's comments then, the main problem for Bookchin was the political naivety of such comments, based on the irrational reading of the ecological situation provided by deep ecology. For Bookchin, as will be fully examined in Chapter 2, when we turn to examine his philosophical foundations, *all ecological problems are ultimately social problems*, and as such require *social* solutions: hence the definition of his work as a *social* ecology. Therefore, he asked—and it is a criticism that ties into the concept of biocentrism in general—how can it be read into the ecological crisis in Ethiopia—the famine of the mid-1980s—that leaving the people there to starve would be "nature finding its own balance?" Were there not social problems that caused this ecological problem? As Bookchin argued, "what does it mean for nature to 'seek its own balance' in East Africa, where agribusiness, colonialism, and exploitation have ravaged a once culturally and ecologically stable area?"[35]

Later, on a lecture tour of the UK in 1992, when asked about his speaking out at Amherst, Bookchin would restate the point to *The Guardian*: "If you look at why they [the Ethiopians] are starving, it is not because of nature. It is because of civil war, agribusiness, social problems. How can I remain silent and be polite about this?"[36] This is why the silence of Devall was so worrying to Bookchin: for the calls for policies of population control and reduction from within the deep ecology framework (made primarily by the Naess-Devall-Sessions work in the Devall and Sessions anthology, as we shall see in more detail Chapter 1) led directly to the "eco-brutalism" of Foreman. If humanity cannot interfere in the natural world, then maybe population control is to be left to famine, viruses, and other "natural" phenomena.

It is difficult for the present author to find a point of disagreement with the initial stance that Bookchin took at Amherst against the comments of Foreman. What seems theoretically uncontroversial in the present, however—the stand against the irrationalities of a cultural arrogance or even racism (a stand, incidentally, that was to bear fruit when

Foreman later retracted his comments)—was to be the generator of the incredible amount of critique and counter-critique, hinted at above and to which we return in more detail below.[37] From this point on, the negative literature surrounding Bookchin's ecology begins to emerge, a literature that, as will be shown, began to cloud Bookchin's contribution and become increasingly focused on Bookchin *himself*.[38]

In terms of the other key strand of Bookchin's work—his anarchism—despite the raging debate with his opponents in deep ecology, by the late 1980s Bookchin's position as one of the pre-eminent anarchist theorists of the twentieth century seemed intact. However, in the mid-1990s, this was about to change dramatically. Here, with the publication of *Social Anarchism or Lifestyle Anarchism: An Unbridgeable Chasm*, the processes that had led to Bookchin's acrimonious split with the deep ecologists were to repeat themselves in full.[39]

In *Social Anarchism or Lifestyle Anarchism*, Bookchin drew attention to and critiqued the increasing trend of a non-socially-engaged anarchism, which he labelled "lifestyle anarchism." Individualist notions of anarchism were singled out by Bookchin as a trend as old as anarchism itself, as exemplified by Max Stirner.[40] However, in the 1990s, Bookchin argued that they were now "supplanting social action and revolutionary politics in anarchism" in general—supplanting, that is, a more "social anarchism."[41] According to Bookchin, anarchism was now profoundly influenced by the bourgeois environment of the socially reactionary 1970s and 1980s, affected deeply by "the narcissism of the yuppie generation," which had infused the movement with an "ad hoc adventurism, personal bravura, an aversion to theory oddly akin to the irrational biases of postmodernism, celebrations of theoretical incoherence . . . and an intensely self-orientated enchantment of everyday life."[42]

Here, the work of prominent anarchist writers (such as Hakim Bey and John Zerzan) and prominent anarchist trends were criticised by Bookchin as stridently as he had criticised the deep ecologists. And just as in the previous debate, the responses to his text were to be equally as strident.[43] Here too, the focus of the critique shifted increasingly to a focus on Bookchin himself, exactly as happened with the exchanges with the deep ecologists, away from the underlying political bedrock of Bookchin's programmatic. Further, Bookchin would himself offer many written counter-critiques, each by necessity increasingly personal in countering the accusations levelled at him, which further entrenched the problematic nature of the literature.[44]

Again, we turn to a full discussion of Bookchin's debate with the deep ecologists and the anarchists in due course, but they are raised at the outset in order to point to the fact that the emergence of the negative literature that surrounds Bookchin stemmed from the polemical exchanges that in a large part were initiated by the forceful argumentative style of Bookchin himself. Moreover, the tone of the critiques and the counter-critiques, hinted at above, were to prove only to raise the temperature in the already heated exchanges, and generated yet more literature that—crucially—became increasingly focused not on the issues raised by Bookchin but on Bookchin himself. It is from this literature that we get the already noted accusations of authoritarianism levelled against Bookchin, of a thinker engaged in an "ideological turf war," or as a thinker "cashing in his chips."[45] It is fair to argue that by the middle of the 1990s, Bookchin was under siege. Not only was his ecology under attack, but so too was his anarchism, and perhaps most confusingly, so was he himself.

What can we take from these introductory comments on the critical literature that surrounds Bookchin? Two things become immediately clear. First, it is clear that in terms of initial causal factors, it was an opening criticism from Bookchin that invoked the ire of both the ecologists and the anarchists. Before Bookchin's critique of the deep ecologists, and before his critique of the "lifestyle anarchists," there is very little critique of Bookchin to be found.[46] As noted at the outset, Bookchin was held in high regard across the board. Therefore, though it cannot be argued that Bookchin's polemics are the *only* reason for the critique he later engendered, it is hard to deny them their importance as a causal factor.

Second, there is a further common factor to both strands of critique stemming from the forthright polemical nature of Bookchin's original critiques themselves. Perhaps the surest thing that can be said about Bookchin at the outset is that his critiques of the sections of the movements of ecology and anarchism he viewed as problematic, or in some cases dangerous, are strident, *to say the very least*. Bookchin, as we shall see, bore no truck with what he viewed as irrationality, and used his lifelong honed skills as a polemicist in critiquing them. From this, the reactions to Bookchin in both strands of his work became, as noted, increasingly concerned with Bookchin himself—concerned with his sinister motives, his "grump-iness," his insecurities—rather than his theories; in short, the critiques become embroiled with Bookchin's polemics.

However, it is argued here that Bookchin the polemicist can quite reasonably be distinguished from Bookchin the social theorist. Moreover, this separation is essential in ensuring that the personal, less-critical busi-ness of political manoeuvre can be separated from a more robust analysis of Bookchin's actual theoretical framework. The problem here is that the critiques do not allow for this separation. As noted at the outset, Book-chin had spent his entire adult life thrashing out a theory of natural and social history, not only a theory for the sake of a theory, but actually a theory cast in terms of revolution. Much like Marx, he forged his theo-retical corpus with a very real practicality in mind: the goal of the radical remaking of society. In this intrinsically theoretical *and* political process, Bookchin had constantly used the tools of the political polemicist and activist: critique, forthright argumentation and the vying for political position (just as Marx had a century earlier against his opponents).

Whether or not the type of polemical approach employed by Book-chin does more harm than good in theoretical and political exchanges is, of course, a valid question. However, this is, and perhaps always should have been, a *separate* question, distinct from the philosophy of Bookchin. Alas, this has not been the case, and the critiques of Bookchin generated by his polemics do not confine themselves to this question but slip over into addressing themselves to Bookchin and social ecology as a whole, drawing connections between his argumentative style (and the possible problems therein) and his theoretical corpus and thus leaving the reader with the notion of Bookchin's work *as a whole* as being contradictory, as containing serious, perhaps terminal failings.

Again, it is argued herein that upon close, critical examination, no such failings can be found within the Bookchin corpus. Worse still, many of the most prominent critiques, after having blurred the separation between polemicist and philosopher, do not even *touch upon* Bookchin's theoretical body of work. That is to say, that a large portion of this critical literature *fails to deal with Bookchin's philosophical and political positions.* Thus can we now argue with greater force that not only do the critiques stem *temporally* from the emergence of Bookchin's critiques of anarchism and ecology but so too do they emerge as a political phenomenon, a reaction to Bookchin's original criticisms. That is to say that the kind of ad hominem, personal, and unsubstantiated nature of much of the critical literature—those critiques noted above that accuse Bookchin of desiring to take over the Left as a whole, those that accuse him of being authoritarian, and so on—stem in the main from his argumentative style and are not substantive enough to give credence to the notion of the contradictory nature of Bookchin and his legacy.

To extend an analogy drawn in one of the more vitriolic critiques, that of Bookchin as the pugilist, picking fights with any thinker who disagreed with him: if this indeed was a fight, then none of his opponents succeed in landing any *serious* blows on Bookchin and social ecology.[47] After all the initial furore one finds when first encountering Bookchin, one reads the critiques constantly anticipating the knock-out punch that will finally put the matter to rest, the one critical insight that will explain the contested nature of Bookchin's reputation, or the problem that started the conflagration in the first place. Alas, the killer blow never comes, and the reams of critique and counter-critique evaporate into a largely non-critical red mist.

That is to say, in short, that after the ensuing battles between Bookchin and his opponents, his theoretical and political programmatic remains intact. Furthermore, it is this vital contribution that needs to be recovered from the controversies and polemics that surrounded his later work. This contribution was always separate from the Bookchin polemics, and its robustness is hinted at by the fact that the critiques fail to deal with it substantially. However, the critiques persist, the red mist lingers, and even though they do not deal sufficiently with his theoretical corpus, they tarnish the legacy of this contribution, tarnish the reputation of this important and relevant political philosopher.

Moreover, it is argued here that in the process of examining the trends that mark not only Bookchin's critique of those parts of the movements he was involved in that he deemed irrational but also the reactions to his critiques, it is revealed to us that Bookchin did little wrong here, theoretically or politically speaking. That is to say, there is *no* evidence for the claims made concerning Bookchin's authoritarianism or malevolence in either thought or deed. What there *is* evidence of, is the constant striving throughout Bookchin's career to refine the ideas and principles to which he was committed, even if this was to bring him into direct conflict

with those who were "on his side." Indeed, as this would even result in
Bookchin's ultimate "break" with anarchism and his move toward "communalism," as we will turn to discuss in full below.[48]

Recovering Bookchin

From our opening discussion then, it is possible to now state the two central, intertwining aims of the present work, its dual purpose:

(1) To offer a reassessment of Bookchin's philosophical and political
contribution through: first, a critique of and response to the critical literature, and second, a restatement of the value of his contribution which thus
far has not been fully appreciated—in short, to "recover Bookchin" from
the more problematic literature that surrounded him in the later years of
his life. The present work is therefore an expansion of the attempt initiated
by White to "advance a discussion of [Bookchin's] work beyond the rather
personalised and vitriolic assessments that have come to predominate of
late."[49] In these personalised responses, three key areas of Bookchin's work
have been lost: his detailed ecological philosophy, the social history which
stems therefrom, and his practical political programme which can be seen
to be a direct expression of these theoretical foundations taken as a whole.
It is to a recovery and reassessment of these three key areas that the present
work is directed.

In the process of this critical defence, of rebutting and discarding
the negative literature that does not warrant its place in the Bookchin
literature, whatever there is worth separating from the more problematic
sections of the negative literature will be taken forward and laid at the
base of the Bookchin theoretic. In keeping with the notion that there are
problems in Bookchin, is there anything we can take from the critiques
in developing social ecology? In fact, as will be shown, there are valid critiques made of Bookchin, there are analyses that stand out and raise some
important questions. Moreover, there are even individual parts of the
more problematic critiques that have merit: they shall not be discounted
here for their failings, but rather will be extracted from the insights they
contribute to Bookchin's work in order to build our critical defence.

(2) In the "recovery" of Bookchin that constitutes the first central
aim of this work, the second central aim is revealed as immanent: the

thesis attempts to demonstrate exactly why this recovery of Bookchin is worth undertaking. It will be shown that Bookchin's contribution to radical social thought proves to be far more insightful and far more useful than the negative literature has historically allowed. The reasons for this are two-fold.

First, Bookchin's contribution, if it could be taken as a body of work in isolation, is substantial and important enough to justify a re-appraisal on its own terms. Here, as already noted, Bookchin provided detailed and robust investigations into: the increasing ecological degradation by capitalism; the irrational nature of the modern city; the failures of Marxism in theory and practice; a detailed reading of the emergence of hierarchy and domination in human society; the centrality of anarchism to any attempt at prefigurative politics; and a thorough practical programme for implementing change within a social ecological framework. All of these facets of his work, taken as a whole, offered something to the ailing Left of the latter half of the twentieth century: an alternative form of opposition to capitalism based not on the "discredited workers'" movements and their many different hues, nor on a "classical" reading of an anarchism that had never really gained a following; but rather, on a more holistic ecological view of society and its place in the natural world—an outlook that offers a detailed understanding of the movement of radical politics over this period and today.

Second, his work today finds a more contemporary resonance than it ever did during the period he was writing. Primarily, it finds resonance in the theories and practice of the alter-globalisation movement, the theories of thinkers like Hardt and Negri, and John Holloway, and in the actions of groups like the Zapatistas and, more recently, the anti-financial crisis movement, Movimiento 15-M, that has emerged so vividly in Spain.[50] Further, in more mainstream academic work, Bookchin's work finds a resonance: the renowned political geographer and Marxist, David Harvey, writes in his most recent analysis of capitalism of a programme of change which has a "socio-ecological" dimension to it, and though he is referring to something distinct from the Bookchin programme, the holistic nature of change that Harvey depicts is strikingly similar to that of Bookchin's, in both theory and practice.[51] Although a full critical examination of the crossover between Bookchin's work and the work of these contemporary thinkers is beyond the remit of the present work, the recovery of

Bookchin we offer here is carried out with these crossovers in mind; it is a political act, as well as a theoretical one, with the hope that readers will pick up from where the present work leaves off.

To carry out this critical exegesis, we begin Chapter 1 by turning to a full discussion of the extraordinary 1987 exchange between Bookchin and the deep ecologists. As noted above, it is in this exchange that the focus in the literature on Bookchin begins to slip from his work and onto Bookchin himself. Moreover, if we want to understand the proliferation of polemics between Bookchin and his opponents throughout the 1990s and the resultant development of the Bookchin caricature, we need to return here first. To do this, we begin by outlining the main principles of deep ecology, specifically, the trends Bookchin critiqued. However, we reserve a full analysis of his critique for Chapter 2. In the remainder of our opening chapter, we explore the immediate response from within deep ecology in order to establish the sheer scale and scope of a highly problematic body of literature that would forever taint Bookchin's legacy.

With the highly problematic response of the deep ecologists in place we then turn to put it to the test: that is, in Chapter 2, we turn to a full examination of Bookchin's 1987 critique and ask if there was any evidence that points to problematic motivations that he was accused of that would plague him throughout the remainder of his life. That is to say, we turn to a task which the deep ecologists abjectly failed to do: to ask what it was that Bookchin said in 1987, to examine the issues he raised. Drawn out in sharp relief to this literature, we are able to show that not only was his critique a rich and detailed examination of the serious problems of deep ecology but further, that the critique stemmed from the philosophical foundations Bookchin had been developing since the 1950s.

It is not, it should be noted, our aim in the present work to inure Bookchin's philosophy from criticism: quite to the contrary, it is to finally offer a criticism of his philosophical foundations *devoid* of the personalistic patterns of engaging with his work established in 1987. After a critical examination of these foundations in the remainder of Chapter 3, we turn to put Bookchin's philosophy to the test by turning to critiques of Bookchin that were slightly more removed from the polemics of the deep ecologists. We find here that there *are* significant questions to be asked of the ecological philosophy of Bookchin. Indeed, we argue that such important questions were asked throughout the 1980s and 1990s but were themselves lost in the furore of the social ecology–deep ecology exchange.

With Bookchin's philosophical foundations recovered from the furore of the late 1980s and finally put to the test on its content (rather than on Bookchin's character) we turn in Chapters 4 and 5 to examine the second key area of our recovery: Bookchin's social history. We find here that Bookchin's version of social history not only offers a further explanation of the reasons for his critique of deep ecology but can also be seen to be the direct theoretical continuation of the philosophical foundations recovered in our opening chapters. Moreover, as will become clear, an understanding of Bookchin's social history is vital to understanding his *political* programme, and the further polemics his particular take on a political programme would provoke throughout the 1990s. Again, we also offer here an examination of the more robust critiques of Bookchin's social history and note the important possible objections.

In Chapters 4 and 5, then, we finally take leave of our engagement with deep ecology and Bookchin's 1987 critique. However, we note that we have devoted considerable attention to the Bookchin–deep ecology exchange for two reasons. First, as Bookchin's critique in 1987 is such a direct expression of his philosophical foundations that was yet so misrepresented within the deep ecology response, to revisit it allows us not only to disprove the Bookchin caricature, but permits us a "way in" to a full analysis of his large theoreticaly corpus. However, second, beyond our use of Bookchin's 1987 critique and the response it engendered in the heuristic sense, we also give it such attention as it can reasonably be argued that the objections Bookchin raised against deep ecology bear revisiting as they offer an excellent discussion of the possible dangers of un-thought out ecological thought, a discussion that provided food for thought to the ecology movements today in light of the social and ecological crises of our time.

It is to Bookchin's practical political project that we begin to turn in Chapter 6. As noted, by the mid-1990s, Bookchin would be embroiled in an exchange with prominent thinkers and writers in the anarchist movement, stemming from his 1995 critique, that would prove to be equal in volume and vitriol to his exchange with the deep ecologists: the caricature of Bookchin as the aggressor, as the authoritarian, out to pick fights with political movements he viewed as a challenge to his own, would be cemented in his exchange with the anarchists. It is argued here that the caricature of Bookchin first established in 1987 infuses the responses to him from within anarchism, and again, the important political programme from which his critique stemmed was lost in the noise.

However, a dissenting note needs to be added here: we also argue in Chapter 6 that although Bookchin's critique *is* explainable as an expression of a coherence of philosophy and practice, it is itself tarnished, perhaps unavoidably, by the nature and extent of the debates that Bookchin had been embroiled in over the previous eight years. In his 1995 critique, Bookchin is at his most scathing; indeed, he is uncharacteristically uncharitable. This development only contributed to the contested nature of his reputation. In this sense, there is a very real need when we turn to his political programme to recover Bookchin *from himself*, a task we also set out to do in Chapter 6. This noted, it is stressed that this problem is a matter of Bookchin's approach, the extremities of his polemics by 1995 that stemmed from his personal experiences, and *not*, as will be shown, a problem with the Bookchin theoretic.

In keeping with the rest of the work, we then turn in Chapter 7 to put Bookchin's politics to the test objectively, turning again to the more robust critiques of his political programme. Importantly, not only does this allow us to see his political project to be the practical manifestation of the same coherent body of work that links his philosophical foundations to his social history, but it also opens the way for us, finally, to start to address the question of what the Bookchin corpus has to offer to today's projects of social and ecological change. We conclude then by looking at Bookchin's work afresh, with, as noted above, a view to opening up new avenues of research on Bookchin that may draw links with the radical Left of the earlier twenty-first century. Here, it is worth re-stressing the overall structure of the present work: our ultimate pointing toward a synthesis of Bookchin's work and contemporary Left thinking would not have been possible without our initial recovery of the full Bookchin project. As will become clear, the sheer scale and scope of the problematic literature has so infused the discussion of Bookchin that only a full re-evaluation of his work permits us to see past the apparent problems and contradictions. Only once this reassessment is achieved can we fully appreciate the potential of Bookchin's work as a valuable addition to present radical thought—a body of work clearly worth recovering and revisiting.

Chapter 1

The Genesis of the Bookchin Caricature

In the June of 1987, Murray Bookchin delivered his keynote address to the inaugural Gathering of American Greens at Amherst and published the article on which it was based, "Social Ecology versus Deep Ecology." From this point on, his reputation, his work, and his standing in the ecology movement would never be the same again. Murray Bookchin the figure was cast in an entirely new light. There was a new way of reading Bookchin's work, of conceiving of him as a thinker, based on a perception of Bookchin as divisive, as authoritarian, as "Old Left," or as set on a mission to dominate the emergent ecology movement—all of this stemming from this one critique.

What was the nature of the critique? As noted in the introduction, it was a forthright critique of the mid-1980's expression of deep ecology. More specifically, in the speech that Bookchin delivered and in the article he published, he railed against the recent proclamations of prominent members of the deep ecology radical action group, Earth First!, which had appeared in recent issues of the group's journal of the same name. For Bookchin, as we shall see, the group had veered into dangerous ideological waters: they had, in trying to formulate an approach to the ecological crisis, developed a particularly misanthropic approach to both the causes of and solutions to that crisis. Perhaps most worryingly, for Bookchin, the new misanthropic bent of Earth First! was the direct result of the philosophical principles of deep ecology as a whole, rather than an aberration, rather than the excesses of perhaps a handful of over-zealous adherents.

The debate sparked by Bookchin's Amherst address was white-hot: in the responses and Bookchin's counter-responses we witness the laying of the foundations of the caricature of Bookchin that would plague him up unto his death. As a result of the nature and volume of the polemics, two vital things were lost: first, the content of Bookchin's 1987 critique of deep ecology itself is obscured and, in fact, was never fully addressed by *any* of the responses; second, and much more importantly for the present work, Bookchin's philosophy of nature as a whole is obscured as the character and motivation of Bookchin himself moved centre-stage. Ultimately, an important philosophy of nature and an important critique of the dangers of uncritical ecological thought were lost as the patterns of critiquing Bookchin established here became personal.

In this chapter, we return to the specifics of the debate. What was Bookchin criticising in '87 and why? Principally, what were the philosophical and political expressions of deep ecology, and the links between the two that led to Bookchin's critiques? And importantly, what happened in the responses that resulted in the focus slipping from the issues raised and turning toward ad hominem argument and personal invective? To do this, we begin by tracing the emergence of the deep ecology movement, intellectually and politically, and the resulting factors that gave rise to Bookchin's critique.

Our next step, though necessary, may appear counterintuitive: we note the outline of Bookchin's critique of deep ecology in this first chapter, but reserve a full critical examination of it until Chapter 2. For the present, we turn to look first at the extraordinary response to Bookchin's critique. This approach is necessary for reasons of both the volume and nature of the response, as will become clear as we go. In Chapter 2, we then return to a full examination of Bookchin's 1987 critique, finding that it is in fact a coherent expression of his wider philosophical programme: a programme that still represents a valuable contribution to ecological thought.

Deep Ecology

As the ecology movement grew in strength and numbers around the world from its beginnings in the 1960s, partly inspired by key writers and activists, but also given impetus by increasing scientific evidence of ecological breakdown, deep ecology had become increasingly popular as a seemingly radical strand within the movement. From the early 1970s onwards, as noted in the introduction, ecology as a distinct movement had been distinguished from the more mainstream, reformist environmentalism, a distinction drawn out by Bookchin and others. This was to demarcate ecology as a *radical* movement, not interested in reform or piecemeal environmental measures but in a wholesale replacement of the destructive social system of advanced industrial statism.

In 1973, the Norwegian philosopher Arne Naess would take the distinction further: there was, for Naess, within the ecology movement itself, a "shallow" and a "deep" version of ecological thought and action. For Naess, the shallow version had failed to shift its thinking sufficiently enough to overcome the ecological crisis. Deep ecology was a way of doing this, as fundamentally it offered an ecological viewpoint that was premised on "a rejection of the man-in-environment image in favour of a relational, total field image."[1] This "total field image," in short, was premised on a rejection of humanity as the marker of value in the human and nonhuman world: in this image, Naess argued, the deep ecologist views the world of life not as a human being at the centre, but as one part of a wider community, stemming principally from "an awareness of the *equal right of all things to live and blossom into their own unique forms of self-realization.*"[2]

In enshrining the right of every lifeform to live and blossom, Naess called for a "biospherical egalitarianism—in principle."[3] Here, the "inherent value" of all life would be acknowledged, as would the reduction of human interference, irrespective of the use of these life forms to humanity. As he would later write, "every living being has a *right* to live," and "nature does not belong to man."[4] Further, not only was the intrinsic value of all beings to be drawn out in defiance of whether or not they were useful to humanity: they were valuable even if harmful to humanity. "Nature is worth defending," wrote Naess, "*whatever the fate of humans.*"[5]

What Naess's theorising about nature and humanity and the equal value of all living beings attempted to do was to reverse the "man-in-environment image" of nature: to rid ecological thinking of the *anthropocentrism*—of the human-centeredness—of its previous shallow interpretations. Under this rubric, the natural world had forever been viewed by humanity as a store cupboard, there to satisfy human needs and, accordingly, all other life forms were evaluated in relation to this need. That is, all value in the natural world is relational only to human value, is subordinate and weighed against human need. What Naess proposed is an ecological philosophy that shifted this view of the natural world toward a *biocentric* interpretation. Here, as noted, value in the natural world was uncoupled from human need, and all living beings were said to have their own "inherent value" or "intrinsic worth."[6]

This central conceptual framework would be more fully elucidated over the decade that followed Naess's original formulation of deep ecology. By 1984, as Warwick Fox argued, the shallow and deep distinction in ecology had been "developed by a number of thinkers . . . to the point where we might reasonably refer to an intellectual 'deep ecology movement.'"[7] Fox then goes on to try and define what that deep ecology movement is and what makes it different from shallow ecology, giving further clarification to Naess's formulation, specifically to the distinction between anthropocentrism and biocentrism.

According to Fox, for the deep ecology movement, shallow ecology was obsolete in the sense that it "views humans as separate from their environment." This anthropocentric view, moreover, sees "humans as the source of all value and ascribes only instrumental (or use) value to the nonhuman world." Deep ecology, in contrast, "strives to be *non-anthropocentric* by viewing humans as just one constituency among others in the biotic community, just one particular strand in the web of life, just one kind of knot in the biospherical net."[8]

This outlook, for Fox, "dissolves not only the notion of humans as separate from their environment but the very notion of the world as composed of discrete, compact, separate 'things.'" More concretely, Fox continues that, "The intrinsic value of the nonhuman members of the biotic community is recognized" in deep ecology, as is "the right of these members to pursue their own evolutionary destinies." Anything short of this standpoint, for Fox, is an "arrogant conceit," and deep ecologists "are concerned to move heaven and Earth in this universe in order to effect a 'paradigm shift' of comparable significance to that associated with Copernicus."[9]

Deep ecology would be given its full theoretical elucidation, however, in an anthology of essays written by the two U.S. academics, Bill

Devall and George Sessions.[10] *Deep Ecology*, dedicated by the authors to Naess, would in fact become the leading text on the movement, and would clarify the central principles first worked out in the early 1970s. For Devall and Sessions, there are two "ultimate norms" of deep ecology.[11] The first is "self-realization," which holds that in attempting to transcend the "modern Western *self*" that is the isolated ego, not only is a recognition of our humanity required through an identification with other human beings, but also a "further maturity and growth is required, an identification which goes beyond humanity to include the nonhuman world."[12]

This further maturity and growth for Devall and Sessions is the realisation of a larger, capitalised "self"—the self that is aware of the nonhuman as well as the human—and the work of the deep ecologist is to foster this self-realisation, to foster "the realization of the 'self-in-Self' where 'Self' stands for organic wholeness." From this, they explain that, "This process of the full unfolding of the self can also be summarized by the phrase, 'No one is saved until we are all saved,' where the phrase 'one' includes not only me, an individual human, but all humans, whales, grizzly bears, whole rainforest ecosystems, mountains and rivers, the tiniest microbes in the soil, and so on."[13]

The second ultimate norm, stemming from and reinforcing the first, is the "intuition of biocentric equality."[14] This, Devall and Sessions's reworking of biospherical egalitarianism, is "intimately related to the all-inclusive Self-realisation in the sense that if we harm the rest of Nature then we harm ourselves."[15] These two, intertwining ultimate norms, form the bedrock of deep ecological thinking, as Devall and Sessions summarise: "The intuition of biocentric equality is that all things in the biosphere have an equal right to live and blossom and to reach their own individual forms of unfolding and self-realization within the larger Self-realization. This basic intuition is that all organisms and entities in the ecosphere, as parts of the integrated whole, are equal in intrinsic worth."[16]

Devall and Sessions then offer a fuller grounding of the basics of deep ecology, stemming from these two ultimate norms, when they tell us that in 1984, "George Sessions and Arne Naess summarized fifteen years of thinking on the principles of deep ecology" by drawing up eight "basic principles" that would form the movement's theoretical "platform."[17] In the first principle, Sessions and Naess would state clearly the principle of inherent worth: "The well-being and flourishing of human and nonhuman life," they wrote "have value in themselves (synonyms: intrinsic value, inherent value). These values are independent of the usefulness of the nonhuman world for human purposes."[18]

Further, they argued that "richness and diversity of life forms [in the biosphere] contribute to the realization of these values and are also values in themselves." From this, humans "have no right to reduce this richness and diversity of life except to satisfy *vital* needs."[19] Therefore, interference into the natural world should be minimal, as "present human interference in the nonhuman world is excessive, and the situation is rapidly worsening."[20] Devall and Sessions do qualify here that a principle of non-interference "does not imply that humans should not modify some ecosystems," but what is at issue rather "is the nature and extent of such interference."[21] Indeed, with this in mind "the term 'vital need' is left deliberately vague to allow for considerable latitude in judgment."[22]

We shall return to the conceptual and practical problems of deep ecology's "vital needs" and "non-interference" when we turn to Bookchin's critique. However, for the present, Naess and Sessions most controversial basic principle was their fourth: "The flourishing of human life and cultures," they write here, "is compatible with a substantial decrease of the human population. The flourishing of nonhuman life *requires such a decrease*."[23] Here, the question of population becomes a central one in deep ecology, and Devall-Sessions-Naess warned that, although "the stabilization and reduction of the human population will take time . . . the extreme seriousness of our current situation must be realized." Moreover, "the longer we wait" in dealing with the population problem, "the more drastic will be the measures needed."[24]

Dave Foreman, *Earth First!* and Earth First!

If Fox was correct in arguing that by the mid-1980s it was possible to point to an "intellectual deep ecology movement," then the same could be said equally of the emergence of a *political* deep ecology movement—a movement, as we shall see, that was premised *explicitly* on deep ecology's philosophical foundations. One of the most prominent activist groups to emerge in this political movement was Earth First!, the radical environmental direct-action group. Formed in 1979, the group was committed throughout the 1980s to taking direct action against ecological degradation; as their slogan read, "No Compromise in Defense of Mother Earth!"[25] One of the co-founders—and the one credited with naming the group—was Dave Foreman. Foreman would be a particular force within Earth First! as editor of the group's journal of the same name, from 1982 to 1988. In these pages, he would outline the principles of the group, which by the mid-1980s had established the link between their own political action and the philosophy of deep ecology.

In a 1987 article in *Earth First!*, Foreman wrote that "some of the things that define Earth First!" included not only "a recognition that there are far too many human beings on Earth (Malthus was Right)," thus expressing the fourth platform principle of deep ecology, but also quite specifically that being a member of Earth First! involves "an enthusiastic embracing of the philosophy of biocentrism or deep ecology." Moreover, reflecting the principle of biocentric equality and the intrinsic worth of the natural world, Foreman would write that being in Earth First! also meant "a refusal to use human beings as the measure of which to value others."[26]

The link between deep ecology and Earth First! had in fact been established a year earlier in the now notorious interview Foreman gave to the Australian journal, *Simply Living*. Foreman was interviewed here by Bill Devall, one of the three leading philosophers of deep ecology—and who is also described in the piece as "an Earth First!er himself," that is, a member of Earth First!.[27] At the outset of the interview, Devall asks Foreman what "is the relationship between deep ecology and Earth First!?" and in response, Foreman states categorically that "deep ecology *is* the philosophy of Earth First!. They are pretty much the same thing."[28]

That Earth First! and its journal were closely linked to deep ecology, then—indeed, that they were expressions of the philosophy of deep ecology—was apparent by 1987. Furthermore, in the interview with Devall, Foreman would go on to illustrate the problematic conclusions that stemmed logically from deep ecology's philosophical premises. When asked by Devall what he would like to see happen to bring about the "best of all possible worlds," ecologically speaking, in the American West over the next twenty years, he argues that there would need to be "an effort to balance the population to the level that can actually be supported. It would be a hell of a lot less than we have now . . . a move toward population reduction is a primary step."[29]

Devall notes that "most environmental groups have avoided talking about population or immigration" and then asks: "do you think population is an important issue?" Foreman replies that it is "extremely important," and describes how previously in his journal he had argued for the problematic policy of "forced sterilization after three children." Continuing in a similar vein, Foreman then tells Devall of his deep ecological approach to the Ethiopian famine of 1986: "When I tell people how the worst thing we could do in Ethiopia is to give aid—*the best thing would be to just let nature seek its own balance, to let the people there just starve there*, they think that this is monstrous. But the alternative is that you go in and save these half-dead children who will never live a whole life. Their development will be stunted."[30] Moving closer to home, Foreman then clarified what particular section of the "population problem" in the U.S. he had in mind when thinking about addressing the issue: "letting the USA be an overflow valve for problems in Latin America," he argued, "is not solving a thing. It's just putting more pressure on the resources we have in the USA. It is just causing more destruction of our wilderness, more poisoning of water and air, and it isn't helping the problems of Latin America"—that is, in addressing the population problem, immigration was a central concern.[31]

Further, Foreman also outlined what he saw as the political action necessary in alleviating the ecological crisis *beyond* a reduction in population. This was "monkeywrenching," the term invented by the writer and activist Edward Abbey (of whom more below), a strategy of direct action to stop the chainsaws of the logging companies, to stop the bulldozers of the mining companies. It would involve destroying industrial machinery, inserting steel rods into trees scheduled for felling that would destroy the logger's chainsaw on contact. Foreman tells us that all that is required for monkeywrenching "is an *individual* who competently goes out and does something, who just steps outside the system, who takes responsibility, *who says I can't change the system but I can defend this piece of land*."[32]

Though this tactic is described by Devall in the interview as redolent of nineteenth-century anarchism, Foreman concedes perhaps one key difference: "changing the system," bringing revolution, and changing the world is not at the forefront of the monkeywrencher's mind: "You can go out and destroy a road. You can go out and trash a bulldozer. You can go out and take out a tractor. Maybe that's not going to stop everything.

Maybe it's not going to change the world, but it's going to buy that *place*, those *creatures*, some time. And maybe that's the best that can be done."³³

The Influence of Abbey

That Earth First! were heavily influenced by the writer Edward Abbey is obvious not only through their wholesale adoption of his tactics for direct action (drawn from his 1975 novel, *The Monkey Wrench Gang*) but also the uniformity of the views on population. In 1986, Abbey had written that "there are many good reasons" to stop immigration into the U.S. from Latin America, but the "one seldom mentioned . . . is cultural." The U.S., Abbey argued, "with its traditions and ideals, however imperfectly realized, is a product of northern European civilization," and its culture must be protected from further immigration. He continues: "If we allow our country—*our* country—to become Latinized, in whole or in part, we shall see it tend toward a culture more and more like that of Mexico."³⁴

Abbey would later write that "it might be wise for us American citizens to consider calling a halt to the mass influx of even more millions of hungry, ignorant, unskilled, and *culturally-morally-genetically impoverished people*."³⁵ Again here, it was immigration from the south that was his main concern: in contrast to Latin Americans, the North Americans "prefer democratic government" and "still hope for an open, spacious, uncrowded, and beautiful—yes, beautiful!—society." The "uninvited millions" from the south "bring with them an alien mode of life," an impoverished people with an impoverished culture unfit for life in the U.S.: "The squalor, cruelty and corruption of Latin America is plain for all to see," he wrote, and then asked, "How many of us, truthfully, would *prefer* to be submerged in the Caribbean-Latin version of civilization?"³⁶

Abbey has also called explicitly for the closing of "our national borders to any further mass immigration, from any source," and perhaps most problematically, he sees the arbiter and executioner of this policy as the U.S. military. "The means are available [to close national borders]," Abbey contends, "it is a simple technical-military problem. Even our Pentagon should be able to handle it."³⁷ Moreover, he argues that if the U.S. were to choose not to close the borders, and not to leave these other nations to it and continues to meddle in their affairs, then perhaps the best thing the

U.S. could do is "stop every *campesino* at our Southern Border, give him a handgun, a good rifle, and a case of ammunition, and send him home. He will know what to do with our gifts and good wishes."[38]

The "Miss Ann Thropy" of Christopher Manes

Elsewhere in *Earth First!*, the commitment to deep ecology's need for population reduction would be taken to the furthest extremes. As the world was beginning to appreciate the deadly nature and full extent of the AIDS pandemic, the writer Christopher Manes, under the pseudonym "Miss Ann Thropy," wrote that as "hysteria sweeps over the governments of the world," he will offer "an ecological perspective."[39] Furthermore, this ecological perspective is to be offered in light of the commitment of deep ecologists to the idea that modern, industrialised society "must give way to a hunter-gatherer way of life, which is the only economy compatible with a healthy land."[40]

For Manes, an "enormous decline in human population" is required for such a social shift, and "is the only real hope for the continuation of diverse ecosystems on this planet." This decline, Manes continues, is in fact inevitable: "through nuclear war or mass starvation due to desertification or some other environmental cataclysm, human overpopulation *will* succumb to ecological limits." However, this is not enough for Manes, as the world which would follow such a cataclysm would be barren, "devoid of otters and redwoods, Blue Whales and butterflies, tigers and orchids"—that is, the natural world would be affected equally seriously in nuclear war as the human world. For the author then, population must be dealt with in a way that preserves the nonhuman world yet decimates the human, and it is here where AIDS is "environmentally significant."[41]

This "significance" for Manes stems from three key characteristics of AIDS: first, it affects only humans; second, it has a long incubation period; third, it is spread sexually. The first of these is the most important for Manes, as "AIDS has the potential to significantly reduce human population without harming other life-forms." The second two characteristics make AIDS "relevant to the global population problem," as the long incubation period means that the disease is not so virulent that it will "kill off the hosts on which they depend," allowing "infection of others, and hence survival of the virus, before death" and because sexual activity "is *the* most difficult human behaviour to control." Taken together, these three characteristics mean that "the AIDS epidemic will probably spread worldwide, especially to cities where people are concentrated."⁴²

From this, the author writes of AIDS that, "Barring a cure, the possible benefits of this to the environment are staggering." "If, like the Black Death in Europe, AIDS affected one-third of the world's population, it would cause an immediate respite for endangered wildlife on the planet." Moreover, "just as the Plague contributed to the demise of feudalism, AIDS has the potential to end industrialism, which is the main force behind the environmental crisis." For all of these reasons, Manes concludes that "if radical environmentalists were to invent a disease to bring human population back to ecological sanity, it would probably be something like AIDS."⁴³

An Outline of Bookchin's Critique

This overview of the direction of deep ecology and its most vocal adherents in the mid-1980s is crucial to our understanding of Bookchin's critique in 1987: it was to these *specific* comments and opinions to which he addressed his criticisms. Bookchin would take to the podium at Amherst and warn of a growing schism in the ecology movement. "It is time to honestly face the fact," Bookchin argued, "that there are differences within the so-called ecology movement of the present time which are as serious as those between the environmentalism and ecologism of the early seventies." Alongside the "deeply concerned naturalists, communitarians, social radicals and feminists" who work in the ecology movement, there was now emerging an ecology movement of "barely disguised racists" and "outright social reactionaries," who adhere to a kind of "eco-brutalism" or "eco-fascism."⁴⁴

For these reactionaries, humanity is seen as an "ugly, anthropocentric thing," Bookchin wrote, "presumably a malignant product of natural evolution . . . that is 'overpopulating' the planet, 'devouring' its resources, destroying its wildlife and the biosphere." Bookchin railed against the social myopia of such a view: humanity to the deep ecologists was "a vague species," one homogenous block that was intrinsically destructive of the natural world; a humanity conceived, in terms of ecological devastation, as an undifferentiated blight in its impact on the world of life. For Bookchin, this papered over the very real distribution of the impact different parts of society have ecologically, and papered over important social differences as such, rendering "people of color . . . equitable with whites, women with men, the Third World with the First, the poor with the rich, the exploited with their exploiters."[45]

Most important in Bookchin's critique, however, was that he addressed it not solely to the comments of Foreman and Manes *et al.*, but just as stridently toward the silence of Devall (and the other academics of deep ecology) at the very moment these views were being expressed in the name of deep ecology: here, as Foreman described the process of leaving Africans to starve in the hope of nature seeking its balance in terms of the population problem, one of the leading intellectual progenitors of deep ecology offered no protest. Bookchin argued that this in fact reflected the conceptual problems in the philosophical foundations of deep ecology, that rendered it "so much a black hole of half-digested, ill-formed, and half-baked ideas" wherein it is possible for its adherents to express the "utterly vicious" notions proffered by Foreman.[46]

As noted, a full explication of Bookchin's 1987 critique will form the opening of Chapter 2, as will be the examination of its roots within Bookchin's philosophical positions: indeed, it will be argued that his critique of deep ecology in 1987 is not only a rich and incisive analysis of the problems of deep ecology but also can be explained as the direct philosophical and political expression of his own theoretical foundations. Central here, as we shall see, is that the philosophy of deep ecology for Bookchin is not only reactionary in its reading of history and ecology, allowing for the "eco-fascism" of Foreman *et al.*, but also that it provides for no social agency in addressing the ecological crisis. For Bookchin, as will be explained, a more thorough reading of the causes of the ecological crisis and of humanity's role therein is required.

However, before we examine how Bookchin provided for this through his own philosophy, we turn to the reaction to his critique of those within deep ecology and Earth First!. This extraordinary reaction, it is argued here, does not allow for the central claim of Bookchin that more analysis is required of humanity's role in the natural world and its future role in averting ecological catastrophe. Moreover, they fail to deal with the specific issues raised by Bookchin at Amherst and in many ways further entrench the problematic logical conclusions of deep ecology philosophy. Again, this loss of focus on the issues raised served not to examine and expand ecological thinking in the 1980s, but rather to establish the problematic caricature of Bookchin that would emerge from the critiques.

Earth First! Responds

In late 1987, *Earth First!* responded to Bookchin's address by including a "special section" in their November 1 issue turned over to articles that offered a reaction. The tenor of the articles in this section was established by an introduction provided by "The Editors."[47] They explained that, in fact, it was "surprising" given the radical nature of their movement, that Earth First! had come under "so little criticism in the last seven years" and how they were relieved to finally sense the stirrings of a critical literature. More surprising for the Editors, however, was the fact that this critical literature included "several inconsequential 'anarchist' punkzines in the US" which had started accusing Earth First! of racism and fascism. They then explained how "These themes were then picked up by the Big Daddy of American Anarchism, Murray Bookchin, in a papal bull he delivered at the Greens Conference in Amherst . . . Lumbering like the WWII German battleship Bismarck, Bookchin delivered his heavy guns toward a variety of targets, including deep ecologists like Devall, Sessions and Naess."[48] The imagery here of war and conflict, of weaponry and targets was in fact the first stone laid in the building of the Bookchin caricature. Not only did this infuse the contemporaneous critiques of Bookchin in *Earth First!* and elsewhere but this imagery would also resurface in the mid-1990s as people reacted to Bookchin's critique of anarchism, when, again, he would be accused of being heavy handed, of being a pugilist, of being out to attack (as will be fully examined in due course).

Returning to the debate in 1987, the first article in the supplement of the November 1 *Earth First!* matches *exactly* those images established by the Editors' introduction. Here, R.W. Flowers, an environmental ethicist from the University of Florida explains that the deep ecology movement has "caught the public attention with amazing speed" and that as with any movement, success spawns envy. One example of this envy is

Bookchin, whose "purpose," Flowers tells us, "is to supplant deep ecology with his own brand of social activism, social ecology," a process which rendered Bookchin's critique "rich in obfuscation, deception, and pointless invective."[49]

Flowers goes on to describe Bookchin's critique as an "attack"—a term, as we shall see, that would recur again and again—directed at the deep ecologists, and describe "Bookchin's attempt to corner the word 'ecology.'" Again, there is no evidence provided, and instead of taking Bookchin's critique on its expressed intentions—of offering a critique of deep ecology and a clarification of social ecology—and instead of dealing with the issues raised, Flowers argues that "Bookchin's real aim" is not a detailed critique of the direction of the ecology movement but is in fact an attempt "to gain ground in his ideological turf war with Naess, Devall and Sessions."[50] Again, Flowers offers us nothing in terms of substantiating this claim and, in truth, resorts to nothing more than ad hominem insinuation and accusation. Like much of the insinuation around Bookchin that originates from this period, one is left wondering quite how Flowers arrived at his conclusions on Bookchin's motivations.

There is *some* passing discussion of the issues Bookchin raised in terms of what social ecology stands for (not, it should be noted, of the criticisms of deep ecology) but unfortunately, it is lost in the constant insinuation that Bookchin's motivations are less than sincere. Indeed, this attitude engulfs the entirety of Flowers's piece, and even in those places where he attempts to discuss issues alone, he gets it badly wrong. For example, in discussing Bookchin's view of humanity's place in the natural world, he argues that Bookchin has "swallowed whole the dogma of humanity as the apex of an evolutionary ladder," and as a result, "human intervention in nature is given blanket justification because it is a 'product of evolution.'"[51]

As will be examined fully in the next chapter, nothing could be more inaccurate than this description of the role Bookchin ascribes to humanity in his overall philosophical programme. Indeed, the notion of humanity having a "blanket justification" for interfering in the natural world is as alien to Bookchin as evidence appears to be to Flowers. Again here he offers no material on which he has drawn this conclusion on Bookchin, no section of text—not even from Bookchin's critique, the piece he is ostensibly responding to. Rather, he appears intent on stating that Bookchin is not only motivated by a "turf war" with the deep ecologists but also that he is wrong theoretically yet cannot see it, as his social ecology "remains mired in the old anthropocentric narcissism: humans self-absorbed with humanity."[52]

It is perhaps in Flowers's concluding remarks, however, that he is at his most problematic. Here, he argues that Bookchin's "fixation" on the destructiveness of capitalism means he "gives scant attention to some of the most acute aspects of the ecological crisis." Further, this focus on capitalism means there is nothing "novel" in Bookchin, simply "a restatement of the old Left/Liberal/Marxist/Progressive social reform ideology," and like those ideologies that went before it, "social ecology is notable for its obsession with 'political correctness'" and fails "to propose concrete solutions to our problems."[53]

It is difficult for the present author to even *begin* to know from where Flowers has drawn these criticisms. Indeed, they are so wide of the mark, it is, at times, almost as if Flowers is offering a critique of somebody else's work. As will be shown, this is not a characteristic peculiar to Flowers: it recurs again and again, increasing over the years as the Bookchin caricature begins to take hold. We return to this issue in Chapter 2, but Flowers's misreading (or more properly, *non*-reading) of Bookchin needs noting here as we examine the initial construction of the Bookchin caricature.

Elsewhere in *Earth First!*, a writer under the name of "Chim Blea" would employ the exact same logic in responding to Bookchin. Blea argued that Bookchin's critique was unsurprising, something to be expected: "Being a cynical Earth First!er of the misanthropic flavor," they wrote, casually advertising their misanthropy, "I have long expected the dogmatic Left to attack the Deep Ecology/Earth First! movements." Again, the description of Bookchin's critique as an "attack" is used as a springboard to accuse him of nefarious motivations and ill-thought-out political manoeuvring. Again also, the fundamentals of Bookchin's critique are overlooked, as Blea focuses on the "vehemence" and "viciousness" of Bookchin's critique.[54]

Overlooking the contradiction of a writer who admits their own "misanthropic flavor"—writing in a journal which had by then a track record of misanthropic leanings—Blea goes on to explain the reasons for Bookchin's "vehemence." First, Blea argues that the "viciousness" of Bookchin can be put down to "sour grapes": "Murray Bookchin has been toiling away for years developing and promoting his 'Social Ecology' and has received little notice," they tell us, and then suddenly, "Deep Ecology and Earth First! appear and steal all the attention that should rightfully be his."[55] The second reason Blea cites to explain Bookchin's "attack" is even more unsubstantiated. Drawing a parallel with the split in the German Greens between the Fundis and the Realos of the same period, Blea contends that Bookchin's "tirade" at Amherst "may have been part of a coordinated attempt by American Redgreens to launch a pre-emptive strike on the Green Greens and engineer a coup in the American Green party," again an accusation based on no evidence, only insinuation.[56]

Of course, what makes this worse, for Blea, is that on top of these motivations, Bookchin is an old-fashioned ecologist, still mired in anthropocentrism. "Wilderness is unimportant" to him, Blea contends, "other species do not have intrinsic value. The world is a collection of resources for human beings. Bookchin is entirely correct—there is a great gulf between his 'Social Ecology' and Deep Ecology."[57] Of course, this outmoded approach made Bookchin a relic of the "Old Left," and riddled with hypocrisy, and then, apparently without irony, they conclude that "Bookchin and other far leftists prattle about their great love for human beings," but in fact, "when they get down to dealing with actual, individual people, they become vicious, spiteful and nasty. Ad hominem arguments prevail."[58]

In his own response to Bookchin, Foreman would restate the principles of Earth First!, and in so doing, further entrenches the philosophical problems of deep ecology and their logical conclusions. "In everything we do," Foreman argues, "the primary consideration should be for the long-term health and native diversity of Earth. After that, we can consider the welfare of humans." Furthermore, "individual human life is not the most important thing in the world," and "has no more intrinsic value than a Grizzly Bear." Perhaps most worryingly, backing up his original quotes concerning the famine in Ethiopia, he contends that "human suffering resulting from drought and famine in Ethiopia is unfortunate, yes, *but the destruction of other creatures and habitat there is even more unfortunate.*"[59]

Indeed, Foreman's "enthusiastic embracing of the philosophy of Deep Ecology or Biocentrism" is taken to the furthest extremes in his response when he argues that biocentrism "states simply and essentially that all things possess intrinsic value or inherent worth." Moreover, "things have value and live for their own sake." This view extends to *all* "things," for Foreman—even inanimate objects, such as "rivers and mountains." Moreover, deep ecology "is an ecological point of view that . . . views Earth as a community and recognizes such heretical truths as that [sic] 'disease' (malaria) and 'pests' (mosquitoes) are not evil manifestations to be overcome and destroyed but rather are vital and necessary components of a complex and vibrant biosphere."[60]

The place this kind of biocentrism plays in the overall schematic of deep ecology is revealed when Foreman argues that ultimately, the "absolute litmus test" for membership of Earth First! is their commitment to the principle that "there are too many human beings on Earth," and that "the refusal to recognize the need to lower human population over the long run clearly defines one as a humanist and places [one] outside the bounds of Earth First!."[61] Of course, this "litmus test," this commitment to the notion that there are far too many human beings on Earth sits nicely next to a commitment to the intrinsic worth of malarial mosquitoes.

The Academy Responds

Outside of the pages of *Earth First!* the response to Bookchin would follow exactly the same patterns. Indeed, the two principal academics of deep ecology, Devall and Sessions, would respond in almost identical (and no less polemical) terms. Devall, for example, responding in a comment on the debate between deep ecology and social ecology, would begin by arguing that the furore stemmed not from the comments that he elicited from Foreman in their earlier interview concerning the famine in Ethiopia, nor from his silence in the wake of them, but from the success of deep ecology itself. "If attacks indicate that a social movement is important," Devall argues, apropos of no such claim, "then the deep, long-range ecology movement has arrived as an important force on the American intellectual scene."[62]

This is confirmed for Devall by the emergence of "long and steamy diatribes" critiquing deep ecology. In particular, Devall continues, "in 1987, anarchists-leftists-Marxists, led by Murray Bookchin, launched an attack on deep ecology."[63] Again here, we see the emergence of the notion—based on no evidence—that Bookchin was "attacking" deep ecology; and again, it is insinuated that he did so on behalf of some greater "Old Left" alliance in the name of political manoeuvre. Despite the paucity of his "anarchists-leftists-Marxists" denomination (a denomination that Devall openly acknowledges is an "over-simplification"), to level the term "Marxist" at Bookchin shows no familiarity with Bookchin's work, much like the criticisms found in the pages of *Earth First!*.[64] But more than this: it shows no engagement with the critique Bookchin offered in 1987, or the reasons why he offered his critique. Again here, the charge of attack is levelled at Bookchin without taking him at his word, and addressing the basis of his criticisms.

Rather, Devall follows the patterns (and language) of the earlier responses by focusing on the emergence, rather than the content, of Bookchin's critique. "Attacks by some leftists," he claims, "indicate that the deep ecology movement is considered the new boy on the block and a *turf war* has erupted." He continues that deep ecology theorists "seek cooperation and have no interest in a turf war."[65] This example of the academic deep ecologists picking up the themes laid down in the pages of *Earth First!* is a common one: Warwick Fox would do the same when, in commenting on Bookchin's critique, he argued that Bookchin launched a "vitriolic attack upon an ideological competitor that was receiving, and that continues to receive, much greater attention from the ecophilosophical community than Bookchin's own ideas," the parallels with Blea's response above being all too obvious.[66]

As well as picking up the "turf war" analogy, Devall also follows the pattern of the earlier responses in stating the importance of "cordial relations" in critical exchanges: "Confrontation, diatribe, denouncing comrades, and factionalism are characteristics of the leftist movements," and not deep ecology.[67] What Devall does not do is tell us what the new characteristics of deep ecology are, but we know from the written record discussed above: they are misanthropy, cultural arrogance, and even racism. Being cordial is not, and should not, always be the right way to proceed against such dangerous ideas.[68]

Devall then goes on to "review the deep ecology movement both for critics of the movement and for supporters confused by the attacks on deep ecology," and here he restates, unknowingly, some of the very reasons that Bookchin offered his critique in the first place.[69] Devall argues that "deep ecologists and their critics *generally* agree that major reconstruction of society is necessary."[70] However, despite a paragraph in which anarchist forms of organisation are posited as "self regulating . . . ecologically aware communities" which "complement" ecological resistance, Devall concedes that "deep ecology theorists have been less interested in political economy and more interested in the causes of anthropocentrism" when dealing with the ecological crisis.[71]

Further, in reversing this anthropocentrism, Devall restates his commitment to the biocentric "inherent worth of all beings," and although he states that "neither Naess nor myself have ever suggested that AIDS is a blessing," he still refused to condemn those in the deep ecology movement who did.[72] Moreover, he simultaneously addresses the "leftist criticism" of population control by arguing that "it is unclear how Bookchin and some leftists view the question of continues [*sic*], rapid population growth" and drawing a parallel with China ("that socialist state," he notes) and its reactionary population control measures, of physically restricting a couple to no more than one child, he asks whether leftists would "accept these policies in Mexico or the US?"[73]

Of course, the insinuation is that, barring the reduction of human population through the operation of natural forces—through famine and disease—the only other options are the draconian measures carried out in the "socialist state" that is China, or some other such measures. Thus, Devall claims independence from the misanthropic extremes of deep ecology philosophy whilst at the same time indicating obliquely that those extremes might provide the *only* resolution of the population problem. It should be noted also that nowhere in Devall's response does he deal with the specific problem raised by Bookchin: Devall's refusal to condemn Foreman's comments on Ethiopia in his interview of him. Nor does Devall deal with the more explicit tracing of the link between his own writings on deep ecology and the misanthropic conclusions drawn by Foreman *et al*.

Finally, Devall argues that "Bookchin has practically nothing to say here about Nature in the sense the ecological movement is interested in. He says little or nothing about the flourishing of non-human life."[74] Furthermore, "For Bookchin and his followers, it seems, Earth is not a sacred place. They do not seem to seek to discover their broader and deeper self but only to change economic and political institutions."[75] Again, the misreading (or more properly, *non*-reading) of Bookchin here is astounding.

As we shall see in our examination of Bookchin's philosophy in the following chapters, his programme of natural and social rationality is built
on a treatise to recover the lost "broader and deeper self," to fully locate it
in the processes of natural evolution, and to create social forms that ensure
the continued endurance of this self and the natural world.

Separately from Devall, Sessions would respond to Bookchin's critique and, again, we see the exact same patterns emerge: there is no taking
of Bookchin's critique at face value, solely the insinuation of ulterior
motives. "In 1987," Sessions tells us, "Murray Bookchin and his Social
Ecology group attacked Earth First! and the Deep Ecology philosophy."[76]
Apart from the now familiar cry of "attack," what is most shocking here
is Sessions's dismissal of the explanation for what gave rise to Bookchin's
critique: "Certain *casual* remarks by individual Earth First!ers (made, to
some extent, for their shock value to drive home the message of how out
of balance contemporary humans are on the planet) concerning allowing
Ethiopians to starve, and AIDS as nature's population control device,
provided Bookchin the opportunity he needed."[77] These "casual remarks,"
made "to shock," get no further treatment from Sessions. They are secondary, reduced to a mere add-on in the debate, despite the fact that it was
Bookchin's main contention in his critique to draw out the connection
between those remarks and the philosophical principles of deep ecology.
This part of Bookchin's critique is overlooked, and the real issue at hand
for Sessions is to prove Bookchin's sinister motives—that Bookchin was
not really interested in the content of the discussion, but was looking for
his "opportunity" to attack Earth First!. In a further misreading of Bookchin, he argues that "in his 1987 attack, Bookchin ridiculed the idea that
humanity was overpopulating the planet and destroying the biosphere."[78]
Following this line of argument in a postscript, Sessions talks of Bookchin's "general dismissal of the relevance of the science of ecology for
humans," and states that "it is not clear why Bookchin refers to his position as social 'ecology.'"[79]

This final proclamation on Bookchin from Sessions, so indicative of the
responses of the late-1980s as a whole, is perhaps the most fitting point
to take our leave of them. In concluding, we need note: as will be shown,
there is nothing in Bookchin's 1987 critique that claimed population

growth was not a problem in humanity's destruction of the biosphere. Indeed, the very idea that Bookchin would oppose, much less ridicule the idea of this destruction, and the idea that this destruction is *in part* down to matters of population, is to put lie to most of Bookchin's written work since 1952.

Moreover, nor would it be an exaggeration to claim that "the relevance of the science of ecology for humans" is in fact one of the central themes of Bookchin's entire catalogue: from his 1964 essay "Ecology and Revolutionary Thought" onwards, Bookchin would constantly write of the explosive implications of ecology, of the radical edge it contained, *as a science*, because not only did ecology expose the extent of the ecological crisis and the need for human action in light of it, but it also pointed to the interdependence, complementarity, the non-hierarchical organisation of ecosystems in the natural world. For these reasons, ecology, for Bookchin, was a "critical and reconstructive science," a science more radical than those that had preceded it.[80]

None of this, unfortunately, seemed important to Sessions, Devall, and the writers of *Earth First!*, and the pattern of dismissing Bookchin's critique and his wider philosophy, all too apparent in this final comment from Sessions, is something we can trace throughout the entirety of responses from within deep ecology. Whilst this literature can easily be shown to be highly problematic, our examination of it here has been important in order to gain a full appreciation of the scale and scope of the patterns of critique that would establish the caricature of Bookchin as dogmatic and authoritarian, patterns that would emerge again and again throughout the next two decades. However, these late 1980s reactions and responses to Bookchin notwithstanding, there *was* a rich and robust critique of deep ecology offered by Bookchin in 1987, and there *was* a rich and robust philosophical foundation on which this critique was built, the explication of which we now turn to directly in Chapter 2.

Chapter 2

The Ecology of Bookchin
The Philosophical Objection to Deep Ecology

After our discussion of the direction deep ecology and its most prominent adherents were heading in the 1980s, our noting of the trends that
Bookchin would critique in 1987, and of our subsequent examination of
the response to that critique, we are faced with a dilemma: was there, in
fact, anything in Bookchin's critique that explains the rise of a body of
literature that would so fundamentally cast a shadow over the soundness
of his motivations? That is to ask, is there anything in Bookchin's critique that would substantiate the claims that he was not interested in the
conclusions of ecology, deep *or* social, not interested in the philosophy
and politics of the ecology movement, but more interested in a political
"turf war"?

Or, alternatively, can Bookchin's critique be explained by something
more substantial than the accusations and misrepresentations of the deep
ecology response? That is, were the criticisms he raised in 1987 not only
grounded in a sound analysis of the failings of deep ecology, but more
importantly, grounded also in his own philosophical principles? We begin
here to build our case for this second position. To do so, it is argued that
Bookchin's critique can be seen to rest on two separate but intertwined
objections. The first is a *philosophical* objection: here, Bookchin critiques
the philosophical foundations of deep ecology and offers in contrast an
outline of his own philosophy of nature. The second is a *socio-historical*
objection: here, Bookchin offers a critique of the history, or more properly, the lack of history in deep ecology, and again draws out his own
historical social theory in contrast. We turn to Bookchin's socio-historical

objection in Chapters 4 and 5 but for the present chapter and the next, it is his philosophical objection to deep ecology and the principles upon which it is based that concerns us.

Vitriolic Attack or Spirited Defence?

Before we begin, however, we need to make a final brief diversion: it is incumbent on us to critically refute the two principal and lingering accusations that emerged from the reaction to Bookchin in 1987. The first: that Bookchin was "vicious" or "vitriolic" in his 1987 critique, indicative of his desire to "attack" deep ecology for political gain; further, that his argument was made up of "pointless invective."[1] Perhaps here, there is a problem: even if Bookchin's motivations are sound, maybe his polemical style overrides the main thrust of his argument (a criticism that would be taken up by later writers in the anarchist debates, as we will see later on)?

On closer inspection, however, there is very little *personal* invective in Bookchin's 1987 critique. To be sure, Bookchin was forthright throughout the article. Further, it must be conceded in parts, he did slip over into outright polemic and, in one or two instances, even into ad hominem argumentation. For example, at the outset, he tells us that "today the newly emerging ecological movement is filled with well-meaning people who are riddled by a new kind of 'spokesmen,' individuals who are selling their own wares—usually academic and personal careers."[2]

Elsewhere in his critique, he would describe deep ecology as having "parachuted into our midst quite recently from the Sunbelt's bizarre mix of Hollywood and Disneyland, spiced with homilies from Taoism, Buddhism, spiritualism, reborn Christianity, and in some cases eco-fascism."[3] Further, he would refer to Foreman as a "patently anti-humanist mountain macho man" and elsewhere, as an "eco-brutalist."[4] In a work that is based on a critique of the ad hominem approach to Bookchin, then the instances where Bookchin does slip into personal invective are inexcusable and must be conceded. However, two things need be noted here.

First, the instances of personal invective are a small portion of Bookchin's overall critique. In a piece over ten thousand words long, the instances of ad hominem reasoning number no more than a paragraph. Moreover, if the rest of the piece made no sense, or contained no detail—it is, in fact, rich in detail and analysis, as we shall see—then of course, the criticisms would stand: Bookchin could be accused of unsubstantiated criticism, motivated by a desire to attack. But this is not the case: Bookchin does occasionally slip into ad hominem argument (the reasons for which we may be able to suggest later in the work), but his 1987 critique is overwhelmingly an analysis of the problems of deep ecology and an outline of his own philosophy.

Second, Bookchin would later concede and defend his forthright approach and his occasional slip into invective. In the first instance, he would concede his awareness of the extent of his own polemics within the original critique itself: "With so much absurdity to unscramble" in deep ecology, he would write, "one can indeed get heady, almost dizzy, with a sense of polemical intoxication."[5] In the second instance, he would later defend the forthright nature of his approach as a whole: as we saw at the outset when asked in an interview with *The Guardian* in 1992 about his speaking out against Foreman's comments at Amherst, Bookchin would respond that: "If you look at why they [the Ethiopians] are starving, it is not because of nature. It is because of civil war, agri-business, social problems. *How can I remain silent and be polite about this?*"[6]

Elsewhere, in a later, published debate with Foreman, he would write that, in the forthright nature of his critique, "I may have seemed very disputatious in dealing harshly with these tendencies in the ecology movement but I think my zealousness is justified. . . . I cannot be 'mellow' on this point."[7] Further, in again noting that not only were these views being expressed by Foreman *et al.*, but more worryingly, they were met with silence by the academics and theorists of deep ecology, Bookchin also argued later that "no one should be silent, in my opinion, when such vicious stuff emerges in what professes to be an ecology movement."[8]

Bookchin would also address the notion of the personal nature of the responses to his critique. Noting those writers who had accused him of envy, Bookchin wrote that, "At seventy years of age, I have neither the energy nor the time to envy anyone about anything. . . . My own life's work is basically finished, and I am reasonably content with it."[9] Further, he decried this slip into personal matters and implored that the *political* issues that fostered the debate remained paramount: "Please let us keep personalities and matters of 'ego' out of the discussion . . . and let us stick to the *politics* that are really involved in the dispute."[10]

The politics of the dispute for Bookchin were still crystal clear: it was a "strictly political fact," he continued, that Ed Abbey warned against "allowing 'our' country to be 'Latinized' . . . that he described Hispanic immigrants as 'hungry, ignorant, unskilled, and culturally-morally-generically impoverished people.'"[11] It was also, for Bookchin a "strictly political fact" that Foreman argued (and later re-entrenched) that the Ethiopian famine was nature taking its course, and that malaria should be respected as a necessary component on the biosphere.[12] It was also a "strictly political fact" that "Miss Ann Thropy" wrote that the AIDS virus could be "ecologically significant," and may have many benefits in reducing human population.[13]

These were the *political* factors that provoked Bookchin's *political* response. And as noted, it is these political and philosophical issues that make up the overwhelming majority of Bookchin's original 1987 critique and his responses to the ensuing debate. Therefore, although undeniably forthright—*harsh*, even, in places—his critique is *absolutely specific* in its targets. It is not an "attack" on deep ecology or on nature philosophy as such, but rather, as we will shortly examine in full, is a spirited defence of humanity—of human reason, human society, and of the role it has to play in averting the ecological crisis—against the inconsistencies and misanthropy of deep ecology.

The Ecology of Bookchin

The second lingering accusation that needs to be refuted is the deep ecologists' claims that "Bookchin has practically nothing to say . . . about Nature in the sense the ecological movement is interested in," that "for Bookchin and his followers, it seems, Earth is not a sacred place," that they seek "only to change economic and political institutions."[14] That, moreover, Bookchin dismisses "the relevance of the science of ecology for humans," that Bookchin "gives scant attention to some of the most acute aspects of the ecological crisis," that his philosophy is solely "a restatement of the old Left/Liberal/Marxist/Progressive social reform ideology."[15]

However, Bookchin had by 1987 been formulating a rich and robust ecological philosophy for over three decades. Contra Flowers, as early as 1952, Bookchin had devoted many pages to the acute aspects of the ecological crisis. In his lengthy article, "The Problem of Chemicals in Food," Bookchin, in discussing the effects of the move to large-scale industrial agriculture, would offer an early statement of ecological principles: "It can never be too strongly emphasized that every tract of soil and every acre of countryside comprises a relatively unique ecological situation. Just as climate, land, vegetation, may vary greatly from one part of the country to another, so every square mile presents in some degree a distinct balance of natural forces."[16] This distinct balance of natural forces needs to be heeded by the farmer of the 1950s, according to Bookchin, and would inform him as to "how far he can interfere in his given situation without causing irreparable damage." Learning this responsible intervention into the natural world, moreover, "can only come with personal familiarity, with fairly extensive experience and understanding" of the ecological situation, an understanding which was lost to large-scale farming, wherein the land was now "to be exploited like any other resource."[17]

A decade later, Bookchin fleshed out his studies of ecology and the ecological crisis into his first full-length book on the subject, and here, we can begin to trace the germination of the very basis of his critique of deep ecology. In 1962, in *Our Synthetic Environment*, Bookchin argued that "Understandably, a large number of people have reacted to the non-human character of our synthetic environment"—that is, reacted to the ecological crisis—"by venerating nature as the only source of health and well-being." This reaction, Bookchin continued, resulted in the view that

> The natural state, almost without reservation, is regarded as preferable to the works of modern man and the environment he has created for himself. The term "natural" tends to become synonymous with "primitive." The more man's situation approximates that of his primitive forebears, it is thought, the more he will be nourished by certain quasimystical wellsprings of health and virtue. In view of the mounting problems created by our synthetic environment, this renunciation of science and technology—indeed, of civilization— would be almost tempting if it were not manifestly impractical.[18]

Clearly, Bookchin had by 1962 begun to see the possible dangers of an improperly thought out nature philosophy, and throughout the 1960s, Bookchin would push his understanding of ecology further, and would begin to formulate a notion of ecology as a possible grounds for a new ethics of society and nature. In 1964, not only would Bookchin offer one of the earliest discussions of global warming, but would describe ecology as an "integrative and reconstructive science."[19] "Broadly conceived" he wrote, "ecology deals with the balance of nature. Inasmuch as nature includes man, *the science basically deals with the harmonization of nature and man.*"[20]

Moreover, an understanding of ecology showed for Bookchin that this harmonization could not solely be the product of human reason, but had to come from an understanding and analysis of the operating procedures of nature, of the lessons therein. "Ecology clearly shows," he continued, "that the *totality* of the natural world—nature taken in all its aspects, cycles and interrelationships—cancels out all human pretensions to mastery over the planet."[21] Nowhere was this clearer for Bookchin than in the diversity that was so apparent through the study of the natural world. "From an ecological viewpoint," he continued, "balance and harmony in nature" is achieved through "organic differentiation."[22] The "mechanical standardization" of modern society was reducing this differentiation, simplifying nature as well as society as an ecosystem. "If we diminish variety in the natural world," he continued, "we debase its unity and wholeness. We destroy the forces for natural harmony and stability. . . . If we wish to advance the unity and stability of the natural world . . . we must conserve and promote variety."[23]

Bookchin argued that these lessons, drawn from the *science* of ecology, had "explosive implications," for the conclusions they pointed to—the need to appreciate the mastery of nature, of the need for the conscious fostering of diversity in the natural world—can only be achieved for Bookchin through the concurrent social development of these very relationships. That is to say, that ecological principles "lead directly into anarchic areas of social thought," as human communities themselves would need to be balanced through diversity: decentralised, spontaneous and variegated.[24]

Throughout the 1970s, Bookchin further developed his notion of ecology, both as a science and as a *radical* movement. Indeed, in his distinguishing of the differences between ecology and environmentalism, Bookchin offered an early outline of an ecological sensibility, no less far-reaching than the later deep ecology view. As he argued in 1971, "environmentalism deals with the serviceability of the human habitat, a passive habitat that people *use*." Environmental issues, moreover, "require the use of no greater wisdom than . . . instrumentalist modes of thought." In contrast, his definition of ecology was of something much "deeper," as it were, and it bears reproducing in full here. Ecology, for Bookchin,

> is an artful science, or scientific art, and at its best, a form of poetry that combines science and art in a unique synthesis. Above all, it is an outlook that interprets all interdependencies (social and psychological as well as natural) non-hierarchically. Ecology denies that nature can be interpreted from a hierarchical viewpoint. Moreover, it affirms that diversity and spontaneous development are ends in themselves, to be respected in their own right. Formulated in terms of ecology's "ecosystem approach," this means that *each form of life has a unique place in the balance of nature* and its removal from the ecosystem could imperil the stability of the whole. . . . Ecology knows no "king of the beasts"; *all life forms have their place in a biosphere* that becomes more and more diversified in the course of biological evolution.[25]

Therefore, two years before Naess would define deep ecology's notion of "intrinsic worth," Bookchin had formulated an ecological outlook equally as far-reaching, which did not place humanity at the apex of a natural hierarchy. Importantly, however, nor did it place nature at the apex of such a hierarchy: into the wide-reaching, "deep" view of ecology Bookchin formulated here, that challenged the mastery of humanity over the rest of the natural world, he inserted a proviso, which, as will be shown, is ever-present in Bookchin's philosophy: this sensibility should never compromise the unique position of humanity in natural evolution—the very mental capacities that make it possible to formulate sensibilities in the first place: "Humans, too, belong to the whole, but only as one part of the whole. They can intervene in this totality, provided they do so on its own behalf as well as society's; but if they try to 'dominate' it, i.e., plunder it, they risk the possibility of undermining it and the natural fundament for social life."[26]

What the above genealogy of Bookchin's ecology makes abundantly clear is that, by 1987, Bookchin had dealt specifically with ecology as a science, that he had clearly also reduced the scope for human interference, that at the very point he would start to formulate his social problem, it was completely infused with and informed by the science of ecology, the claims of Devall, Sessions, Flowers et al. to the contrary notwithstanding. However, so too was it infused with an unavoidable truth: the distinctiveness of humanity as one species in the biological whole. It is the development of these principles since the 1950s, as we now turn to examine, that would form the basis of his 1987 critique of deep ecology.

Bookchin's Philosophical Objection to Deep Ecology

At the outset of his critique, Bookchin would make his intentions clear. After surveying the progress the ecology movement had made since its beginnings in the late 1960s, Bookchin argued that it was time for those in the movement to define what ecology meant. "The question that now faces us," he wrote, "is: What do we really mean by an ecological approach? What are a coherent ecological philosophy, ethics and movement?"[27] For Bookchin, there was now a choice for the ecology movement, between "a vague, formless, often self-contradictory, and invertebrate thing called deep ecology and a long-developing, coherent, and socially oriented body of ideas that can best be called social ecology." Moreover, this was not only "a quarrel with regard to theory, sensibility, and ethics" but rather has "far-reaching practical and political consequences [concerning] not only the way we view nature, or humanity, or even ecology, but how we propose to change society and by what means."[28]

The notion of how we propose to change society will be a matter we return to when we examine Bookchin's socio-historical objection to deep ecology, but for the present, our focus will be philosophical. For Bookchin, the very basis of the philosophy of deep ecology contained the seeds of its terminal contradictions. To re-cap, in the deep ecology schematic, the generative cause of the ecological crisis can ultimately be reduced to one thing: the impact on the world as a whole of an anthropocentric, overly-populous humanity. As such, the reversal of the ecological crisis is predicated on the reversal of this "population problem" through not only a reduction of human numbers, but also by humanity learning to live in accord with the rest of nature through the new principle of "biocentrism."

Here, as we have seen, humanity would learn to respect the right of all life-forms to live and blossom through a biospherical egalitarianism, in which humanity would eventually come to recognise itself as just "one constituency among others in the biotic community, just one particular strand in the web of life, just one kind of knot in the biospherical net."[29] This process, as was shown, is the expression of the two ultimate norms of deep ecology: the move toward "self-realization on the larger Self," where the larger Self is the organic whole of both humanity and nature, and the commitment to non-interference in nature by humanity in a state of "bio-centric equality."[30]

For Bookchin, however, the conceptual framework that rested on these two norms represented a "deadening abstraction" of humanity from its evolutionary history and its place in the natural world.[31] The process of human "self-realization" in the larger "self" of the natural world tells us nothing about humanity's evolution from the natural world, according to Bookchin, tells us nothing about how humanity came to be so ecologically destructive. Nor does it say anything specific about humanity's future role. To define this ultimate "self-realization," the "growth and maturity" of humanity—this seemingly final intellectual, spiritual and political resting point—as the attainment of an undefined "organic whole" is, for Book-chin, to erase "all the rich and meaningful distinctions that exist not only between animal and plant communities but above all between nonhuman and human communities."[32]

Indeed, as Bookchin argued in 1987, "a 'Self' so cosmic that it has to be capitalized is no real self at all." Rather, it is "a category as vague, faceless, and depersonalized as the very patriarchal image of 'man' that dissolves our uniqueness and rationality."[33] If this is to be the philosoph-ical and political striving of the ecology movement, if this is the way it conceives of itself and the action it takes is to be toward the instigation of a political and social settlement that is based on a biospheric egalitarian-ism, "broadly defined as a universal 'whole,'" then for Bookchin "a unique function that natural evolution has conferred on human society dissolves into a cosmic night that lacks differentiation, variety, and a wide array of functions."[34]

Further, Bookchin argued, in this deadening abstraction of humanity into a humanity "that accurses the natural world," and of the realisation of individual selfhood into a process that "must be transformed into a cosmic

'Selfhood'" *nonhuman* nature, too "is not spared a kind of static, preposi-
tional logic." That is to say, under the deep ecology rubric, once humanity
is abstracted from nature as a whole as a destructive element, defined as
separate from the natural world, the natural world *itself* becomes separate
and abstracted. It thus "becomes a kind of scenic view, a spectacle to be
admired around the campfire," a static image, revered as a place humanity
must somehow attempt to return submissively to. However, for Bookchin, this obscures the important fact that nature is not static, but is rather
"an *evolutionary development that is cumulative and includes the human
species.*"[35]

After raising these conceptual objections to deep ecology, Bookchin outlined his own view of humanity and nature, and elaborated on
the "unique function" that natural evolution has produced in humanity.
Like every other living species in the natural world, Bookchin contends,
human beings adapt the natural environment that surrounds them, and
in this sense, the communities they form are no different from any other
animal community. However, human societies are "consciously formed
communities." That is, in contrast to other animal communities, they "are
not instinctively formed or genetically programmed."[36]

That is to say, humanity's adaptation of their environment is (or more
properly, *could be*, a point to which we return below) *conscious*, a unique
evolutionary step. Indeed, Bookchin continues, human societies consist
of "an enormous variety of institutions, cultures that can be handed down
from generation to generation" and "technologies that can be redesigned,
innovated, or abandoned." What makes them "particularly unique" is
the fact that "they can be radically changed by their members—and in
ways that can be made to benefit the natural world as well as the human
species."[37]

For Bookchin, this distinctly human development, the evolution of
consciously formed communities, means that human communities cannot, as the deep ecologists argued, be conceived of as solely one part of a
larger "organic whole," or a larger "self." Rather, humanity's social evolution
is distinct as a "*second* nature," a new evolutionary pathway in natural evolution, distinct from nonhuman "*first* nature." However, as we have seen,
Bookchin did not deny that human society remains a product of natural
evolution, "no less than beehives or anthills."[38] To the contrary, for Bookchin, the very things that make humanity a distinct evolutionary path—"a

brain that can think in a richly conceptual manner and produce a highly symbolic form of communication," rendering humanity highly adaptive— are themselves a product of natural evolution. As Bookchin summarised: "Taken together, second nature, the human species that forms it, and the richly conceptual form of thinking and communication so distinctive to it, emerges out of natural evolution no less than any other life-form and nonhuman community. This second nature is uniquely different from first nature [however] in that it can act thinkingly, purposefully, willfully, and depending upon the society we examine, creatively in the best ecological sense or destructively in the worst ecological sense."[39]

This was, then, Bookchin's primary, philosophical objection to deep ecology: that despite the deep ecology claims of working toward an "organic whole" or a "oneness," in which each life-form is valued equally, at its base, this philosophy abstracts humanity from the natural world and natural evolution, and in the process, deifies the natural world into a static, "scenic view." As a result, all of the processes, connections, and indeed the operating procedures of the natural world that produced the human species are lost, rendered unimportant in our understanding of nature as a whole, and the evolution of society in particular.

That is to say, for Bookchin, an understanding of the unfolding of natural evolution as a whole is rendered unimportant in deep ecology, as is (perhaps more importantly) the most advanced expression of this pro- cess as a whole: human society. As Bookchin argued, "a cardinal feature of this product of natural evolution called society is its capacity to intervene in first nature—to alter it . . . in ways that may be eminently creative or destructive."[40] What the deep ecologists failed to see, for Bookchin, was that although human intervention currently *is* destructive, this does not mean it must forever be so. Nor does it lessen humanity's capacity to be creative, and to reduce this creative capacity in the name of biocentrism is to divest humanity of its unique place in natural and social evolution.

A Non-Antagonistic Philosophy of Nature

The claims of Bookchin's "turf war" and disinterest in ecology notwith- standing, by the mid-1980s, Bookchin's thirty-year project of building a philosophy of nature amply qualified him to raise his philosophical objection to deep ecology. Moreover, in the years immediately leading up to Amherst he had fully theorised his view of humanity's place in the natural world. In his essays, "Toward a Philosophy of Nature" (1984), "Freedom and Necessity in Nature" (1986), "Rethinking Ethics, Nature and Society" (1986), and "Thinking Ecologically" (1987), Bookchin had begun to draw together a robust natural philosophy. It is in these works, and his major work, *The Ecology of Freedom* (1982) that we can fully explain his philosophical critique of the deep ecologists and begin to draw out his important contribution to ecological thought.

Traditionally in social thought, Bookchin argued, the relationship between nature and humanity has been conceptualised as antagonistic, the two realms being a priori pitted against one another. First, nature in this traditional view is seen to have "dominated" a pre-historic, pre-agricultural humanity. Subsequently, humanity, in its move toward agriculture and "civilization," increasingly learned the necessary skills and created the necessary technology to dominate nature, to tame nature. "The counterpart of 'domination of nature by man,'" in this view, Bookchin argued, "has been the 'domination of man by nature.'"[41] Marxism and liberalism, for example, "see the former as a desideratum that emerges out of the latter"—that is, the domination of nature by man is seen traditionally as a necessary step toward progress: the "taming" of a wild nature, which has ultimately led to the destruction of nature as a whole by humanity, has forever been seen as the necessary by-product and progenitor of progress.[42]

For Bookchin, deep ecology—although expressly an attempt to overcome this dualistic approach in their calls for biocentric egalitarianism—essentially reproduces this antagonistic view of the nature/humanity relationship. Undoubtedly, as the current extent of the ecological crisis proves, humanity *is* antagonistic to nature, humanity *does* (in some senses at least) dominate the natural world; ultimately to the extent that human exploitation of the natural world leads to the threat of ecological collapse. Moreover, there is no doubt that this requires a radical approach to resolve. However, under the rubric of deep ecology, with its focus on an overly populous humanity, this antagonistic relationship is never really challenged: it simply *is*, and in trying to overcome it, they reduce the uniqueness of both nature and humanity and collapse the two realms into one biotic community in the name of biocentrism.

Both of these viewpoints, therefore, are flawed for Bookchin, not solely in terms of the results they yield, but in the way they are "philosophically structured and worked out," based as they are on an a priori antagonism between human and nonhuman nature.[43] And as noted above, even from his earliest writings, what Bookchin had attempted to do was to formulate a philosophy that would dissolve the dualism which pitted humanity against nature and help to theorise a conception of natural evolution as one mutually cooperative process, of which humanity was at once both a part and a unique differentiation thereof.

For Bookchin, a mode of conceiving of this evolutionary process is required that is ecological, that can ascertain the ecological principles that have produced humanity, a viewpoint that can show that it is "eminently *natural* for humanity to create a second nature from its evolution in first nature," and that these two distinct natures need not be antagonistically opposed in thought or practice, that they are in fact part of one creative evolutionary process.[44] A conceptualisation of a natural philosophy along such lines allows the transcendence of the centricity of biocentrism *or* anthropocentrism and rather sees nature and humanity *holistically*, as distinct parts of one evolutionary continuum.

Though conceding the world "is indeed divided antagonistically, to be remedied by struggle, reconciliation—and transcendence," Bookchin argued that if natural evolution "has any meaning," it is in the fact that it is a continuum "that is graded as well as united," a process of cooperation as well as competition.[45] Fundamentally, for Bookchin, the one approach that can draw out this evolutionary continuum, this notion of a continuity of process from the simplest form of natural evolution to the most complex can only be provided through a *dialectical conception of ecology, and an ecological conception of dialectic.* Here, Bookchin offers a rethinking of both evolution and dialectic, and it is crucial to understanding his philosophy as a whole.

A Dialectical Conception of Ecology

By way of an explanation of his conception of dialectic, Bookchin traces the kind of thought processes required by drawing an analogy with the way "rational and humane" people conceptualise the maturation of the child: there is "a flow" in the child's life, one which is respected to the extent that adults do not put unnecessary demands on the child whilst they are maturing. Moreover, it "requires no unusual perceptive qualities to recognize the infant that lingers on in the child, the child that lingers on in the adolescent, the adolescent that lingers on in the youth, the youth that lingers on in the adult—in short, the *cumulative* nature of their development."[46]

Therefore, the mature adult, for Bookchin, is not a static "inventory of test results and measurements," but in fact is "an individual *biography*, the developmental embodiment of wholly or partially realized qualities."[47] This very same dialectical outlook is required to examine the *cumulative* evolution of nature, and the evolution of society out of that nature, an outlook that clearly identifies the growth, differentiation, maturation, and wholeness of that evolutionary unfolding; in short, an outlook that identifies the "biography" of natural and social evolution.

For Bookchin, this dialectical understanding of the processes of natural evolution allows us to see the evolution of nature and society *as a whole*. This stems from "the power of the dialectic tradition," that "lies *in building up* the differentia of natural and social phenomena from what is implicit in their abstract level." That is to say, that dialectic helps to conceive of the underlying processes of natural evolution as it "tries to *elicit* the development of phenomena from their level of abstract "homogeneity," latent with the rich differentiation that will mark their maturity."[48] In short, this process of differentiation, conceived dialectically, reveals "a 'logic' of evolution," that although producing differentiation, can be conceived of as a unified process.[49]

This dialectical interpretation of the science of ecology, therefore, opens up the possibility of "a concept of evolution as the dialectical development of ever-variegated, complex, and increasingly fecund *contexts* of plant-animal communities" as opposed to "the traditional notion of biological evolution based on the atomistic development of single life forms."[50] These "contexts," more properly, these ecosystems, via the differentiation of the life-forms therein, become increasingly complex and in so doing, "open a greater variety of evolutionary pathways due to their increasingly flexible forms of organic life."[51] This process, again, is conceived of *holistically*, as the holistic differentiation of nature as a whole, not as the evolution of individual species. Here, as nature as a whole differentiates in its evolution, there is for Bookchin a "unity of diversity" in natural evolution as the more complex and flexible life forms result in greater ecological stability.[52]

Moreover, Bookchin argues, through the opening of this greater variety of evolutionary pathways, individual life-forms within an ecosystem, beginning with the very simplest, are presented with "a dim element of choice," and from this, they begin to "exercise an increasingly *active* role in their own evolution."[53] That is to say, as life in general becomes more differentiated within an ecosystem, the individual life-forms begin to *participate* in their further differentiation by "choosing" the newly opened evolutionary pathways: life forms become increasingly complex as a result of their increased participation in their own evolution.

From this, the two key concepts of natural evolution for Bookchin become "participation and differentiation." Rather than the "competition," or the "survival of the fittest" that permeates earlier conceptions of the natural world, Bookchin sees ecocommunities first and foremost as "participatory communities," as "the compensatory manner by which animals and plants foster each other's survival, fecundity, and well-being surpasses the emphasis conventional evolutionary theory places on their 'competition.'" For ecological participation, no matter what form it takes—even on prey or predation—automatically posits a compensatory manner between species of an ecosystem.[54]

This participation, in turn, is the key to fostering the further development of the second key concept, differentiation. Indeed, "the two concepts [participation and differentiation] cannot be raised without leading to interaction with each other."[55] As evolutionary science has shown, the more differentiated an individual ecosystem, the more complex it becomes, and the more stable. Moreover, the more complex and stable the ecosystem, the more complex the individual life-forms themselves become. "The more differentiated a life-form and the environment in which it exists," Bookchin argued, "the more acute is its overall sensorium, the greater its flexibility, and the more active its participation in its own evolution."[56]

In short, this "participatory evolution" for Bookchin, "is the source of an ecosystem's fecundity, of its innovativeness, of its evolutionary potential to create newer, still more complex life forms and biotic relationships . . . a multiplicity of life-forms and organic interrelationships in a biotic community opens new evolutionary interactions, variations, and degrees of flexibility in the capacity to evolve."[57]

Here, for Bookchin, this awareness of participation and differentiation in natural evolution helps us to see that, *"Life is active, interactive, procreative, relational and contextual. . . .* Ever striving and always producing new life-forms, *there is a sense in which life is self-directive in its own evolutionary development."*[58] However, most importantly for his conception of a dialectical evolution, not only does the ever striving toward diversification and complexity instil stability into individual ecosystems, but it can also be seen to be the general thrust of evolution *as a whole.* That is, natural evolution as a whole can be seen to be united by the very "logic of differentiation" and increasing complexity of life itself. As Bookchin argued, "The thrust of biotic evolution over great eras of organic evolution has been toward the increasing diversification of species and their interlocking into highly complex, basically mutualistic relationships, without which the widespread colonization of the planet by life would have been impossible."[59]

Once natural evolution is seen as united by this "logic of differentiation," Bookchin argues that we can begin to trace the dialectical development of increasing complexity that, stemming from the simplest life-forms, would eventually lead to humanity's distinct evolutionary path. As Bookchin explained, in the "ever striving" of life noted above,

> The possibility of freedom and individuation is opened up by the rudimentary forms of self-selection, perhaps even choice, if you will, of the most nascent and barely formed kind that emerges from the increasing complexity of species and their alternate pathways of evolution. Here, without doing violence to the facts, *we can begin to point to a thrust in evolution that contains the potentialities of freedom and individuation.*[60]

In these rudimentary forms of self-selection, moreover, Bookchin maintained that we find the emergence of a "sense of self-identity, however germinal, from which nature begins to acquire its rudimentary subjectivity."[61] This "rudimentary subjectivity," derives first from any life-form's "metabolic process of self-maintenance"—that is, from its participation in evolution as a matter of biological survival. However, this subjectivity extends itself beyond self-maintenance "to become a *striving* activity, not unlike the development from the vegetative to the animative, that ultimately yields mind, will, and the potentiality for freedom."[62]

For Bookchin, this "striving of life toward a greater complexity of selfhood—a striving that yields increasing degrees of subjectivity—constitutes the internal or immanent impulse of evolution toward growing self-awareness." This evolutionary dialectic, moreover, "constitutes the essence of life as a self-maintaining organism that bears the potential for a self-conscious organism."[63] Here, ultimately finding its (current) most complex expression in humanity, the thrust of natural evolution—its "biography," to return to our opening analogy—can be seen to be a thrust toward a nature that is rendered increasingly self-reflexive and self-conscious. Ultimately, then, for Bookchin, the application of dialectic to ecology, freed of any earlier interpretations, "explains, with a power beyond that of any conventional wisdom how the organic flow of first into second nature is a re-working of biological reality into social reality."[64]

An Ecological Interpretation of Dialectic

Before turning to examine what this dialectic of evolution means for Bookchin's conception of humanity's place in nature, we need to examine Bookchin's counterpart to dialectic understanding of ecology: that is, the effect of ecology on dialectic as a method of thought. For Bookchin, evolution itself, now understood dialectically as an ever-present continuum, provides a new ground on which to base an ethics for society and nature.[65] That is to say, that in nature's striving toward increasingly complex and ultimately self-conscious life-forms, natural evolution provides a *potentiality* on which norms can be built. This striving, originating from the "dim choices" faced by the simplest of life-forms and flowing through to complex, conceptual thought and the conscious forming of human communities, provides a *dialectical potentiality* on which to ground these norms. These norms, in fact, can then be formulated as "the actualization of the potential 'is'" of natural evolution "into an ethical 'ought' . . . anchored in the *objective reality of potentiality itself.*"[66]

For Bookchin, dialectic is a speculative philosophy that is "creative by ceaselessly contrasting the free, rational, and moral actuality of 'what-could-be'... with the existential reality of 'what is.'"[67] That is to say, present "reality" can constantly be compared, contrasted, and critiqued in light of the acknowledgment of an existential, objective potentiality. Under an *ecological* interpretation of dialectic, this potentiality, which provides the grounds for an ethical notion of the "what could be," is seen to inhere most fundamentally "in nature's thrust toward self-reflexivity," which now provides a radical and far-reaching contrast to the current "is" of the irrational anti-ecological society.[68] Therefore, the unity in diversity, the logic of differentiation—elicited from a dialectical understanding of ecology and evolution, as discussed above—reflects back onto dialectic itself, providing the grounds for "an ecological ethics in the actualization of the potential . . . the grounds for a genuinely objective ethics" in the objectification of this evolutionary potential.[69]

Furthermore, Bookchin argues that not only does ecology provide the ground for dialectically situating an objective ethics on the potentialities therein, but in its focus on the basic premises of natural evolution—that growth, change, diversification never reach an endpoint but are ever-present—it divests dialect of its earlier teleological interpretations. The evolutionary reality that "the mature and the whole are never so complete that they cease to be the potentiality for a still further development, represents an *ecological change* in dialectic."[70] In this ecological dialectic, therefore, based on a logic of constant differentiation, there is "no terminality that could culminate in a 'God' or an 'Absolute'" as dialectic did for Hegel, nor for that matter, in a more material endpoint as was the case for Marx and Engels.[71] Therefore, for Bookchin, by bringing "nature into the foreground of dialectical thought, in an evolutionary and organismic way," ecology, "can ventilate the dialectic as an orientation toward the objective world by rendering it coexistent with natural evolution."[72]

For Bookchin, then, this ecological dialectic differs from its idealistic or materialistic predecessors because it neither sees the ultimate subsuming of the contradictions of being in a perfect absolutism, as did Hegel, or in a mechanical resolution, as did Marx and Engels. Rather, it sees the contradictions of being as an ever-present continuum in the ever-increasing diversification of life forms, in the ever more forms of complexity, and in the increasing participation of life forms in their own evolution, a process stemming from the most unconscious of beings to the conscious ability of humankind—not, in fact, a striving toward perfection in an ultimate absolute.

The Lessons of Ecology Lost

What, therefore, does our examination of Bookchin's detailed philosophy of nature tell us of his philosophical objection to deep ecology in 1987? For Bookchin, under this conceptual marriage of ecology and dialectic—under this *dialectical naturalism*—our conception of humanity and its relationship to nature begins to change. Nature and humanity are no longer conceived of as largely antagonistic: nature is no longer the stingy necessitarian world which dominates humanity unless humanity dominates it. Although never a "realm of freedom," Bookchin argues, "nature is not reducible to an equally fictitious 'realm of necessity.'"[73] Rather, the natural world begins to open itself to the dialectical ecologist as the creative and ever-present continuum of humanity, historically and in terms of future action. Equally, humanity must no longer, by necessity, dominate and exploit nature in the move toward civilization. Rather, the unique capabilities of humanity, derivative of the natural world, become a realm of potentially creative interaction with nature.

This view, for Bookchin, permits a focus on "nature's fecundity, on its thrust toward increasing variety, on its limitless capacity to differentiate life-forms and its development of richer, more varied evolutionary pathways that steadily involve ever more complex species," rather than the combative nature that confronts humanity in earlier social theories.[74] The emergence of humanity for Bookchin is no longer premised on an escape from this harsh natural world, but is a direct product of it. These factors of natural evolution, indeed, "extend from nature directly into society," as looking back in time "we find that the history of society deliciously grades out of the history of life without either being subsumed by the other."[75]

This process of natural evolution as a whole, then, ultimately provides "certain premises" for the emergence of social life, "the institutionalization of the animal community into a potentially rational, self-governing form of association."[76] Moreover, it contains the potentialities for freedom and individuation, and further, this thrust in humanity itself, "owing to the ever-greater complexity of the nervous system and brain," also contains the necessary processes for *"the emergence of reason itself."*[77] For Bookchin then, this "ensemble of ideas" provides "the basis for an ecological ethics which sees the emergence of selfhood, reason, and freedom *from* nature—not in sharp opposition *to* nature."[78]

All of this forms the basis of Bookchin's philosophical objection to deep ecology: that humanity, the human intellect and human reason, and the rest of the characteristics that make humanity unique, are not alien to natural evolution, but are solely one end of the continuum of evolution that inheres in all of nature: that is, that humanity in all its forms, creative *and* destructive, is a direct product of natural evolution. In the reduction of this important process in deep ecology, where humanity *as such* is seen as a blight on the natural world, humanity is removed from its place in natural evolution, and this abstracted humanity is subordinated to a static nature. Here, all of the attendant lessons of the processes of natural evolution are lost as humanity is divested of its potentiality to play a continuing part is this evolutionary continuum.

Ultimately for Bookchin, the most important lesson lost under the rubric of deep ecology is the unique ability of humanity not only to play a passive role in the continuum of evolution but in fact, the unique ability that humanity has *to now be aware of that continuum and guide it toward the fulfilment of its own latent potentiality*. That is to say, that although not fully developed, the human ability to be aware of the processes of evolution represents a nature that is aware of itself, that can grasp its own movement from the simple to the complex, a development that "renders humanity *potentially* the most self-conscious and self-reflexive expression of that natural development."[79]

This potentiality, of course, represents no "predetermined inevitability" for Bookchin, only ever a potentiality. This potentiality is the latent capability of all life forms to develop to their fullest: from the potential of an acorn to become an oak tree, or for the human embryo to become a mature adult. However, it still remains only one potentiality among many; it contains only "a message of freedom, not of necessity; it speaks to an immanent striving for realization, not a predetermined certainty of completion."[80] Further still, though this natural potentiality is the ground on which Bookchin proposes to build his ecological ethics, there is no certainty *as such* of the ethical value of nature for Bookchin. Nature is not ethical or unethical; moreover, nor does it "possess the power of conceptualization" in the way humanity does (and which is the only way to formulate an ethics) and therefore nature can only ever be "a ground for ethics, not ethical *as such*."[81]

However, *if* this potential was fully realised, *if* an ethics could be built thereon that would enable the fulfilment of this potentiality, human intelligence could become fully aware of its own natural evolution and the potentiality therein. In so doing, Bookchin argued, human intellection would "'fold back' upon the evolutionary continuum that exists in first nature. In this sense—and in this sense alone—second nature would thus *become* first nature rendered self-conscious, a thinking nature that would know itself and could guide its own evolution," a society and culture that could "consciously express the abiding tendency within first nature to press itself toward the level of thought and conscious self-directiveness."[82]

Finally, natural evolution, fully aware of itself in the form of a humanity that had fulfilled its potentiality, could create a fully ecological society, wherein humanity and nature retained their specificity yet mutually reinforced each other: nature would re-enter humanity in the lessons of a full understanding of natural evolution, and humanity would re-enter nature as the most conscious guide of its immanent striving.[83] In this sense, for Bookchin, a human-led,

> ecological society would be a transcendence of both first nature and second nature into the new domain of a *free* nature, a nature that could reach the level of conceptual thought—in *short, a nature that would willfully and thinkingly cope with conflict, contingency, waste and compulsion.* . . . Humanity, far from diminishing the integrity of nature, would add the dimension of freedom, reason and ethics to first nature and raise evolution to a level of self-reflexivity that has always been latent in the emergence of the natural world.[84]

It is this potentiality of humanity to create a transcendence of the separation between humanity and the natural world, wherein humanity is seen as separate from nature *only in the sense that it is its most conscious expression*, and can thus serve as a guide of nature as a whole—can build an ecological ethics, can construct a society on these ethics, can "fold back" its consciousness as an expression of the creative processes that created it—that characterises the entirety of Bookchin's ecological philosophy.

Under this schema, humanity is conceived of not as sat at the apex of evolution as a whole as a *dominating* force, but by dint of its position as the most complex expression of, as a potential conscious guide of nature as a whole. Both human and nonhuman nature conceived in this holistic sense, according to Bookchin, points to the fact that a genuine ecological ethics, a genuine project to build an ecological society, "definitely involves *human stewardship of the planet,*" in an attempt to construct "a radical integration of second nature with first," and an "abiding ecological sensibility that embodies nature's thrust toward self-reflexivity."[85]

On closer inspection of Bookchin's exchange with the deep ecologists, then, two things become immediately clear. First, and despite the existence of the extraordinary body of literature that makes up the deep ecology response to Bookchin, discussed in Chapter 1, it is clear that Bookchin's critique in 1987 was not only a rich and detailed critique of the conceptual problems of deep ecology but was also a coherent expression of his own philosophical principles, principles he had formulated over the previous three decades. Therefore, rather than explainable as the result of "sour grapes" on Bookchin's behalf, or as an attempt to corner the ecology movement, as his deep ecology critics would have it, it makes much more sense to view his critique as such an expression and to put it to the test objectively. Unfortunately the nature of the responses in 1987 obscured this possibility and as such, prevented a genuine engagement with Bookchin's ideas.

Second, as our discussion has shown, these philosophical principles in fact render Bookchin's version of ecology much "deeper" than deep ecology itself. Bookchin's philosophy of nature, as we have seen, allows us to conceive of humanity and nature as separate but complementary differentiations of nature as a whole. That is, Bookchin allows for a transcendence of the antagonistic relationship between humanity and nature in both thought and practice. He does so through a dialectical focus on the "graded continuum" of evolution, a constant unfolding of increasing complexity and diversity that links the simplest life forms to the same process that produced complex human society. As such, humanity becomes neither pitted against nature nor subsumed in the name of biocentrism: humanity is solely one part of nature, but has a potentiality to be a fully conscious expression of that nature, and as such has the capacity to create a free nature in the form of a rational ecological society.

We turn to a full examination of precisely how Bookchin argues this is to be achieved in due course. For the present, however, we need now turn to a task that the literature that surrounded Bookchin and his philosophy of nature since 1987 has precluded in the past: a full and critical examination of Bookchin's ecological philosophy. To do so, we turn to some of the more robust critiques of the ecology of Bookchin, critiques themselves that have also not received sufficient attention, lost as they were in the noise of the initial exchange between Bookchin and the deep ecologists.

Chapter 3

Reassessing Bookchin's Philosophy of Nature

Despite the problematic nature of the response to Bookchin's 1987 critique of deep ecology, despite the clear lack of engagement with Bookchin's ideas therein, and despite the fact that, as we have seen, his critique pointed to the very real wider problems of the deep ecology movement, based on his own rich and robust formulation of an ecological philosophy, when one first encounters Bookchin, none of this is immediately apparent. Indeed, the accusations of Bookchin's desire to attack, his initiation of an ideological turf war, and perhaps most problematically, his outdated, old fashioned "Leftist" sectarianism, permeate not only the literature of the time, but also shaped and formed the literature that would emerge throughout the 1990s. We turn to this in Chapter 6, but it is worth noting here that the same terminology—of attack, of turf war, of Bookchin's "Old Leftism"—is everywhere to be found, and consolidates the caricature of Bookchin as a divisive and flawed theorist.

For the present however, there is another sense in which the deep ecology response affects Bookchin and his work: such was the force and tone of the response (and of Bookchin's response thereto), such was its elevation of Bookchin's personal failings above theoretical engagement, that the opportunity to ask the very real and pressing questions of his philosophy was lost in the noise. Indeed, in some places, these questions *were* asked, as will be shown, and have indeed been asked since, but it is argued here that a full appreciation of them has been denied as the fundamental debate that lies at the heart of Bookchin's disagreement with the deep ecologists—the question of how to conceive of humanity's place not only in the world of life but in a response to the ecological crisis—was largely subsumed over what was passed off largely as an ideological turf war.

The current chapter is an attempt to redress this imbalance in approaches to Bookchin and his philosophy of nature. Returning to the more robust philosophical critiques of Bookchin that were offered at the time and that have been offered since, we attempt to extricate them for the more problematic literature on Bookchin and the caricature it engenders. Moreover, we point out as we go that even though the critiques we look at here are more robust than the 1987 response to Bookchin, there is still evidence that they are partly infused by the ad hominem approaches to Bookchin, showing clearly the extent of the Bookchin caricature. That said, there are indeed valuable contributions to be found amongst the critical literature, contributions that help to shed light on Bookchin's positions. Ultimately, however, we find that his unique philosophical programme as a whole, after having been put to a rigorous test, still stands as a unique and important contribution to ecological thought.

To do so, it is argued here that across the more robust critiques of the philosophy of Bookchin as a whole, we can discern two main strands. The first is a matter of methodology: there are important questions raised about the validity of Bookchin's particular use of dialectic, his *dialectical naturalism*. The second is a matter of content: questions concerning Bookchin's conception of natural and social evolution. In the first strand, Bookchin's projection of a future ecological society, of a "free nature" based on the creative potentiality he sees in natural evolution is called into question. In the second line of critique, it is the actual *content* of this potentiality: serious questions are asked of Bookchin's notion of a complementary and creative nature that leads to increasing complexity, and ultimately produces humanity as its most advanced form. As such, his central notion of human stewardship of the planet as a whole is also called into question. We return to this second strand below, but we start here with the questions of methodology.

Questions of Methodology

As discussed in Chapter 2, at the heart of the Bookchin dialectic lies the potentiality Bookchin sees in natural evolution upon which we can base an objective ecological ethics, a blueprint for a new, ecological society. For Bookchin, this potentiality is evidenced by the diversity, mutual relationships, complementarity and the tendency toward increasing complexification found in the natural world. This nexus of relationships links natural and social evolution into the one "graded continuum," from the most simple to the most complex. Moreover, this process has produced humanity itself, as the most complex and adaptable life form; has produced a "second nature" that can reflect upon itself and the processes from which it emerged.

It is this "directionality" in nature—this movement of nature as a whole from the simple to the complex—that Bookchin traces throughout natural and social evolution and uses as the basis on which to build his normative philosophical and political programme. It is in this tendency in the natural world that Bookchin identifies an objective *potentiality* for an ecological society, and the place where norms can be situated in the bringing about of this society. As Bookchin explained, "from the ever-greater complexity and variety that raises sub-atomic particles through the course of evolution to those conscious, self-reflexive life forms we call human beings, we cannot help but speculate about the existence of a broadly conceived *telos* and a latent subjectivity in substance itself that eventually yields mind and intellectuality."[1]

From this, Bookchin formulates his normative philosophy as the process of the intellectual and political development of this *telos*, "the actualization of the potential 'is'" that inheres in this nexus of processes of natural evolution, "into the ethical 'ought' . . . anchored in the *objective reality of potentiality itself*," and it is here where we can examine some key problems with this position, as outlined by more sober critiques of Bookchin that would emerge throughout the 1990s.[2] The most challenging of these critiques would raise objections to the very way in which Bookchin formulated this normative basis for his ethics. As argued by Eckersley, Bookchin's "claim that his ethics has discerned the true telos of nature is highly contentious and cannot perform the work of shoring up his ethics in the way he would like."[3] This contentiousness, moreover, "is apparent from his very method of reasoning." As she explains,

> Bookchin's ethical naturalism rejects the sharp fact/value divide of hypothetico-deductive logic by insisting that ethics *is* part

of, or at least implied by, the natural world. Judgements about
the "goodness" of an action are seen to be factual or objective
judgements about what is conducive to the fulfilment of certain
natural ends or tendencies. Evolutionary biology and ecology are
treated as both objective and normative sciences in that they not
only tell us what reality is like, but also provide a "deep wisdom" as
to what we ought to value.[4]

In this sense, Eckersley continues, Bookchin is untroubled by the "Achilles'
Heel" of academic environmental ethics," namely, "the logical difficulties associated with deriving an 'ought' from an 'is.'"[5] That is, in reading
into nature to find the "is" of natural evolution, Bookchin has derived an
"ought"; from the science of natural evolution, Bookchin derives values.
However, these two things—the operating procedures of nature and a
set of human ethics—are distinctly different, and worked out in different
ways. The operating procedures of nature can never be an a priori guide
on which to base a set of values: the often "blind" choices of the natural
world cannot be equated or linked to the conscious establishing of values
and ethics in the human world: traditionally, this nature has been conceived as holding no moral direction.

Indeed, this is a problem that Bookchin seems to have himself
engendered, yet not addressed in his own philosophical programme. As
discussed, Bookchin's attempt to transcend the separation (and antagonism) between humanity and nature is based on the notion of natural
evolution as one continuous movement from the simple to the complex.
However, this single process has produced the differentiation of the social
world out of the natural world, of second out of first nature, and Bookchin continually points out that it is only this complex and self-conscious
second nature that can conceptualise so thoroughly its own behaviour,
can reflect consciously on the values of the societies they form. As we have
seen, there may be rudimentary choices in the natural world, yet they are
only ever "dim" choices for Bookchin. Thus on the one hand does Bookchin draw out the complexity of human second nature in explicit contrast
to the "muteness" of the nonhuman first nature, yet at the same time,
appeals to this mute realm for the place to situate an ecological ethics.

Does Bookchin therefore transgress his own central conceptualisation of value in the natural world by claiming it contains directionality

or a striving for complexity whilst at the same time viewing nature as the realm of the relatively simple? Is it theoretically sound to invoke the facts of natural evolution as a ground for an objective ethics if, as Bookchin claims, that natural evolution is largely unaware of itself? Even if Bookchin's nexus of relationships in the natural world can be proven to be true, the non-conscious element of the natural world which Bookchin describes renders these relationships *valueless*. That is, if nature is as "dim" as Bookchin claims, then the existence of a nexus of complementary relationships in fact tells us nothing about the *value* of these relationships: they exist "unconsciously," and follow no plan. As Eckersley points out, "it is not enough to invoke the authority of nature as known by science, since even if Bookchin is right in his argument that there is a telos in nature, this discovery in itself does not tell us why we ought to further it."[6]

As such, it is argued, Bookchin's "ought," derived from the "is" of the operating procedures of the natural world, has no basis in fact. However, to make this criticism is to misunderstand Bookchin's particular use of dialectic, both as a way of reasoning and as a political tool. For Bookchin, the dialectic is a speculative philosophy, that, when applied to natural evolution, can "elicit the development of phenomena from their level of abstract homogeneity" toward "the differentiation that will mark their maturity."[7] That is, out of the "blind" homogenous abstraction that is nature as a whole, an ecological dialectic draws out from living beings in their multifarious differentiations the processes that unite them, the shared characteristics of their evolution. In this sense, Bookchin's use of the dialectic is purposively set toward blurring the differences between the "is" and the "ought": it looks at the "is" of natural evolution and *purposively* pulls out the "ought" from the unity inherent in nature's continuous differentiation and complexification.

Moreover, Bookchin was explicit in his use of dialectic, this purposive subversion of the logical problems that surround the is/ought separation, his wilful and direct challenge to this apparent "Achilles' Heel" of environmental philosophy. This separation, for Bookchin,

> would deny speculative thought the right to reason from the "what-is" to the "what-should-be." This positivistic mousetrap is not a problem in logic as it is a problem in ethics and the right of the

ethical "ought" to enjoy objective status. . . . Speculative philosophy
is by definition a claim by reason to extend itself beyond the given
state of affairs, whether one refers to Plato's exemplary domain of
forms or Marx and Kropotkin's visions of a co-operative society.
To remain within the "is" in the name of logical consistency is to deny
reason the right to assert goals, values, and social relationships that
provide a voice to the claims of ecology as a social discipline.[8]

That is to say, that Bookchin's methodology *as such* is carefully chosen to
subvert this apparent problem in logic: his use of the dialectic to investigate the potentialities in natural evolution is based both on an objective
reading of the science of ecology *and* on the political act of providing a
theoretical way around the problems of philosophy that remains solely
within the "is" and not the "ought." Indeed, Bookchin argues that to raise
this methodological criticism of dialectic misses the fundamental point
that dialectic itself "is an ongoing protest against the myth of methodology; notably, that the techniques for thinking out a process can be
separated from the process itself."[9]

In this sense, we must keep in mind Bookchin's holism in terms of
his view of the natural world and the social, his view of the graded continuum of natural evolution. As will be discussed in more detail below,
Bookchin's differentiation between the most complex expression of
nature in the consciousness of humanity in contrast to the most simple of
life forms does not privilege one or the other. They are inseparable parts
of the same processes, and therefore under the Bookchin schema, the "is"
of their existence, and the "is" of the processes that join them together,
created not only their material reality but the ability of nature's most conscious expression (humanity) to identify this reality and ground a value
thereon. That is, that the ability to think and theorise and value facts is as
an important part of the same process that produced these facts, and cannot be denied its importance in the name of methodological consistency.

Therefore, Bookchin's philosophical basis does not solely reject this
is/ought separation in natural philosophy, as Eckersley argues, but offers
a conscious and direct challenge to it. As Albrecht has argued here, Bookchin's entire project "runs counter to the central elements . . . that create the
logic and structure of the problem," and as such, he does "not find the is/
ought problem intimidating."[10] Out of the processes of natural evolution

and the potentiality discernible therein, Bookchin speculates as to what these could and should mean for the creation of an ecological society, and in doing so attempts to form an objective ground for his ethics.

Indeed, under this image, nature is denuded of its traditional static image, as a strictly "blind" nature. Yes, Bookchin notes that there are largely "unconscious elements in the natural world, but when viewed as part of the same cumulative process that ends (for the time being) with the consciousness of humanity, Bookchin argues, this earlier blind nature, under the cumulative processes of evolution, can be seen not to be "a static vision of the natural world but the long, indeed cumulative, *history* of natural development . . . toward ever more varied, differentiated, and complex forms and relationships."[11]

In this sense, the view of a mute or blind nature—which *does* exist for Bookchin—does not come to represent the *whole* of nature, nor does it float free of the rest of evolution as a whole. On the contrary, the most simple, the most dimly subjective elements of the natural world are placed on the continuum where blind nature, lacking any moral direction, eventually "turns into "free nature," a nature that slowly finds a voice and a means to relieve the needless tribulations of life for all species in a highly conscious humanity and an ecological society."[12] Therefore, these facts of natural evolution, as unthinking as they may be in the most simple of life forms and evolutionary processes, are directly linked to the ethics Bookchin places on this evolutionary process *as a whole*.

It should, however, be noted here that Bookchin does not see the *telos* of nature in itself as ethical. That is to say, that because Bookchin draws out the cumulative process of evolution as evidence of a *telos*, a tendency of increasing complexity and creativity in natural evolution on which to base his ethics, this does not automatically posit ethics *in* nature itself. Bookchin is not reading his ethics as a *fact* of nature, but solely as *grounded* on a *potentiality*, elicited by speculative thought, that can be found in its natural processes. That is, contrary to Eckersley's claim that Bookchin is "insisting that ethics *is* part of, or at least implied by, the natural world," nature for Bookchin can never be a "source" of ethics, as it does not possess the "volition . . . does not have will in the human sense of the term nor does it possess the power of conceptualization" needed to form an ethics.[13] In this sense, Bookchin stressed that nature can only ever be "a ground for ethics, not ethical *as such*."[14]

However, if it can be argued that Bookchin successfully circumvents the criticism that he blurs the is/ought separation in the way he uses his speculative philosophy to discern the continuum of natural evolution from natural fact to human formulations of value, the criticism itself raises a secondary, potentially more substantial problem. Briefly put, if Bookchin is justified in basing his ethics on the potentiality found in natural evolution, then so too is anyone else. That is to say, what makes the potentiality that Bookchin discerns *the* potentiality of nature? Could it be argued that there is a tendency not only for increasing complexity, subjectivity, consciousness, and reason in the natural world but also for the predation, conflict, and tendency for destruction so characteristic of natural, but particularly social history?

In this sense, it can be argued that Bookchin's dialectical method-ology falls down more fundamentally in its claims to objectivity, of its elevation of *his* version of the way natural evolution unfolds above any other version. As Eckersley asked, "can it be said that there exists some objective standard of fulfilment latent within human society itself, urging it toward mind and truth [as Bookchin contends]?" If this is the case, then what of the other possibilities latent in natural evolution, "why are not *all* of the myriad potential paths of human development also objective and desirable ones in Bookchin's sense?" "What is it," she continues, "about Bookchin's evolutionary path of mutuality, diversity, and advancing sub-jectivity that makes it the good and true path?"[15]

For Eckersley, there is nothing to validate Bookchin's claim of a liberatory potentiality in natural evolution over the more destructive tendencies that can be seen in the natural world: as she argues, "the actu-alisation of Hitler's potential is no less 'real' than that of Mother Teresa's," as attested to by the historical record.[16] This same criticism was also lev-elled at Bookchin by Alexander, who argues that Bookchin's defence of his use of "speculative philosophy" and his concurrent claim that through this he can discern an objective ground for an objective ethics "fails to acknowledge that there is no authoritative and 'objective' tribune which can render judgment as to the authentic nature of potentiality and rea-son." Indeed, he argues that Bookchin's insistence in rooting his ethics in an objective potentiality of natural evolution "would be just as imag-inable as coming out of the mouth of Stalin," albeit to radically different ends.[17]

Moreover, Alexander argues that when Bookchin writes that "past, present and future are cumulatively graded processes that [only] thought can truly interpret and render meaningful," just exactly *"whose* thought" will be assigned this role "is a relevant question to ask." He continues that "different individuals and groups—not to mention people in different historical epochs—will interpret past and present phenomena in various ways, depending on their socially constructed and historically relevant experiences." From this, to claim, as Bookchin does, that solely the interpretations of processes in evolutionary history as Bookchin understands them is, like the Marxists before him, to claim that only his dialectical naturalism—impervious to time—presents "the one true dialectical creed," and therefore "endowing dialectical naturalists with a superior understanding of natural and social reality."[18]

It is true indeed that Bookchin could not claim divinity over what is the "one true path" of natural evolution; but importantly, he did not claim to. Throughout his philosophical works, he would draw analogies with developmental processes in natural evolution as indicative of his conception of the latent potentiality in nature. As discussed in the previous chapter, Bookchin often drew an analogy with the development of a child, and the acknowledgment of the potentially rounded adult that is latent within (see Chapter 2). Elsewhere, Bookchin would extend the analogy to include the potentiality for a conscious human being that inheres inside the human embryo; in other places, he follows Hegel and uses the analogy of the latent flower that lies dormant in the bud; and elsewhere still, he draws the similarities between the potentiality of reaching an ecological society and the oak tree that objectively exists as a potentiality inside the acorn.[19]

However, in all of these cases, Bookchin stresses that the existence of the potentiality does not automatically mean it will necessarily be fulfilled. As he argued in 1996, "that what may be brought forth [through dialectical reason] is not necessarily developed: an acorn, for example, may become food for a squirrel or wither on a concrete sidewalk, rather than develop into what it is potentially constituted to become—notably, an oak tree."[20] However, the continual unfolding of increasing complexity that inheres in all of nature and is common to the analogies Bookchin draws still remains as one potentiality amongst many. As such, it contains *only* "a message of freedom, not of necessity; *it speaks to an immanent striving for realization, not a predetermined certainty of completion.*"[21] Society too, for Bookchin is, like the acorn, "potentially constituted to become" an ecologically rational society—but only *potentially*. It is only through the conscious grounding of an ethics on this potentiality that what is latent has a chance of becoming a reality.

Moreover, Bookchin was even more specific about the existence of counter trends in natural evolution: he argued that, of course, in the natural world "coercion does exist . . . so does pain and suffering."[22] Furthermore, the capacity for the emergence of these conditions could be termed a potentiality and an ethics built thereon, as has happened in the past, most vividly, for example (and returning to Eckersley's example), with the fascism of Hitler. But as far as a *telos* is concerned, as far as a *continuum* of development, the act of being as a process of becoming that lies at the heart of dialectic interpretation, these characteristics cannot be seen to form a complex nexus of relationships that represent the development of one stage of being to another. As the coercion of one particular ecosystem by a pest will lead to its collapse, the policies of a Hitler or a Stalin will lead to social collapse: not regeneration, rebirth, or transcendence.

Therefore, the existence of other potentialities is conceded by Bookchin. However, as he explains in an unpublished manuscript, Bookchin argues that the very "task of dialectical thinking is to separate the rational from the arbitrary, external, and adventitious in which it unfolds, an endeavor that demands considerable intellectual courage as well as insight."[23] In comparison to the continuous natural and social directionality toward increasing complexity and cooperation, the instances of coercion in the natural and social world appear sporadic: they do not provide enough material, according to Bookchin, from which a potentiality can genuinely be elicited. He argued, therefore, that coercion can more properly be thought of as a *capacity* that inheres in natural evolution, rather than a potentiality.

Moreover, according to Albrecht, the discipline of evolutionary science seems to bear the Bookchin thesis out. Here, it can be seen that even if there is contradictory evidence of alternative capacities, or even potentialities, in natural evolution it is not enough to weaken the potentiality that Bookchin appeals to. For Albrecht, evolutionary science points to the fact that although Bookchin's theoretical claim could be contradicted by evidence of opposing examples, "the historical totality of life and the process that generates it are what the claim is about." In this sense, "Particular instances in evolutionary and ecological relationships that seem to contradict the [Bookchin] thesis can be overcome by *a more powerful general and long-term tendency of increasing complexity and diversity*. Not even occasional catastrophes in nature that produce, for example, mass extinctions of species can negate the long term direction. When evolution recommences, it can be shown that it again moves in the direction of increasing complexity and diversity."[24] Therefore, the movement of evolution as a whole, based on the science of evolution, according to Albrecht, closely matches Bookchin's description of the graded continuum of increasing complexity and diversity. It should be noted that there *are* problems with Bookchin's presentation of the complexity thesis for Albrecht—his conceptual basis for his thesis is "inadequate," as Bookchin offers no detailed discussion "of how complex structures emerge and are reproduced over time."[25] Moreover, Albrecht continues, "it is evident that Bookchin does not provide enough detail about the foundations of, and crucial terms in, his directionality thesis" as a whole.[26] However, these do not negate his theory for Albrecht: that is, although Bookchin fails to produce enough evidence for his complexity theory, it does not mean it does not exist. On the contrary, "there is continuing general support from within science for the view that there is directionality in nature toward the increasingly diverse and complex."[27]

Indeed, Albrecht continues that, based on evidence from the fossil record, it is clear that there is an "increasing diversity and complexity of species and ecosystems over time," matching perfectly Bookchin's two central evolutionary concepts. In terms of *complexity*, "the fossil record shows that there has been a sequence of developments on life from the simple to the complex."[28] Albrecht continues:

> The Monera, or single-celled organisms, have evolved into other, more complex kingdoms, such as the Fungi, Plantae, and Animalia over great time. From the Triassic through to the Pleistocene epochs, life has manifested a tendency to produce more complex organisms. The genetic and anatomical structure of mammals represents the most complex form of life that has been known; humans, while they share 98% of the their genes with their closest relatives, the great

apes, are the leading edge of the evolution of the brain into new dimensions of complexity.[29]

In terms of *diversity*, Albrecht argues that, "according to our best information at the present time, there are between 5 and 100 million species existing on the planet" and because, despite the periods of mass extinction, there has been over time an increase in the rate of speciation as compared to the rate of extinction, "we can therefore conclude that biodiversity has increased over evolutionary history." Moreover, Albrecht continues that "increasing complexity and diversity in nature is not simply a philosophic assertion; *it is supported by the best scientific evidence available.*" This evidence, stemming largely from the emerging scientific discipline of "complexity theory," Albrecht argues, can be used in "a potentially fertile union" with social ecology "that begins to counter the major objections to Bookchin's work."[30]

Although it is beyond the remit of the current work to offer a full examination of this scientific backing, it is important to note: to the arguments addressing why Bookchin's potentiality should be any more evident than any other potentiality, one would be hard pushed to find such a consistent *pattern* in natural evolution other than complexification and diversification. Again, although Albrecht concedes that Bookchin does not adequately address the scientific backing for his claims, this doesn't mean he can be so easily dismissed. Indeed, Albrecht implores critics of Bookchin to look at the science "before any comprehensive dismissal of Bookchin's position is attempted," as "the combined insights of Bookchin's dialectical naturalism, eco-evolutionary science, and complexity theory provide an expanded foundation on which to build a more theoretically sophisticated social ecology."[31]

However, Bookchin's lack of an adequate conceptual basis, identified here by Albrecht, is indeed a criticism that needs to be taken into account: a more detailed reasoning from Bookchin on the empirical basis of the directionality he sees in nature could have, in many ways, preempted the criticism that he had no grounds for his dialectical naturalism and that as such, like the teleologists of the past, that he simply stated his position as "the one true dialectical creed," based on nothing but what *he* felt society *ought* to be. In truth, as we have seen, Bookchin *does* have the grounds for that which he bases his ethics on, but it can be argued that he failed to convey these grounds sufficiently in his work. For example, to return to Bookchin's analogous approach to explaining the processes he saw as making up his dialectical potentiality, various critics would pick up on the non-scientific simplicity of such an approach.

According to Eckersley, Bookchin's analogous approach is "both telling and problematic."[32] Eckersley argues that the analogies Bookchin draws are too simplistic: "the similarities between an acorn and a human embryo," she contends, "are essentially confined to the growth patterns of the physical organism; they tell us nothing about consciousness or about what humans may properly value or do with their hands and tools." For Eckersley, "The analogy thus begs the question as to what characterises a mature and fulfilled adult psychologically, intellectually, and ethically. More importantly, there are very real limits to the extent to which the 'objective' developmental path of an acorn can be reasonably compared with that of the human species as a whole and, in particular, with the immensely more complex and open-ended phenomenon we call human society."[33]

In a later critique, John Clark would make the same claim, albeit using yet another analogy sketched by Bookchin.[34] In the Introduction to the second edition of his collection of philosophical essays, Bookchin argued that "an egg patently and empirically exists, even though the bird whose potential it contains has yet to develop and reach maturity. Just so, the given potentiality of any process exists and constitutes the basis for a process that should be realized. Hence, the potentiality does exist objectively, even in empirical terms."[35]

Of course, the implication here is that the immanent unfolding of an ecological society can also be said to objectively exist as a potentiality, even in empirical terms. However, Clark argues that "it does not seem to have occurred to Bookchin that there is a crucial difference between determining the potentialities of a bird's egg and determining those inherent in a social phenomenon, a social practice, a social institution, or a social order." Moreover,

The biological development of members of various bird species has been observed innumerable times, and certain well-grounded generalizations can be made based on observed regularity. And of course there is the fact that we know quite a bit about ornithology and reproductive biology. On the other hand, specific social phenomena are historically conditioned in enormously complex ways . . . there are no strictly analogous cases that can be observed as a basis for empirical generalizations, and there is, in fact, no science of society with the predictive powers of natural science.[36]

For both Clark and Eckersley then, there is nothing within the Bookchin analogies that can tell us about the potentiality for society to evolve at all, let alone along rational lines: the simple biological reality of natural evolution cannot help to explain the extremely complex processes of social evolution. Such "groundless speculation," for Clark, is at best a "description of certain apparent tendencies abstracted from the context of a vast multitude of variables and of complex and often mutually contradictory developments," and as such, Bookchin "presents no evidence of how he would establish a normative basis on which to judge that any particular development of humanity constitutes what 'should be.'"[37]

Again, the criticism of Bookchin's simplicity in explaining the basis of his dialectic potentiality is conceded here, but two qualifications must be made. First, as argued by Biehl, these types of botanical illustrations were never "the centerpiece of Bookchin's philosophy"; rather, they were drawn out as one small illustration in discussion of the general idea of dialectic.[38] For Bookchin, drawing out the process in society that followed this general idea—as his entire body of work on anthropology, history, and political forms shows (as we shall see)—was the important task in his work, not drawing out the evidence of it in particular examples in the natural world. For Bookchin, natural science had already achieved this, and the point now was to draw the social lessons from it.

Second, Bookchin's philosophical work can never be separated from his politics: Bookchin was at one and the same time equal parts theorist *and* activist, as his biography attests to. Therefore, Bookchin never solely wrote for the academy: he wrote for the people who both populated the movements he had been involved in all his life and for his intended audience: the citizen, not the academic. In this sense, as Biehl argues, Bookchin tried to explain his theory in the most simple of terms, and "to illustrate what he meant by development. . . . Bookchin found it helpful to use simple analogies from plant growth."

However, it would be a mistake to give these illustrations too much prominence, to make them the centrepiece of his work. Indeed, Biehl continues, "the growth of an acorn into an oak is in fact an instance of hard teleology," wherein the acorn "contains DNA for an oak and nothing else . . . . Absent genetic mutations, there's no room for variation." Moreover, "Bookchin clearly understood that social and historical processes do not act this way," and the analogy he draws between this and social development are solely to illustrate the developmental nature of his dialectic.[39] As we have seen, Bookchin talks continuously of this development only ever being a potentiality, or a tendency, in nature: the bird or the acorn are not predetermined end points, but existing potentialities. Thus to criticise Bookchin's illustrative use of analogy as a claim that he saw an ecological society as the *fixed* DNA of human society as such, as its kind of biological endpoint, when he saw no such endpoints in nature as a whole, is surely overdrawn. As Biehl argues, Bookchin "devoted his life to developing and advancing a program, history, philosophy, and politics for the creation of a free, rational, ecological, and above all *socialist* society. Are people going to create such a society inevitably? Of course not. Is its achievement a fixed and determinate end of social evolution? No. But do human beings have the potentiality to create such a society? Indeed."[40]

And as Bookchin himself would explicitly state, the ecological society that does lie dormant in society as *one* potentiality is never a fixed or predetermined end—and indeed, at present, only a distant possibility: "What is clear is that human beings are much too intelligent not to have a rational society; *the most serious question we face is whether they are rational enough to achieve one*."[41] Yet despite Bookchin's ever present qualifications about the absence of a predetermined endpoint in dialectical naturalism, criticisms of a kind of "biological determinism" in Bookchin—and again, in part stemming from his overly-simplistic use of analogy—would persist throughout the 1990s. Indeed, according to Leff, Bookchin's "project to root an ecological society and the political philosophy of environmentalism in natural dialectics and an "ethical ontology" faces problems of theory and praxis."[42] Leff argues that Bookchin errs in "inscribing dialectical reason in the material movement of nature, instead of grasping dialectics in power strategies and discursive formations that emerge from conflicting social interests in the appropriation of nature."[43]

Therefore, Bookchin, in apparently placing the movement of history in natural processes, is "ignoring culture and cultural theory" in the movement of history and reason, and as a result, "the sources of human rationality and social change are grounded in nature, not (as they should be) in critical reason and strategic action."[44] Moreover, because Bookchin "roots his ecological dialectics in a naturalist view of society" and because he views human subjectivity and knowledge "as extensions of natural evolution to its ultimate state of self-consciousness . . . he offers no strategic thinking to guide this social reconstruction, other than the spontaneous development of natural ethics."[45]

The criticism here, then, is that, like the economic determinism of the "vulgar" Marxists, Bookchin has slipped into a teleological conception of natural evolution, a kind of naturalistic/biological determinism, wherein no social action is required but simply the "waiting" for an ecological consciousness to spontaneously arise, for the natural conclusion of Bookchin's dialectic of the increasing complexification (and ultimate perfection) of natural evolution. Indeed, the majority of Leff's critique is based on this position: for Leff, Bookchin's philosophy is actually based on "deep ecological roots [and] can only result in passivity, awaiting the forces of nature to be actualized in society by natural self-consciousness and spontaneous transformations." Leff chides Bookchin on this basis, and points out that the ecological utopia that Bookchin aspires to "is accomplished through political theory and strategic action, rather than by the simple actualization of the real."[46]

Further, in rooting the emergence of this ecological consciousness in natural evolution, Bookchin also "ignores the mechanisms of ideological, technological and economic manipulation that impede the internalization of ecological conditions and principles of social equity and political democracy in new forms of productive and social organization."[47] Bookchin has overlooked this for Leff, and in the process "ignores . . . the strategic theory and practice necessary to deconstruct the prevalent dominant system and to construct an alternative social order."[48] Leff concludes his critique with the following dictum for Bookchin: "the social order cannot be reduced to the biological organism, nor power and knowledge subsumed in the laws of evolution."[49]

It is hoped that from our discussion thus far, it is clear that Bookchin did not "subsume" power or knowledge in "the laws of evolution," nor did he ever propose that "the sources of human rationality and social change are grounded in nature," as Leff claims here. This simplistic rendering of

Bookchin has been refuted above in our explanation of precisely *where* Bookchin *grounds* his ethics of social change, and we need not revisit it here. But even aside from this plainly inaccurate picture of Bookchin's philosophy: nowhere has Bookchin's entire programme been more poorly represented than in Leff. Though not the place to deal fully with Bookchin's "strategic theory and practice . . . to construct an alternative social order"—which is the explicit remit of the latter part of the present work—it should be noted in passing that perhaps no other thinker of the twentieth century provided so detailed a practical political plan for the enactment of his theoretical positions.

Tellingly, there is no reference in Leff's piece to any of Bookchin's *political* works. There is only reference to his collection of philosophical essays.[50] Naturally, for a piece that offers a critique of Bookchin's dialectical naturalism this would make for passable research (although even here, any serious critique that wants to deal with social ecology must deal with his major work, *The Ecology of Freedom*, something Leff fails to do). However, as noted, Leff offers an explicitly *political* critique of Bookchin: that Bookchin offers no strategic thinking or action; that Bookchin argues for the spontaneous emergence of an ecological consciousness and ultimately an ecological society. Again, we will disprove this notion fully in due course, but suffice to say here, this is a claim made in direct contradiction of a substantial body of evidence.

But more than this, even staying with the philosophy of Bookchin, the reverse of the Leff position is more than apparent: dialectic for Bookchin is the unceasing critique of that which exists by that which could or should exist; the critique of present society by the image of an ecological society that can be discerned as a *potentiality*. As Biehl noted above, this was Bookchin's goal: Bookchin attempted to formulate a philosophy based on all that had been before that would allow the actualisation of his political changes, of a socialist society. The philosophic, for Bookchin, was also political: it was to try and devise a processual way of thinking that would not only elaborate our understanding of the world but also point to ways to act upon that understanding. Indeed, Bookchin was explicit as to how a philosophical potentiality would translate into a political reality: "The actualization of humanity's potentiality for a rational society—the 'what should be' that is achieved by human development—occurs in the fully democratic municipality, the municipality based on a face-to-face democratic assembly composed of free citizens, for whom the word *politics* means direct popular control over the community's public affairs by means of democratic institutions. Such a system of control should occur within the framework of a duly constituted system of laws, rationally derived by discourse, experience, historical knowledge, and judgment."[51] This detailed system of organisation was the process through which Bookchin actualised his dialectical potentiality of an ecological society, not, as Leff claims, through an appeal to allow a spontaneous unfolding of natural evolution.

Questions of Content: The Problems of Human Stewardship

The second main philosophical critique of Bookchin would, as noted, concern the *content* of his philosophy. These critiques relate, in the main, to the natural conclusion of Bookchin's dialectic of increasing complexity discussed above: that humanity represents the most complex expression of natural evolution thus far and as such is bestowed special responsibilities in the potential elaboration of an ecological society. As discussed, for Bookchin, the lessons to be drawn from a natural dialectic prove conclusively that "human intervention into first nature is inherently inevitable," and moreover that the move toward an ecological society "definitely involves human stewardship of the planet."[52]

Of course, criticisms of Bookchin's notion of the role humanity has to play in reversing the ecological crisis and the remaking of society are, as we shall see, based in part on the deep ecology philosophy of biocentrism, of the equal value of all life forms that we discussed in our opening chapter. However, it is stressed here that the critiques examined below are distinct from the problematic body of literature associated with deep ecology that we examined at the outset: again, the critiques here are the more robust, more objective than (and slightly more removed from) the largely ad hominem critiques that stemmed from the principle actors in deep ecology. Therefore, is there anything in these critiques that point to Bookchin being erroneous in his version of increasing complexity in natural evolution, culminating in the particular attributes of human beings?

To return to Eckersley: as shown, Eckersley offered a robust challenge to the methodology of Bookchin and argued that it is impossible to discern and act upon the potentiality he claims in the natural world. However, Eckersley went further, and argued that even if Bookchin's methodology *was* sound, the content of his thesis is self-negating. For Eckersley, "Bookchin's enticing promise that his ecological ethics offers the widest realm of freedom to *all* life forms is undermined by the way in which he distinguishes and privileges second nature (the human realm) over first nature (the nonhuman realm.)"[53]

In drawing this distinction between humanity and the rest of nature, Eckersley argues that Bookchin's "graded continuum" of natural evolution, joining the most basic of life forms to human consciousness and ultimately freedom, is negated: Bookchin is at one and the same time lauding the creative and holistic characteristics of the natural would whilst separating humanity from the rest of nature by privileging second nature and by inference denigrating first nature. As such, according to Eckersley, "there is a certain arrogance in his claim that humans have now discerned the course of evolution, which they have an obligation to further," as this ultimately "favours human attributes over the attributes of other life forms and therefore cannot deliver his central promise of freedom or self-directedness writ-large."[54]

The main concern for Eckersley is whether or not, in the fostering "of diversity and mutualism along the lines urged by Bookchin," wherein humanity is appointed as the stewards of such a project, "the potential for self-directiveness in nonhuman life forms [will] expand along with that of humans."[55] From this, she argues that Bookchin's philosophy "reveals serious cross purposes that tend to undermine his central premise."[56] These central problems, for Eckersley, "stem from the way in which he [Bookchin] distinguishes and privileges second nature over first nature and from his presumptuous conclusions concerning the state of human understanding of ecological and evolutionary processes."[57]

As discussed in Chapter 2, for Bookchin, humanity is indeed distinguished from the rest of the natural world as its most complex and adaptive species, and through this, humanity has the *potential* to act in a consciously elaborated future society as nature rendered self-conscious: that is, a potential to act as an expression of nature as a whole that is able to reflect back and act upon itself rationally. However, according to Eckersley, "what is troubling in this stance is that Bookchin's vision of human stewardship does not qualify how and to what extent our responsibility is to be discharged."[58] "Where is the line to be drawn?" she continues. "Should we enlist the aid of computers and the latest biotechnology and step up the selective breeding of plants and animals so as to foster the development of more complex ecosystems and more intelligent species?"[59]

Extending the criticism further, she argues that under Bookchin's call for diversity "one can envisage the greening of deserts to enhance ecosystem diversity, the speeding up in the international trade of seeds and sperm, the growth of 'gene banks' and gene splicing, and the proliferation of 'exotic' flora and fauna in the native ecosystems"—all of which are "troubling scenarios . . . that can be reasonably drawn from his [Bookchin's] theoretical position" on the fostering of diversity.[60] Of course, the implication here is that, no matter how much Bookchin attempts to integrate second and first nature through his concepts of diversity and complementarity, he cannot avoid providing an anthropocentric position, wherein the natural world would still be manipulated and dominated by humanity.

From this, Eckersley refers Bookchin back to the deep ecologists' approach, and argues that he has misunderstood the central premise of biocentrism. Eckersley explains that biocentrism, or ecocentrism as she reformulates it, is, through its commitment to biological egalitarianism, "a *prima facie orientation* of nonfavouritism" in the natural world, an ecological policy of "live and let live." For Eckersley, however, and contra Bookchin's critique of deep ecology, "this does not imply the passive surrender of humans to the natural order as Bookchin has claimed, since humans, like any other organism, are recognised as special in their own unique way and are entitled to modify the ecosystems in which they live in order to survive and blossom in a way that is simple in means and rich in ends. In this orientation, it is not inconsistent for humans to act in their own self defence by keeping in check or eradicating life-threatening organisms *where there is no alternative* (and when the action is taken with reluctance)."[61]

However, despite this ceding by Eckersley of the fact that even under a biocentric approach, humanity is given a fairly wide leeway in intervening in the natural world (eradicating "life-threatening organisms," albeit "with reluctance," allows for wide interpretation, a point to which we return below), she argues that the biocentric orientation "*is* inconsistent when the activities of humans wantonly or needlessly interfere with or threaten the existence or integrity of other life forms, when humans no longer see themselves as plain members of the biotic community, but assume instead the role of planetary directors who have discerned the true path of evolution and hence determined what should be the destinies (or nondestinies!) of other life forms and entities."[62]

Though clear that this is a critique of the picture she has established of Bookchin's "stewardship," it is hard to know on what material she has based it. There is nowhere in Bookchin where he allows for any of the above, for the planetary direction of the destinies of all life forms. Indeed, the very commitment to diversity, mutualism, symbiosis, and complementarity mean that a rational ecology precluded this caricature of Bookchin's philosophy. Indeed, Eckersley acknowledges that Bookchin has done much to dispel the overly anthropocentric approach she outlines above, but again, she then draws no conclusions here but shifts the argument sideways. Whilst noting that Bookchin is not calling for the instrumental management of nature as a whole, and is rather calling for a stewardship based on *ecological processes* (thus partly refuting the criticism she has just made), she then moves on to argue that the problem in fact is not Bookchin's anthropocentrism, but "arises in Bookchin's claim that we know enough about these processes to *foster and accelerate* them." She continues:

> are we really *that* enlightened? Can we really be sure that the thrust of evolution, as intuited by Bookchin, is one of advancing subjectivity? In particular, is there not something self-serving and arrogant in the (unverifiable) claim that first nature is striving to achieve something that has presently reached its most developed form in us—second nature? A more impartial, biocentric approach would be to simply acknowledge that *our* special capabilities (e.g., a highly developed consciousness, language, and tool-making capability) are simply *one* form of excellence alongside the myriad others (e.g., the navigational skills of birds, the sonar capability and playfulness of dolphins, and the intense sociality of ants) rather than *the* form of excellence thrown up by humanity.[63]

The possible problems of Bookchin's notion of "human stewardship" were also picked up on by Alexander. Based on the same objection to the way in which Bookchin apparently privileges the knowledge of humanity above the rest of nature, Alexander argues that "the fossil record shows [that] there are many extraordinary potentialities that exist in nature, not all of which endure."[64] Therefore, although he agrees (tentatively) with the broad outline of the movement of natural evolution that Bookchin discerned, he argues that Bookchin might have overemphasised the particular importance of humanity as distinct due to its current complexity, as it is solely one version of complexity among many complexities (actually existing, potential, and those which have not endured): "given the highly localized (so far as we know) nature of life and mind on Earth," Alexander argues, "are we at risk of making too much of a potentially insignificant and transient phenomenon?"[65]

As such, Alexander continues, whilst he has "no problem with humans valuing themselves . . . above slugs and termites," in terms of currently existing notions of complexity, this is not enough to appoint humanity as *the* expression of nature's thrust or striving for freedom. Not only does this not pay sufficient attention to the process of *continuous* unfolding of complexity that Bookchin is committed to, but it also underplays, according to Alexander, the interdependencies, the diverse interactions between the "higher" form of nature that is humanity and these "lower" forms. Alexander reminds Bookchin that although slugs and termites may have less value than humanity, "that does not meant that the function of such "lower" species is any less important ecologically." In this interdependent, ecologically diverse world—a world Bookchin himself appeals to—wherein the highest life form is dependent on the lowest, "we should remember," warns Alexander, that instead of viewing humanity as a distinct and complex species who can guide the world of life, "it is we [humanity] who are, ultimately, fleas on the dog."[66]

Of course, and as noted, these objections to Bookchin's differentiation of second human nature from first nonhuman nature are based on the principle he would criticise the deep ecologists for: the principle of biocentrism (or ecocentrism as reworked by Eckersley and others). Moreover, the "arrogance" that Eckersley accuses Bookchin of above can also be read as a synonym for anthropocentrism: the notion that Bookchin's approach, despite its claim to "speak" for ecology as a whole, cannot get beyond the human centeredness so characteristic of post-Enlightenment philosophy. On their commitment to biocentrism alone, the arguments above can be both shown to falter, but before we turn to examine this, it should be clear by now that in fact, Bookchin's entire programme transcends the distinction between the two *isms* of biocentrism and anthropocentrism. Under the Bookchin schema, humanity *is* differentiated from nonhuman nature as something distinct, as the most complex and evolutionary advanced element therein. However, *nowhere* does Bookchin argue that this distinction places humanity *above* nature in any other sense than biological fact (i.e. the complexity of human life and mind).

As discussed throughout the present work, Bookchin's ecological dialectic allows for a view of a diverse yet unified nature as a whole, wherein "the natural world and the social are interlinked by evolution into *one nature that consists of two differentiations*: first, or biotic nature, and second or social nature."[67] But as the description suggests, the fact of these two differentiations does not negate the overall concept of "one nature." As Bookchin argues elsewhere: "non-human and human nature are as inextricably bound to each other as the ventricles of the heart are bound to the auricles," and the instances in his work, some of which already covered, where he calls for humanity's "recovery" of nature and an ecological sensibility are manifest to such an extent that the holism of the two distinctions of first and second nature can be seen as one of his central philosophical positions.[68]

As such, *nowhere* did Bookchin argue that "lower species" were "any less important ecologically" than humanity, as Alexander suggests here. On the contrary, Bookchin would detail in many places the whole point of his entire project: again, to recover the participatory and creative operating system of natural evolution, to situate humanity in this system as steward *and* student of nature's interdependent and complementary relationships. As Bookchin argued, his call for an ecological ethics and sensibility stems not solely for the need of humanity to take control of nature but for nature to inform the human world too: "Our re-entry into natural evolution is no less a humanization of nature than a naturalization of humanity."[69]

Indeed, it is true that Bookchin *does* draw out the important differences between humanity and nature, between first nature and second nature, that render humanity "the *sole* ethical agents that exist" in the world of life and thus imparts to humanity a distinct role to play in the reversal of the current ecological crisis.[70] However, as Bookchin himself would ask, is his differentiation of first and second nature "an argument for the belief—imputed by many 'biocentric' ecologists to social ecology—that the human species is 'superior' to or 'higher' than all other life-forms?"[71] The answer is emphatically no: there is *nothing* in the entirety of Bookchin's writings that argues for the lower or higher ranking of individual life forms. Bookchin was explicit about this, in far too many instances across his work to cover in full; one example will suffice here. In the new introduction to the second edition of his major work, *The Ecology of Freedom*, Bookchin wrote that,

> Given the constellation of differences that distinguish human from non-human life-forms, indeed, differences that have been produced by natural evolution itself, it is fair to say that some species are more flexible than others in their ability to adapt and that they possess more complex nervous systems that endow them with the capability to make more suitable choices from among evolutionary pathways that promote their survival and development. In short, they can be said to be more advanced in dealing with *new* situations than are other, less flexible and less neurologically developed species.[72]

Drawing on our exposition of his notion of natural evolution in Chapter 2, we can see that this principle stems from the idea of evolution as participatory, as different species "choose," no matter how dimly, the paths to take in their own evolution. That humanity has made the right choices, as it were, that it has developed into the most complex, adaptive, and flexible, *is* one of the cornerstones of the Bookchin thesis, *"but in no sense does it follow that a more advanced life-form will or must dominate less advanced life forms."*[73] The notion that humanity is "higher" ecologically than other species is nowhere apparent in Bookchin's work, and to offer a critique of him in this sense, as Alexander does, is further evidence of the way in which Bookchin's basic premises were lost in discussions of him post-1987 as the general conception of his philosophy became increasingly distorted by the caricature.

To return to the problems of the biocentrism on which the critiques of Bookchin's notion of human stewardship rest, it is clear from the preceding discussion that there is *no* anthropocentrism in the Bookchin model, no ecological privileging of humanity. Crucially, however, nor did Bookchin ascribe to or allow for a biocentric approach. Although it is clear that Bookchin was explicit about the rejection of the ranking of life forms, he also refused to be drawn into notions of biocentrism: "Why must I be forced to choose," he asked, "between 'biocentrism' and 'anthropocentrism?'"[74] The distinction made no sense to Bookchin: under his own rubric of natural evolution as a graded continuum of increasing complexity and diversity, humanity can neither be opposed to nature in an anthropocentric sense, nor subsumed into one undifferentiated "whole," in which there is no difference but rather a "biospheric egalitarianism," as the biocentric position suggests.

Indeed, as evidenced by his original 1987 Amherst address, for Bookchin, the biocentric or later ecocentric position is riddled with inconsistencies—inconsistencies that spill over even into the more scholarly works on the topic represented here by Eckersley and Alexander. In a general sense, to downplay the very distinct differences and capabilities of humanity in the name of a biocentric outlook is not only equally dangerous, according to Bookchin, as the ecological degradation that results from an extreme anthropocentric outlook, but moreover is built on a glaring contradiction: to downplay the significance of the emergence of second nature, of human society and all it contains that is distinct from the natural world is, in fact, to denude humanity of the skills which go up to make the ability to formulate *any* conception of humanity (and nature) in the first place. That is to say, that to formulate the concept of any "centrism," to be able to identify oneself or another as any type of centrism, and finally, to attempt to build a philosophical and political programme on any type of centrism is *strictly* human skill. Yet under a biocentric approach, this skill is invoked yet immediately debased as indistinct from the skills of other life forms as simply "one knot in the biospherical net."[75]

More specifically, returning to Eckersley, this glaring contradiction can be seen to manifest itself throughout her critique. Primarily, this contradiction is expressed in Eckersley in the qualification she makes about precisely what humanity *is* allowed to do in terms of its intervention in the natural world: although committed to the notion that humanity must live "in a way that is simple in means and rich in ends," the deep ecology leitmotif, she argues that in doing so, humanity is "entitled to modify the ecosystems" in which they live. Moreover, as discussed, it is not inconsistent for Eckersley under a biocentric position "for humans to act in their own self defence by keeping in check or eradicating life threatening organisms *where there is no alternative* (and when the action is taken with reluctance.)"[76]

Of course, Devall and Sessions's notion of vital needs, noted in the introduction, resurfaces here: the qualification that in essence brings the whole structure of biocentric philosophy crashing down. The notion of "eradicating life-threatening organisms," only when there is "no alternative"—and *with reluctance*, of course—begs a set of obvious questions: how and from where would this "reluctance" emerge? Who would be the judge of when and where a "vital need" outweighed the "reluctance?" Who would be the judge, jury, and executioner of the "eradication of life-threatening organisms?" Who will decide exactly when or how an organism becomes life threatening? Of course, it is possible to provide answers to these questions, but crucially, when one does, one finds the answer to forever be the same: *humanity* would decide. That is to say, that to *ask* these questions—or even simply to conceive of their possibility, as Eckersley does here—is to draw upon the unique ability of humanity to conceptualise and generalise value in both the human and the nonhuman world.

Moreover, in the defence that both Eckersley and Alexander make of their biocentric position, in which humanity should not be elevated in any sense above the other species in the world of life, this same central contradiction of calling for the reduction of humanity's distinctiveness whilst using the very tools that make it distinctive is everywhere apparent. Take, for example, Eckersley's knowledge of myriad other forms of excellence in the natural world she notes above: "the navigational skills of birds, the sonar capability and playfulness of dolphins, and the intense sociality of ants."[77] Or, take Alexander's notion that humanity is, in cosmological terms, a transient phenomenon, or that humanity is, in fact, the "fleas on the dog" in their time and place on earth.[78] In both cases, it can quite reasonably be asked: how have these writers arrived at their individual positions?

In the case of Eckersley, her knowledge of these other forms of excellence is premised on the one thing she attempts to denigrate: that is, the uniquely advanced state of human intelligence and consciousness. The dolphins, the birds and the ants, it is fair to argue, are all "unaware" of the "excellence" of their instinctual drives. Moreover, they are unaware of the capabilities of other species. Perhaps most importantly, they are unaware of the *value* of either their own capabilities in relationship to the other species or vice versa. Finally, and obviously, even if they *were* aware of them, they would be unable to communicate them to each other and between each species, in verbal or written form. So too with Alexander: his notion of humanity as transient, as "the flea on the dog" is again formulated by that very transient being, by that very "flea." The actual—as opposed to metaphorical—flea, and the actual dog, are unaware of their respective cosmological roles (or, for that matter, their secondary use as an analogy in the written word of humanity). Not so with humanity, as evidenced by Alexander's very building of his own case.

In short, in both critiques, we see the expression of the fundamental contradiction of deep ecology which Bookchin critiqued in 1987: they fail to acknowledge (or even *see*) that the way in which they argue, the methods and tools they use, are the skills solely of humanity. In both cases, we can see that the ultimate argument is the preservation of life forms other than humanity, but, as argued by Fromm at the height of the polemics between Bookchin and the deep ecologists, the one thing that is missing from the biocentric position is an awareness of the seemingly obvious fact that "no life *except the human* has any regard for the preservation of anything but itself."[79] Indeed, Bookchin makes the point even more clearly: if a life form needs eradication or preserving, only one species has the capability to do so: "Whatever rights or other ethical formulations that we develop in an ecological ethics, the fact remains that *we* as a species are the sole ethical agents on the planet who are able to formulate these rights, to confer them, and to see that they are upheld. Whether these rights are formulated and upheld, I must insist, depends overwhelmingly upon the kind of society we create and the sensibility it fosters."[80]

Herein lies the fundamental failing of Eckersley's critique of Bookchin: while the major complaint is that Bookchin privileges second nature and the human characteristics that render second nature "arrogant," in the very moment she makes the complaint, she appeals to those same characteristics, albeit unwittingly. That is, it appears that Eckersley applies these values piecemeal: on the one hand, she denies them their importance and potential as a grounds for the human ordering of the world along ecological lines, while simultaneously on the other hand, appeals to them in determining what would make up the characteristics of a "life-threatening organism" and when and where to eradicate such organisms. However, it should be noted that there is *no* difference in her notion of deciding whether there is "no alternative" in eradicating organisms in the natural world, or that it must be carried out "with reluctance" from Bookchin's own notions of human stewardship of nature as a whole.

Or perhaps, more correctly, there *is* one fundamental difference, but not the difference Eckersley had in mind. To put it bluntly, the position Eckersley outlines above *is* stewardship, it is stewardship of the certain aspects of nature by humanity in order that humanity can "live and blossom." However, unlike Bookchin's notion of stewardship, Eckersley's, paradoxically, seems more narrowly conceived, more centred on the human: Eckersley's stewardship is for the right of *humanity* to live and blossom—and eradicate anything that might threaten this life and blossoming—and *not* for the continuation of the creative potentiality that Bookchin spent years eliciting from the processes of natural and social evolution. Therefore, through an express attempt to undo the anthropocentrism or arrogance she sees in Bookchin, Eckersley, *due to the glaring contradiction of biocentrism which denigrates humanity's ability to formulate value while employing that very same ability*, cannot help but reinforce such anthropocentrism.

Again, such a terminal failing is characteristic not only of Eckersley's critique of Bookchin but of deep ecology in general: deep ecology cannot help but reinforce the one concept—anthropocentrism—that it expressly set out to overturn. To be clear: in Bookchin's explicit calling for a form of human stewardship, his social ecology was acutely conscious of the possible problems this entailed, of the capacity of humanity to develop along highly irrational, anthropocentric lines, not only historically, but in the future as well. As such, his philosophical and political programme (as we shall see) can be seen as a detailed way to try and manage not only the natural world, but first and foremost, humanity's impact upon it. Thus can it be claimed that Bookchin dealt almost exclusively with the reversal of the problems of humanity's anthropocentric plundering of the natural world.

In contrast, however, Eckersley, and deep ecology in general, obliquely concede not only that humanity is currently destructive of the natural world, but that it might always have to be so in certain circumstances, i.e., in the destruction of "life-threatening organisms." Yet at the same time, a biocentric approach refuses to face the logical conclusions of such a position: namely, that this destructiveness, no matter what form it takes, would need to be managed, and would require large and complex structures of value and institutionalisation to make it practically applicable. In short, it would require a form of *human stewardship* of, in the first instance, the human impact on nature, and in the second, of the impact of nature on humanity (in its "life threatening" forms).

But rather than acknowledging this, deep ecology argues for the biocentric notion of the intrinsic worth of all living beings, and thus for the non-interference of humanity into nature, as represented here by Eckersley's conclusion that "the wisest course of action" in light of the ecological crisis, is a matter of, "wherever possible, simply to let beings be."[81] However, *even this position is itself a form of human stewardship.* To decide collectively as a species to "let beings be" in the natural world is in fact a form of interference: it is to take a position against the natural world as humanity as such. Again, this is based on the exact same logical processes which Bookchin uses to reach his opposing interpretation of the relationship humanity should have with the natural world. But while on first appearance the deep ecology approach may seem radical, it is actually far narrower than the one proposed by Bookchin. If it can be conceived that humanity can take a position of "letting beings be" toward the natural world, then it can equally be argued on the same grounds that humanity can take the far more nuanced and far reaching position argued by Bookchin of *helping beings be.*

It is this second position it is argued here that is *less* anthropocentric: a call for an extensive and wide ranging construction of a human consciousness and society which, conceiving of the rational management of both human and nonhuman nature along ecological principles, *by definition* deals more directly with the interests of nature as a whole than does the kind of social and natural disengagement that would be required by the policy of non-interference that stems from a commitment to biocentrism. Indeed, to argue for this position is based more on human needs than any other approach, as it simplifies the complex processes humanity would have to go through to build a genuinely ecological society. As Fromm noted in his commentary on the debate between Bookchin and the deep ecologists, the truth is that "the "biocentric" notion of "intrinsic worth" is even more narcissistically "anthropocentric" than ordinary self-interest because it hopes to achieve its ends by denying that oneself is the puppeteer-ventriloquist behind the world one perceives as valuable."[82]

Indeed, it was to this central philosophical contradiction of deep ecology to which Bookchin addressed his 1987 critique, and, as has hopefully become clear thus far in the present work, it was this critique that was lost in the furore, the polemics, and the construction of the Bookchin caricature that emerged from the initial response of the deep ecologists. Moreover, it is clear from the discussion in the present chapter, that the critiques discussed here do raise important objections to Bookchin's philosophy—in particular, his lack of detail on his notion of the unfolding of complexity and diversity in natural evolution, and his particular use of dialectic—and indeed, these criticisms also suffered from the extraordinary nature of his exchange with the deep ecologists as they themselves have forever been bound up with the more problematic literature. It was the express attempt of the present chapter to extricate them from that literature, giving them a full theoretical airing and using them in putting the philosophy of Bookchin to the test.

In so doing, it is argued here that with the problems duly noted, Bookchin's philosophy emerges relatively unscathed. Yes, there are challenges that can be made on Bookchin's unscientific "simplicity." Further, there is scope for perhaps an even more extensive discussion of Bookchin's dialectic, with considerable leeway for a wide range of criticisms (and in fairness, for a defence from this criticism). However, there is no one *terminal* failing in Bookchin as suggested by the highly contentious literature discussed in our opening chapter, there is no fundamental flaw in Bookchin, a notion of which seemed to hover round him as the caricature of a divisive and conflicted thinker cemented throughout the post-1987 years. Rather, Bookchin's philosophy can be seen to be a genuine attempt to theorise a way that humanity can *act* decisively in re-imagining an ecologically rational world and its own place therein. Problems aside, this philosophy—which imparts a coherence to the Bookchin project as a whole, as will be demonstrated in due course—has yet to be fully appreciated in and of itself and perhaps more importantly, in its practical manifestation of Bookchin's project, an elucidation of which is the immanent aim of the present work, and an aim we move ever-closer to.

Chapter 4

On Hierarchy and Domination
The Political Objection to Deep Ecology

It should be clear to the reader by now that—notwithstanding the critical literature that emerged after Amherst 1987—Bookchin, by the time
of his exchange with the deep ecologists, had theorised a rich philosophy
of nature. His ecological dialectic—dialectical naturalism—is a complex conceptualisation of humanity's place in the natural world, which
helps to conceive of humanity and nature as existing *non-antagonistically*.
It was from this philosophical base that his opposition to deep ecology
stemmed: there was no "sour grapes" here, no "turf war" but rather a
defence of the specificity and complementarity of humanity as a distinct
part of natural evolution as a whole. Moreover, it should also be clear that
Bookchin's philosophical foundations can be subjected to critical ques-
tioning, and indeed, can be seen to require further elucidation in parts.
However, also clear is that as a philosophy of nature, it may prove to be
a far deeper, far more nuanced and far more coherent body of work than
the literature on Bookchin up to the present has allowed for. It is this
under-appreciated philosophy we have thus far attempted to draw out
from more problematic literature that emerged from Bookchin's exchange
with the deep ecologists.

In the present chapter, we turn to the other key area of Bookchin's
theoretical foundations, his notion of social history, a thorough analysis
and full appreciation of which has also been lost since 1987, subsumed
in the wider polemics of Bookchin's later life. To do this, we open with
our final encounter with the deep ecologist: we return briefly to outline
Bookchin's *political* objection to deep ecology in 1987. We do so not

solely as a heuristic tool in allowing us to frame our discussion of his large corpus and draw out his history in contrast to the positions of deep ecology, but also because the issues Bookchin raised in his Amherst critique go right to the heart of fundamental questions of ecology which will be vital in formulating a response to the ecological crisis. Today more than ever, the revisiting of such debates is a necessary exercise. Again, at the risk of repetition, these issues were also lost in the ensuing controversy post-1987.

After examining Bookchin's political objection to deep ecology, we then turn to a full elucidation of that upon which it is based: Bookchin's own version of social history. Here, we find not only is this social history a coherent expression of Bookchin's philosophical foundations, but that it in turn forms the basis of his *practical* political programme. We turn to a full examination of this practical political programme in Chapters 6 and 7, but not until, just as we did with Bookchin's philosophy, we have exposed it to a critical account, examining the robust critiques that challenge Bookchin's notion of history, a task we carry out in Chapter 5.

Bookchin's Political Objection to Deep Ecology

In a very real sense, and as will become clear, Bookchin's political objection to deep ecology and the social history upon which it is based *are the direct expressions of his philosophical* foundations, of his ecological dialectic. Specifically, and to recap briefly on our discussion thus far, what this ecological dialectic shows for Bookchin is that "the universe bears witness to an ever-striving, developing—not merely moving—substance, whose most dynamic and creative attribute is an unceasing capacity for self-organization into increasingly complex forms."[1] This capacity for self-organisation in nature eventually produces its most complex (current) form: human society. As we have seen, this ecological dialectic allows for a non-antagonistic view of humanity and nature, allows for a view of a diverse yet unified nature as a whole, wherein "the natural world and the social are interlinked by evolution into *one nature that consists of two differentiations*: first, or biotic nature, and second or social nature."[2]

This key conception of "one nature, two differentiations" permits an evolutionary outlook that allows for the very distinct, adaptive capabilities of human society to be recognised as different but not intrinsically antagonistic toward the rest of the natural world. Rather, it shows human society to be *the very expression* of "nature's fecundity" and its underlying "thrust" toward increasing diversity and complexity, a thrust nonetheless that inheres unity to the evolutionary process as a whole.[3] Therefore, "humanity's second nature is not simply an external imposition of human society on biology's first nature" for Bookchin, but rather, this second nature "is the result of first nature's inherent evolutionary process."[4]

Most importantly in terms of Bookchin's political objection to deep ecology is that this ecological dialectic, in placing humanity at the centre of nature's evolutionary thrust, allows the ecologist to see, through the focus on the gradations of nature from the simple to the complex, from the inorganic to the organic, and ultimately, from nature to society, that "*human intervention into first nature is inherently inevitable*," and the debates as to whether it should or should not intervene are "utterly obfuscatory." The key *political* question, therefore, and especially in light of the ecological crisis, is not whether humanity *should* intervene in the natural world, but *how* humanity should intervene, and what form this intervention should take. As Bookchin argues, "what is at issue in humanity's transformation of nature is whether its practice is consistent with an objective ecological ethics."[5]

Moreover, Bookchin continues, "such an ecological ethics *definitely involves human stewardship of the planet*," and "a humanity that fails to see that it is the embodiment of nature rendered self-conscious and self-reflexive has separated itself from nature morally as well as intellectually." Formulated in this sense, Bookchin argues that this human "stewardship of the planet" can represent "a radical integration of second nature with first nature along far-reaching ecological lines, an integration that would yield new ecocommunities, ecotechnologies, and an abiding ecological sensibility that embodies nature's thrust toward self-reflexivity."[6]

For Bookchin, this is the key political failing of deep ecology: in the name of a biocentrism, deep ecology denies the "active presence" in nature as a whole that has produced human society. It denies nature's thrust toward increasing complexity, denies the continuum of differentiation and increasing self-awareness that ultimately "reaches a degree of unity-in-diversity such that nature can *act* upon itself rationally, defined mainly by coordinates created by nature's potential for freedom and conceptual thought."[7] Rather, the distinctiveness of humanity as the most complex expression of the consciousness of nature is collapsed under the deep ecology rubric in the name of creating a larger "organic whole," a realm in which humanity returns as a non-active presence to the natural world as simply one knot (amongst many) in the biospherical net.[8] For Bookchin, this would "cut across the grain of nature," would deny humanity's "heritage in its evolutionary processes, and dissolve our legitimacy in the world of life."[9] In short, deep ecology denies human agency to act upon nature as its most self-conscious element: the sole way for Bookchin that the ecological crisis can be resolved.

Furthermore, Bookchin argues that deep ecology not only denies human society any agency in guiding nature as a whole to an ecologically rational society, but also denies an examination of social history. That is, although the entirety of the deep ecology project is an attempt to reduce the destructive nature of human society through an appeal to a biocentric equality, wherein humanity is prohibited from interfering in the natural world, there is no explanation of *why* such a philosophy is needed. That is to say, there is nothing in deep ecology to explain why humanity in its current form is so ecologically destructive. All there is, for Bookchin, by way of an explanation of ecological degradation in deep ecology is the accusation of a humanity that is "anthropocentric," that values the world solely in terms of its owns needs. Further, this is compounded by the deep ecology focus on the population problem (as outlined in Chapter 1). The result is a view of humanity as the self-centred, overly populous *cause* of the ecological crisis.

For Bookchin, however, this is a gross simplification not only of humanity's emergence out of nature as a distinct social phenomenon, and the complex relationships between society and nature, but is a simplification of society and the causes of the ecological crisis itself. That is, what *exactly* is it about society that makes it so destructive? Which particular sections of society and, just as importantly, which particular social relationships render it (in the present) a pest in its own environment? As we turn to examine shortly, this is *precisely* what Bookchin tries to ascertain through his own examination of social history. However, in deep ecology, these developments are nowhere given sufficient analysis. Rather, the ecological crisis is presented as a matter of an idealized, near-perfect realm of nature being confronted by "a vague species called humanity."[10]

However, for Bookchin, this is to collapse the many different facets of human society into a naturally exploitative species, "as though people of color were equatable with whites, women with men, the Third World with the First, the poor with the rich, and the exploited with their exploiters" in terms of their impact on the world of life.[11] That is, there are detailed and important reasons for society's ecological destructiveness, reasons of class and gender, of domination and exploitation *within* society that render society so problematic. As Bookchin asked of Foreman's comments on the famine in Ethiopia and Latin American immigration into the US, "what does it mean for nature to 'seek its own balance' in East Africa, where agribusiness, colonialism, and exploitation have ravaged a once culturally and ecologically stable area? Or who is this all-American 'our' that owns 'the resources we have in the USA?'"[12]

Moreover, Bookchin continued, "is it the ordinary people who are driven by sheer need to cut timber, mine ores, and operate nuclear power plants," actions that so contribute to ecological degradation in the present? Or rather, is it the "giant corporations that are not only wrecking the good old USA but have produced the main problems these days in Latin America that send largely Indian folk across the Rio Grande?"[13] These fundamental and far-reaching differences across humanity have to be acknowledged (and ultimately disposed of) for Bookchin in dealing with ecological problems, rather than all of humanity being embraced in "a realm of universal guilt."[14] As Bookchin would perhaps most vividly express in a later exchange with Foreman, what or who is this species from which the natural world has to be protected? Bookchin continues: "Is it 'humanity'? Is it the human 'species,' *per se*? Is it people, as such? Or is it our particular society, our particular civilisation, with its hierarchical social relations which pit men against women, privileged whites against people of color, elites against masses, employers against workers, the First World against the Third World, and ultimately, a cancer like, 'grow or die' industrial capitalist economic system against the natural world and other life forms?"[15]

To circumvent these questions in the simplistic dualism that posits humanity *as such* as destructive of the natural world, and sees resolution of this problematic relationship as being achieved through a world where population must be drastically reduced and a stance of non-interference in nature denigrates the roles and responsibilities, the guilt and innocence that exists across these key social differentiations. "Let's face it," Bookchin argued, "when you say a black kid in Harlem is as much to blame for the ecological crisis as the President of Exxon," which blaming humanity *as such* surely does, "you are letting one off the hook and slandering the other."[16] For Bookchin, this is the *key* political failing of deep ecology, and as a result, not only does it contain no history "of the emergence of society out of nature," as discussed in Chapter 2, but also, "presents no explanation of—indeed, it reveals no interest in—the emergence of hierarchy out of society, of classes out of hierarchy, of the State out of classes—in short, the highly graded social as well as ideological development that gets to the roots of the ecological problem in the social domination of women by men and of men by other men, ultimately giving rise to the notion of dominating nature in the first place."[17]

As such, deep ecology for Bookchin, in its absence of an analysis of the profound natural and social developments that saw society grade out of nature, and later hierarchy, domination, classes, and the state grade out of society, "essentially *evade[s] the social roots of the ecological crisis.*"[18] This, Bookchin's political objection to deep ecology, is based on perhaps his most important theoretical commitment in terms of the political project he proposes to initiate the radical remaking of society: the fact that *all ecological problems are in fact social problems*, thus requiring social solutions. We turn to examine this more fully below when we trace Bookchin's own detailed social history, but we need to deal first with one final issue raised by Bookchin in 1987.

Bookchin and the Population Problem

According to Bookchin, and as represented by the comments of the deep ecologists discussed thus far, there is one particular manifestation of their simplistic ahistorical worldview that is most problematic. "Nothing more clearly reveals deep ecology's crude, often reactionary, and certainly superficial ideological framework, than its suffocating biological treatment of the population issue," Bookchin argued in his Amherst critique.[19] Here, as manifest not only in the comments of the Earth First!ers but also in the basic principles of Naess and Sessions—the theoretical bedrock of the movement—the notion of humanity as one homogenous entity that afflicts the rest of the nonhuman natural world by sole dint of numbers is cemented, as is the reactionary policy formulations that these point toward.

However, as discussed in Chapter 1, the moment Bookchin raised these issues, he was accused of having nothing to say on the population issue. Indeed, in his direct response to Bookchin, Sessions claimed that "in his 1987 attack, Bookchin ridiculed the idea that humanity was overpopulating the planet and destroying the biosphere."[20] But Sessions could not have been more wrong here, both in terms of the entirety of the written corpus of Bookchin but perhaps more problematically, in terms of the content of his 1987 critique; perhaps Sessions can be forgiven for an unfamiliarity with Bookchin's wider work, but not for such a clear misrepresentation of the 1987 critique to which he was supposedly responding.

In truth, Bookchin offered a lengthy discussion of population in 1987 and has a long intellectual history of dealing explicitly with the problem. Nowhere in his treatment of human population does he underestimate the effects of its continuing exponential growth. Rather, Bookchin would constantly stress that to focus on human population numbers as the cause of the ecological crisis is to confuse cause with effect, to focus on a symptom of the ecological crisis instead of the root causes. As he wrote in 1964, in a clear precursor to his critique of the deep ecologists: "Obviously, man could be described as a highly destructive parasite, who threatens to destroy his host—the natural world—and eventually himself. In ecology, however, the word *parasite*, used in this oversimplified sense, is not an answer to a question but raises a question itself ... a destructive parasitism of this kind usually reflects a disruption of an ecological situation ... What is the disruption that has turned man into a destructive parasite?"[21]

For Bookchin, it is not enough to simply state that humanity *is* a parasite, overpopulating a resource-finite environment. An examination of the *causes* of this parasitism is required, not the effect of parasitism itself. This effect, for Bookchin, was not a product of humanity *as such* but can only be explained by social factors, primarily, the "destruction of pre-industrial family forms, village institutions, mutual aid, and stable, traditional patterns of life" wrought by the move to industry and urbanisation. Moreover, "the decline in social morale ushered in by the horrors of the factory system, the degradation of traditional agrarian peoples into grossly exploited proletarians and urban dwellers, produced a concomitantly irresponsible attitude toward the family and the begetting of children. Sexuality became a refuge from a life of toil on the same order as the consumption of cheap gin; the new proletariat reproduced children, many of whom were never destined to survive into adulthood, as mindlessly as it drifted into alcoholism."[22]

These were the immediate cause of population growth: the emergence in society of increasingly hierarchical forms that would eventually manifest into the horrors of the factory system in modern capitalism. Again, Bookchin was always keen to stress that *all* ecological problems are first and foremost *social* problems, and thus requiring social solutions. Any approach that failed to appreciate the deep social roots of the ecological crisis was far wide of the mark. As Bookchin wrote in 1969, of the growing focus on populations, "this thesis is perhaps the most disquieting and in many ways the most sinister" of the emerging notions in ecology, as here, "an *effect* called 'population growth' . . . is turned into a *cause*. A problem of secondary proportions at the present time is given primacy, thus obscuring the fundamental reasons for the ecological crisis."[23]

Again, it should be stressed that Bookchin nowhere denies the extent of the problem. Again, he was explicit in his acknowledging of the problem, so much so that he would warn in 1969 that "if present economic, political, and social conditions prevail, humanity will in time overpopulate the planet and by sheer weight of numbers turn into a pest in its own global habitat."[24] This point Bookchin would never deny, but to blame humanity as such for these expressly "economic, political, and social conditions" is to blame the victim. Moreover, in an early outlining of the "barely disguised racism" of the deep ecologists, he would point to the theoretical and political problems of Western academics and activists raising population as a problem. "There is something obscene," he argued, "about the fact that an effect, 'population growth,' is being given primacy in the ecological crisis by a nation [the U.S.] which has little more than seven percent of the world's population [and] wastefully devours more than fifty percent of the world's resources."[25]

Moreover, and again, evidence of his longtime engagement with the population problem, Bookchin partly forewarns of the dangerous policies that would later be espoused by deep ecologists like Foreman and Manes.

"Sooner or later, the mindless proliferation of human beings will have to be arrested, but population control will either be initiated by 'social controls' (authoritarian or racist methods and eventually by systematic genocide) or by a libertarian, ecologically oriented society."[26] Indeed, it was from the emergence of such "authoritarian and racist methods," those suggested by deep ecology in the 1980s, from which his critique of population stemmed, and not from any attempt to ridicule the issue as Sessions contends.

However, as noted, the evidence for Bookchin's position on population lies not solely in the distant articles from Bookchin's past, but in the actual critique of 1987. Rather than ridiculing population, the same commitments are expressly evident throughout his discussion of the matter. "Human beings are not fruit flies," who mindlessly reproduce *as a genetic trait*: rather, "their reproductive behavior is profoundly conditioned by cultural values, standards of living, social traditions, the status of women, religious beliefs, socio-political conflicts, and various socio-political expectations."[27] Moreover, Bookchin again in '87 stresses the social roots (rather than biological) of population growth: "smash up a stable pre-capitalist culture and throw its people off the land into city slums," Bookchin pointed out, "and due ironically to demoralization, population may soar rather than decline." "Reduce women to mere reproductive factories, and population rates will explode. Conversely, provide people with decent lives, education, a sense of creative meaning in life, and above all free women from their roles as mere bearers of children—and population growth begins to stabilize and population rates even reverse their direction."[28]

Indeed, as with the accusations already noted that Bookchin was not interested in ecology, that he was "Old Left," anthropocentric, or out solely to attack, the notion that he ridiculed the effects human population growth was having on the world of life is completely unfounded. As with the earlier accusations, this is not simply a matter of redressing this woeful misrepresentation of Bookchin's version of ecology, but it is to finally rid discussions of Bookchin's ecological outlook of misrepresentations that have obscured a full appreciation of his theoretical foundations. The central commitment of Bookchin to the social roots of all ecological problems, so evident in his discussion of human population growth, was never really taken on board, critically or otherwise, due to such misrepresentations. It is the way in which Bookchin formulates this notion out of his detailed and unique social history to which we now turn.

Bookchin's Social History

If, for Bookchin, all "our ecological problems have their ultimate roots in society and in social problems," then considering the creative and complementary view that Bookchin holds of natural evolution as a whole, then the question of "what went wrong?" emerges.[29] That is, if evolution is a process of a continual striving for increased complexity and self-awareness, and ultimately freedom, why has society developed along such ecologically problematic lines? For Bookchin, the answer lies somewhere "in the intermediate zone between first nature and second that saw the graded passage of biological evolution into social," from where "social evolution *began to assume a highly aberrant form.*" Here, "social evolution was diverted from the realization and fulfillment of a cooperative society into a direction that yielded hierarchical, class orientated, and Statist institutions."[30]

It is an examination of the highly aberrant forms in this intermediate zone in the evolution of the biological into the social that forms the basis of Bookchin's social history. What, for Bookchin, is the cause of humanity's antagonistic relationship to the natural world? What developments led to humanity's domination and exploitation of the natural world? Specifically, it is the emergence of *hierarchy* in this intermediate zone from which stems the social and ecological crises of our time. In his major work, *The Ecology of Freedom*, Bookchin would detail at length the systematic emergence of hierarchy from within early organic society and then trace the vast "legacy of domination" that has ensued from this development right up to present day, statist societies.

As will become clear, Bookchin's focus on hierarchy as the principal concern for a project to radically remake society renders his project wide-reaching in its focus: hierarchy *as such* would need to be challenged in a full social revolution, hierarchy on every front. But more than this, what Bookchin's examination of social history also does is to suggest a rethinking of our understanding of the emergence of modern society, as traditionally understood. That is to say, the emergence of "civilisation" from prehistory, the emergence of agricultural society from tribal, then industrial from agricultural, and all the attendant benefits and problems this brought forth, is rethought out schematically.

For Bookchin, the theorisation of these developments "touch on one of the major social problematics of our time—the role of scarcity, reason, labor, and technics in wrenching humanity from its 'brutal' animal world into the glittering light of 'civilisation,' or in Marxian terminology, from a world dominated by 'necessity' to a world dominated by 'freedom.'"[31] That is, for Bookchin, the traditional Enlightenment approach to the move toward civilisation, predicated as it is on the notion that a "pre-civilisation"—primitive humanity—was dominated by a harsh, stingy natural world and thus had to learn to dominate nature in order to progress—to change the *realm of necessity* into the *realm of freedom*—does not provide the whole picture in terms of the "aberrant forms" of social development. As he argued in his major work, our conceptualisation of these actual developments "are worth re-examining—not so much to refute them but to place them in a larger perspective than nineteenth-century social theory could possibly attain."[32]

What was the larger perspective to which Bookchin aspired? Well, for Bookchin, the traditional view of social development outlined above led to the view that "history's onward march from the stone age to the modern," occured for reasons primarily related to "technological development: the development of advanced agricultural techniques, increasing material surpluses, and the rapid growth of human populations."[33] The emergence of the surplus and economic history is everything, as is the technology that made it possible. Bookchin continues that under the traditional version of social development, "we owe the advent of 'civilisation' to the early arts of systematic food cultivation and increasingly sophisticated tools like the wheel, kiln, smelter, and loom. All these provided an increasing abundance of food, clothing, shelter, tools, and transportation. With this basic reserve of food and technics, humanity acquired the leisure time to gain greater insight into natural processes and settled into sedentary lifeways from which emerged our towns and cities."[34]

However, under this traditional schema, Bookchin argues, this social development "has not been free of a Janus-faced ambiguity, of its dark treacherous aspects. The stream of human progress has been a divided one: the development toward material security and social complexity has generated contrapuntal forces that yield material insecurity and social conflict unique to 'civilisation' as such."[35] That is to say, that traditionally, the move out of a primitive state has often been thought of as a double-edged sword. "On the one side," Bookchin contends, "without the agrarian economy that the early Neolithic introduced, society would have been mired indefinitely in a brute subsistence economy living chronically on the edge of survival."[36] This society would be confronted, as it had been for the entirety of its pre-Neolithic history, according to this traditional account, by a "stingy" nature, a nature that dominated humanity, as it would never have produced the early agricultural surpluses that did so much to change the forms of human consociation.

On the other hand, however, there is in humanity's move away from this primitive condition, a "negative side of its [humanity's] progress." "Technical progress," Bookchin continued, is seen to exact "a penalty for the benefits it ultimately confers on humanity."[37] This penalty is the subordination of large parts of humanity to the project of progress itself, as this move through civilisation requires coordination by elites and centres of power, themselves shored up by the control over growing surpluses, who coordinate growing numbers of people in large civic centres. This would take the form of slavery at the extreme or of simple subordination to the elites of history that coordinated such a project. That is to say, that to "resolve the problem of natural scarcity," the technological development necessary to create the surplus and all it brings with it,

> entails the reduction of humanity to a technical force. People become the instruments of production, just like the tools and machines they create. They, in turn, are subject to the same forces of coordination, rationalization, and control that society tries to impose on nature and inanimate technical instruments. Labor is both the medium whereby humanity forges its own self-formation and the object of social manipulation. . . . Self-repression and social repression form the indispensable counterpoint to personal emancipation and social emancipation.[38]

Thus does the move away from primitive human sociality through early agricultural forms to increasingly urban conurbation and ultimately to industrial society—conceived of traditionally—consist of the subjugation of a large part of humanity in the name of progress. The larger the conurbation, the more sophisticated and numerous the technology, the more subordination and domination of the labour force required. As such, in this schema, domination is posited as an a priori side effect of progress, one that, in part, is to be welcomed: progress away from basic animality would not have been possible without it. Although beyond the scope of the present study, it should be noted that this view permeated post Enlightenment social theory, both radical and conservative, from Hobbes through to Marx.

In his own treatment of this social problematic, however, Bookchin offers a reformulation of this double-edged historical development. Is this process really "an inescapable drama," Bookchin asks, "a dialectic that is woven into the human condition as the very substance of history?"[39] Moreover, does the move toward "civilisation," the move toward "our human fulfillment involve a penalty—the domination of human by human as a precondition of the domination of nature by human," that is, as a precondition of humanity's attempt to control the forces of nature in the production of increasing surpluses and material security?[40] Further, Bookchin would challenge whether the very basis of this supposed historical movement holds true. "Is it a given that nature is 'stingy' and that labor is humanity's principle means of redemption from animality?"[41]

If this traditional view does hold true, then, for Bookchin, it cannot help but posit the emergence of hierarchy and domination in society as an inevitable by-product of the processes of societal development in the quest to dominate this stingy nature, and this hierarchy eventually leads to the utmost bifurcation of society into classes. Therefore, Bookchin asks further whether class societies must also be viewed as inevitable, once "enough technics, labor, and 'manpower' exist so that society can plunder nature effectively and render exploitation possible."[42] Or did something else happen here? Can it not be argued, Bookchin contends, that an already formed, pre-economic-history elite usurped the new post-surplus economic strata of society, usurped the fruits of technics and labour, later to consolidate themselves into clearly definable ruling classes? If this *can* be argued, then it fundamentally challenges the traditional notion of the emergence of hierarchy, as, for an elite to usurp the emergent surplus suggests that hierarchy had bifurcated society *before* the technological advance of the agricultural revolution.

In *asking* this series of questions, Bookchin argues that he is

deliberately reversing the way in which Victorian social theorists
have typically oriented such inquiries. *I am asking not if the notion
of dominating nature gave rise to the domination of human by
human but rather if the domination of human by human gave rise
to the notion of dominating nature.* In short, did *culture* rather
than technics, *consciousness* rather than labor, or *hierarchies* rather
than classes either open or foreclose social possibilities that might
have profoundly altered the present human condition with its
diminished prospects of human survival?[43]

Bookchin asks therefore, in contrast to Enlightenment social theory
(Marxism included) whether the antagonistic relationship between
humanity and nature stems not from early organic society's need to dominate a natural world that has thus far dominated it, but rather if it stems
from the emergence of domination that existed *previously in society itself.*
That is to say, did domination already exist, between the sexes, between
the ages, between the exploiters and the exploited *before* humanity conceived of the notion of dominating the natural world? Indeed, did the
notion of dominating nature stem directly from the emergence of relations of domination in social form?

In attempting to *answer* these questions, Bookchin opens up a whole
new realm of early human experience that has to be taken account of in
the formulating of the emergence of hierarchy. That is, Bookchin opens
the realm of pre-history to analysis, the deeply embedded changes in the
relations of society that expand beyond the parameters of class. Indeed,
he argues that "we must fix this *pre*class, indeed, *pre*-economic, period in
social development clearly in our minds," as traditionally, an analysis of
the central concepts with which all ideologies ascribe to the period has
been "papered over by a *less fundamental* critique," the critique of the
private property and the hierarchical forms of society that, as noted, are
posited as inevitable.[44]

It is in the developments in this under-examined, pre-economic
period, that Bookchin finds the historic turning point, the moment
that social evolution, up until then complementary and creative, began
to assume its "highly aberrant form." Crucial here is that despite the

traditional view, in this pre-historic period, the natural scarcity of a stingy natural world which confronted humanity was not necessarily the common experience. Bookchin argues that early human "organic societies," are actually characterised by "their intense solidarity, internally and with the natural world."[45] Of course, these societies are the direct expression of the unity of natural evolution that Bookchin sees as complementary and creative (as discussed in detail above). In *The Ecology of Freedom*, Bookchin offers a detailed study of the anthropological and ethnographic literature on existing tribal peoples to argue that the natural world is not viewed as a harsh realm of necessity to people untouched by the move toward "civilisation," but is in fact "a *participant* that advises the community with its omens, secures it with its camouflage, leaves its tell-tale messages in broken twigs and footprints, whispers warnings to it in the wind's voice, nourishes it with a largesse of plants and animals, and in its countless functions and counsels is absorbed into the community's nexus of rights and duties."[46]

We return to the validity of Bookchin's picture of organic society in the next chapter, but for our exposition of his social history, it is important to note that in organic society, there exists, according to Bookchin, *no* antagonism between humanity and the natural world. Moreover, Bookchin contends that as "people of all ages have projected their social structures onto the natural world," then it follows that "organic society's harmonized view of nature *follows directly from the harmonized relations within the early community*" itself.[47] Therefore, there exists no hierarchy between humanity and nature, no antagonistic attempt to dominate nature because there exists no hierarchy of domination whatsoever in organic society itself.

Where then, if not from the changes in agriculture and the resultant surplus, did this hierarchy begin to emerge? Of course, Bookchin does agree with traditional social thought that there were fundamental changes around the time of the Neolithic Revolution, as the actual changes wrought by agriculture were indeed vast and increasingly hierarchical. Indeed, in the Bookchin model, the growing surpluses of the early Neolithic retain their historical importance, but they are not elevated to the position of *the* causal factor in the emergence of classes, just because they rendered the existence of classes possible. As Bookchin argued, to ignore the changes of the early Neolithic "would be as simplistic as to make them the all-important factor that changed early society's complementary values into later society's egocentric ones."[48]

However, for Bookchin, structures much more fundamental than the growing surplus had to be in place for the emergence of class; structures much more ingrained in the material and the psychological recesses of early society than the surplus. Bookchin contends that "even before material surpluses began to increase significantly" the roles of members of organic communities began to shift away from egalitarian forms into "systems of obedience and command."[49] What were these structures? What, exactly, was it that crystallised hierarchical values and brought them forth from the non-hierarchical relationships found in organic society? "What social substance gave them reality long before classes and states emerged to give them almost unchallenged power?"[50] For Bookchin, this "social substance" was the nascent emergence of "hierarchies rooted in age, sex, and quasi-religious and quasi-political needs," which in turn would create "the power and the material relationships from which classes were formed."[51]

More specifically, although the continuous historical differentiation between the male and female spheres of early human societies is important in the emergence of this hierarchy, in terms of the first genuine, non-biological, strictly *social* hierarchy (of which more below), the difference between the sexes is not the defining factor for Bookchin. The fact that the male did have very different capabilities from the female, which earmarked him for a very different role, does not automatically posit the notion that his role was more important, or domineering, than the female's in organic society. For Bookchin, in organic society, "both sexes occupy a distinct sovereign role in their respective spheres" and their roles are complementary.[52]

This is not an attempt on Bookchin's part to sublimate the very important differences between the roles of the sexes in organic society: there were clearly key differences that affected the make-up of these societies. "The primal division of labor," Bookchin argues, "that assigned hunting tasks to the male and domestic tasks to the female is based on hard biological reality: A woman, coupled to a noisy infant, can scarcely be expected to practice the stealth and athleticism needed to hunt large animals."[53] This biological difference undoubtedly forged the widening gulf between the male and the female in organic society as the dependency of the human infant would force the female into an increasingly sedentary lifestyle.

Moreover, the growth of the human population would ensure that the role of the male began to outstrip that of the female, as differing tribes and clans began to grow, to collide with one another, bringing forth both cooperation and conflict, war and trade. Thus did society begin the slide toward *patriocentricity*. However, for Bookchin, "there is no intrinsic reason why a patricentric community, merely because it has a masculine temperament, must be hierarchical or reduce women to a subjugated position. The economic roles of the two sexes are still complementary; without the support that each sex gives to the other, the community will disintegrate."[54]

Here, and in line with his notion of natural evolution as complementary, and of the biological differences therein being complementary, we can see that Bookchin's particular use of the concept of hierarchy takes on a unique meaning. Hierarchy, for Bookchin, is "a strictly social term . . . an exclusive characteristic of second nature."[55] As such, it is something outside of the differences in society that stem from biological fact: it is the development of interests that are strictly social, that exist outside of the nexus of relationships of natural evolution. In its most advanced form, hierarchy for Bookchin "refers to institutionalized and highly ideological systems of command and obedience."[56] It does not exist in the natural world: interactions within distinct ecocommunities and food webs do not constitute hierarchy, do not constitute ranked patterns of behaviour. Rather, for Bookchin, there are dominant and submissive individuals, and individual acts in the natural world, and these must be seen as part of the entire ecosystem or food web: everything therein has a specific role, whether as predator or prey.

The early differences between the sexes, Bookchin argued, should also be seen as part of the complementary ecosystem of early human society: they are part of the participatory evolution of that ecosystem as a whole, which, like any other ecosystem, contains different actors and individuals with distinct roles. However, for Bookchin, these roles and the individuals that execute them—be it dominant animals in a food web or the male in early human society—do not constitute a hierarchy, which "is guided by a social logic that goes beyond individual interactions or inborn patterns of behavior." The strata or classes that go to make up the nodes on a social hierarchy "are made of sterner stuff" than the interactions of a food web: "They have a life of their own apart from the personalities who give them substance."[57]

For Bookchin, then, although the primordial division of labour between the sexes did provide the "raw materials from which hierarchical society will raise its social and moral edifice," it was not until a sub-group of society emerged that had its *own distinct social interests* that hierarchy began to emerge.[58] This sub-group, he contends, was the community elders, a nascent *gerontocracy*, a group "that forms the point of departure for a separate social interest."[59] From within this strata, needs and interests gradually emerge that do not necessarily fit in to the complementary and participatory relationships that had characterised the evolution of human society thus far. "To be born, to be young, to mature and to finally grow old and die is natural fact," Bookchin points out, "but the older one becomes, the more one acquires distinct interests that are not 'natural.'" These interests, for Bookchin, become something different, they become "uniquely social." He explains that

> The later years of life are a period of diminishing physical powers; the declining years a period of outright dependency. [Therefore] the aging and the aged develop interests that are tied neither to their sexual roles nor to their lineage. They depend for their survival ultimately on the fact that the community is social in the fullest sense of the term; that it will provide for them not because they participate in the process of production or reproduction, but because of the *institutional* roles they can create for themselves in the social realm.[60]

These "institutional roles" for Bookchin, are borne of need: the elders of an early organic society become increasingly disconnected from their society due to their waning powers of production and reproduction, and must form new uses and skills for themselves that help them to remain useful to the wider communal group. Although the sexes "complement each other economically," Bookchin argues, "the old and the young do not." Initially, the elders thus compensate for their decline in productive and reproductive power by becoming "a vital repository of knowledge and wisdom," but for Bookchin this very process "merely underscores the fact that their capacities [those of the elders] belong largely to the social and cultural sphere," by way of the fact that their roles become a matter of the social contribution they can make, and not the economic in the sense of production or reproduction.[61]

Therefore, for Bookchin, even more than the increasingly powerful male in preliterate communities, "the aging and the aged tend to be socially conscious as such—as a matter of survival."[62] They somehow have to prove their continued worth to the community. "They have the most to gain," Bookchin continues, "by the institutionalization of society and the emergence of hierarchy," for it is here that they can "retain powers that are denied to them by physical weakness and infirmity." Bookchin continues that the elders' "need for social power, and for hierarchical social power at that, is a function of their loss of biological power. The social sphere is the only realm in which this power can be created and, concomitantly, the only sphere that can cushion their vulnerability to natural forces. Thus, they are the architects par excellence of social life, of social power, and of its institutionalization along hierarchical lines."[63]

This is the point, for Bookchin, at which social evolution began to assume its "highly aberrant form." Of course, nowhere was this development rapid or even uniform. Indeed, it would take centuries for the elaboration of these early hierarchies into fully accoutred systems of social domination. Again, this would be aided in large measure by the technological innovation of the Neolithic. However, the central claim from Bookchin is that these nascent forms of hierarchy were already in place by the time of the Neolithic, to varying degrees across different societies. Generally, however, by the time the effects of agriculture began to cement social differentiations, the early social domination by the gerontocracy had been further removed from the complementary social nexus of a participatory community by the rise of the shaman, who would create even more distant social interests. Later still, the rise of the male warrior-chief, who would further elaborate the realm of the shaman, pushed hierarchical forms further, and ultimately, the emergence of the collective that would group around the warrior-chief, provide us with our earliest forms of classes, the wholly social form of hierarchy.

It is here then, starting with the gerontocracy, that the "social substance," the "raw materials" of hierarchy and domination first appear in the physical and psychological world of early "civilisation." It was these raw materials that were to eventually create what Bookchin calls the "vast legacy of domination," which passes through various guises and finds its ultimate expression in class society and the State.[64] Important here is that the emergence and elaboration of the legacy of domination has a dual effect: a material effect and a subjective effect.[65] On a material level, the shift from hierarchical society to class society was "embodied by the emergence of the city, the State, an authoritarian technics, and a highly organized market economy."[66] On a subjective level, this shift "found expression in the emergence of a repressive sensibility and body of values—in various ways of mentalizing [sic] the entire realm of experience along lines of command and obedience." These types of sensibilities and mentalities Bookchin labels "epistemologies of rule," to denote the emergence of a body of knowledge that normalises the characteristics of bifurcated class society. Bookchin contends further that "as much as any material development, these epistemologies of rule fostered the development of patriarchy and an egoistic morality in the rulers of society; in the ruled, they fostered a psychic apparatus rooted in guilt and renunciation. Just as aggression flexes our body for fight or flight, so class societies organize our psychic structures for command and obedience."[67]

Thus in this sense does Bookchin further reduce the economism of the problematic of the rise of hierarchy and domination. That is to say, by stressing the subjective side of the emergence and concretisation of domination in society, the psychological aspects of the rise of hierarchy, Bookchin moves our conception of dealing with these problems further away from the notion of them as strictly economic factors, as strictly the by-product of the necessary project to control the natural world and render it productive in the move through human history. As we shall see in the remainder of the work, this is essential to Bookchin's widely conceived notion of what a revolutionary project must address to affect deep and lasting social change.

But to finish here, and to stress again: all of these developments, according to Bookchin, were in place *before* the emergence of the surplus. They are thus in the Bookchin programme *not* the inevitable by-product of the move to an economic world; they are not, perhaps most importantly, the by-product of a human project to dominate a stingy, harsh natural world. This, it is argued here, is the *central motor* on which Bookchin's entire historical and philosophical programme revolves. This is *the* critical insight of the Bookchin programme that explains the social focus of his philosophy and politics. There is much more that can be said about Bookchin's social history—some of which we turn to in the next chapter—but to understand the Bookchin project as a whole, philosophically, historically, and politically, it is this central motor we need to focus on.

Bluntly put, from this central motor stem: (1) the notion that social evolution veered off track from its up-until-that-point complementary and creative evolution in the world of life as a whole in large measure because of changes in *social* forms and relationships and not because of the *natural* reaction to a harsh and necessitarian natural world; (2) the notion that hierarchy as such is perhaps *not* the inevitable by-product of humanity's historical move through civilisation; (3) the commitment to an analysis of hierarchy and domination in society that is more far-reaching and more fundamental than the class analysis has traditionally allowed for; (4) that the dissolution of such social hierarchy and domination would require a social project that reached into the very recesses of this hierarchy in society; and finally, most important in terms of the operating system of Bookchin's social ecology as a whole, (5) the notion that *all ecological problems are social problems*, which stem in the first instance from the emergence of hierarchy in its nascent form in the gerontocracy.

On this final, central point, it is important to emphasise the particular conclusion it itself brings, which relates directly in the approach to the ecological crisis and its resolution. If, as Bookchin maintains, hierarchy and domination emerged in society first, that they were posited as a material and subjective reality *before* the notion of dominating nature in the quest to wrest increasing surpluses and material security therefrom, then the exploitation of natural forces becomes something far more entrenched, requiring a much deeper ecological and social response to the ecological crisis that stems from such exploitation. Moreover, and crucially, it uncouples the notion of dominating nature from the notion of human progress, and of course, it nullifies and reformulates the traditional conceptions of a stingy necessitarian natural world and permits a view of the natural word as non-antagonistic to human society.

As Bookchin argued, "I cannot emphasis too strongly that the concept [of man dominating nature] emerged very gradually from a broader social development: the increasing domination of human by human," and the notion of domination of human by human was fostered by the rise of social hierarchy.[68] Indeed here, a stingy nature plays no role in the emergence of hierarchy, and this emergence is stripped of its a priori status. Again, this is the central motor of the entire Bookchin project, and as we move closer toward an elucidation and examination of the political manifestation of this theoretical bedrock, we need to note the two primary effects of this reversal of the traditional view of the social problematic that is the move toward civilisation.

First, the notion that humanity's domination and destruction of the natural world stems from the domination and destruction within human society suggests that to reverse this process, social domination as such has to be challenged. As we have seen, this forms the theoretical grounds for Bookchin's ecological leitmotif: *that all ecological problems are first and foremost social problems*, thus requiring social solutions. Second, the placing of these social problems at the point not of the emergence of economic strata and classes but at the emergence of the much more socially pervasive material and subjective hierarchies necessitates the widest possible conception of a programme of social overhaul. That is to say, if the social problems that are the root cause of the ecological problems are problems that reside in the recesses of everyday life—the domination of the young by the old, women by men, people of colour by whites, and the poor by the rich—then the transformative project required to address this is extensive: this is why Bookchin argues that the solving of the ecological crisis required the full remaking of society.

Before we examine this widely conceived project of radical social change, based on the two preceding conclusions, we turn in the next chapter to the question of whether Bookchin's historical schema as outlined above stands or fails when exposed to the serious and robust analysis that has been denied it since the fall-out from his 1987 critique. However, this much can be said at present: what we have here called the "central motor" of Bookchin's theoretical framework fully rounds out his criticism of deep ecology in the first instance, as it places ecological problems firmly in the realm of social relations and *not* as the inevitable impact of humanity as such, and in the second instance, gives a historical working out of his philosophical commitments to the idea of a complementary nature as a whole, to the creative process of evolution. As we have seen, humanity was a part of this complementary and creative nexus until the emergence of hierarchy as a social problem. Moreover, and most revolutionary, if this social problem is identified as inhering in the most entrenched hierarchical relationships of society, as inhering in the deeply entrenched everyday social relations, the ventricles of society writ-large, then their resolution necessitates the most wide-ranging social revolution possible as a means to avert ecological collapse. This is Bookchin's revolutionary force, the "explosive implications" of his version of ecology, stemming both from his philosophy and his social history. But do they stand up to robust critique?

Chapter 5

Reassessing Bookchin's Social History

If the central motor of Bookchin's social history is the switching of the emergence of hierarchy, as discussed in the previous chapter, and if it is in the historical development of this hierarchy that Bookchin traces a "legacy of domination" of human by human—and just as fundamentally, of the natural world by humanity—then the genesis of his critique of deep ecology can clearly be seen to be an expression of these principles, raised in the face of deep ecology's direct rejection of or lack of focus on both of them. It hardly needs repeating by now that theoretical and philosophical differences generated Bookchin's controversial critique, and that these were based on a richly elaborated set of theoretical principles.

In this chapter then, we complete our recovery of Bookchin from the rancorous late 1980s exchange with the deep ecologists. As we did with our treatment of Bookchin's philosophy, we have shown in the previous chapter the rich social history in Bookchin, examined its conceptual bases: now, we put it to the test, with sources more robust and more removed from the materials of the original exchange, and examine its validity as a theoretical basis. Here, through an examination of these robust critiques, we find that there *are*, in fact, significant problems in Bookchin's social history that need to be addressed. However, the first thesis of the present work still stands: that the caricature generated in 1987 represents not only the loss of Bookchin's more concrete contribution but also a missed opportunity for a full discussion of where his body of work can be properly critiqued and even improved.

In the present chapter then, we take the opportunity previously denied for a full discussion of these problems. Then, with the recovery of Bookchin's philosophy and social theory from the more problematic literature complete, in the next part of the present work, we turn to the practical and political consequences of Bookchin's philosophical and theoretical foundations. Shorn of the caricature of a theory hopelessly flawed, it can be seen that Bookchin's entire programme, as manifest in the political practice he calls for, offers a valuable and viable avenue for attempting to reverse the social and ecological crises of our time.

Résumé

To recap briefly on our discussion thus far: for Bookchin, the unity in diversity that inheres in natural evolution would, until the move toward "civilisation," inhere too in human society. Even though early human society would of course be biologically differentiated, as are all ecosystems, resulting in different roles for the male and female for example, they were not, according to Bookchin, hierarchically structured. As such, they were "organic societies," living in harmonious balance with each other and with the natural world. Hierarchy, for Bookchin, then—nowhere to be found in early societies and nowhere to be found in the natural world—is made of "sterner stuff": it is "a strictly social term . . . an exclusive characteristic of second nature. It refers to institutionalized and highly ideological systems of command and obedience."[1]

Therefore, for Bookchin, the central social question is *how* this hierarchy emerged; and, moreover, the consequences it has resulted in for humanity's relationship with itself *and* its relationship to the natural world. Tracing this emergence from, first, within the age group, then through the shaman, the warrior chiefs, the early priesthood and ultimately leading to the emergence of economic classes and ultimately the State, Bookchin identifies a vast "legacy of domination" that is the root not only of the social crisis of our time, but of the ecological crisis too. Importantly, and as will be discussed more fully in the remaining chapters, the emergence of hierarchy and this legacy of domination also brought forth a counter legacy, "the legacy of freedom," which has been the ever present (if subordinate) counterpart of domination since the moment hierarchy emerged.

Just as importantly for Bookchin is *when* this hierarchy emerged, and from our discussion in the previous chapter, we can see that it emerged for Bookchin before society started to bifurcate into economic classes around the emergence of the surplus from the early-Neolithic onwards. As such, the action required for the dissolution of hierarchy—the *only* way to reverse the ecological crisis for Bookchin—requires a social project far wider than one that focuses on the economic reformation of society, even one as radical as Marxism. As Bookchin argues in numerous places, hierarchy is "an even more fundamental problem than social classes," and the resulting domination is "an even more fundamental problem than economic exploitation."[2]

Taken together, this *how* and *when* concerning the emergence of hierarchy and the resultant legacy of domination is, as noted, the central motor on which the entire Bookchin project turns. Not only does this explain, philosophically, why the creativity and fecundity of natural evolution has been diverted—and in particular, why social evolution has taken a "highly aberrant form"—it also provides the basis for Bookchin's wide-ranging political programme—his communalism—which is set in its entirety to the dissolution of this hierarchy: the programme built on an attempt to institutionalise the "legacy of freedom" and dissolve the "legacy of domination." Again, we turn to a full examination of this political project in due course. For now, however, we put to the test the base on which it is constructed—Bookchin's social history.

It is argued here that although Bookchin's version of social history as a whole offers an alternative approach to understanding the emergence and persistence of forms of hierarchy and domination in society, and an approach to addressing them, there are three significant objections that can be raised. First, there are questions of the historical accuracy of Bookchin's view of the emergence of hierarchy from within organic society, stemming from a lack of anthropological evidence in Bookchin's work. Second, and more problematically, on closer examination, Bookchin's thesis of the *how* and *when* can be seen to be inadequately explained, and as such, containing a contradiction that strikes right at the heart of the central motor of his social history as a whole. Third, that even with these problems aside, Bookchin's historical dialectical drama between the legacy of domination and the legacy of freedom does not provide adequate grounds on which to understand the movement of history. At the outset of our examination of

these three significant problems, it needs to be noted that while none of
the three problems raised here can be successfully refuted in their entirety,
that they do however require significant qualification.

Historical Accuracy and Anthropological "Evidence"

As has hopefully become clear throughout the present work, Bookchin's
project was indeed grand in scale: it can quite reasonably be argued that
Bookchin was a "generalist" in the widest possible sense. His was a project
that, in trying to elicit the dialectic of natural and social history, was by
necessity interdisciplinary: it involved sociology, anthropology, ethnology,
political theory, and even psychology. As Bookchin himself conceded at
the outset of *The Ecology of Freedom*, his overall project had an "unabashed
messianic character."[3] However, it is this very messianic character, it could
be argued, that resulted in Bookchin spreading himself too thinly: a work
of speculative philosophy whose primary aim must be the outlining of its
own philosophical theoretical foundation leaves little space for empirical
evidence and the full treatment of the many varied themes he touched
upon. We shall return to the question of the validity of Bookchin's overall
approach below, but a related criticism here is that in his major treatment
of social history and the emergence of hierarchy in *The Ecology of Freedom*,
Bookchin fails to produce sufficient evidence for his conception of both
society *before* the emergence of hierarchy—i.e., of organic society—and
of the actual transition to hierarchical society. As argued by White, when
examining Bookchin's social history, "it is difficult to avoid being struck by
the sheer vagueness and imprecision that seem to linger around this whole
enterprise." More specifically in terms of Bookchin's notion of organic
society, White argues that beyond Bookchin's references to "early-Neolithic" village societies, "it is never made very clear by Bookchin when or
where this early form of human association actually existed."[4]

A further problem here concerns not only the "when or where" of
Bookchin's organic society, but also the "what." That is, on what does
Bookchin base his conception of organic society as based on "intense solidarity, internally and with the natural world," the contention that organic
society is in ecological balance with a participatory and fecund natural
world?[5] In truth, as argued by Rudy, "Bookchin provides no climatological

or epidemiological data—because none exist—to support such an assertion of perpetual social ecological fecundity in prehistory."[6] Rudy further
criticises Bookchin's notion of the sexual division of labour in organic
society as the latent (if outwardly complementary) base on which hierarchy would eventually emerge, pointing out that his conclusions are based
on "two (and only two) anthropological studies from the 1950s" which by
1982 (the year his major work was published) had been "superseded" by
later research.[7]

Moreover, the anthropological data that Bookchin does use can also
be questioned. As White argues, Bookchin's historical speculations are
based in the main on twentieth century ethnographic studies of existing
tribal peoples, from which he draws conclusions about the make-up of
organic society. As such, White points to the problems this raises in terms
of "the implicit (and highly questionable) assumption . . . that tribal people
have lived in a permanently static state, without change or social development."[8] Furthermore, according to Rudy, "to extrapolate from . . . studies
of modern, long post-European contact, tribal entities to a uniform theory
of social organization within preliterate societies is to practice an extreme
form of unevolutionary thinking." While the use of contemporary ethnographic research *is* acceptable for Rudy, unlike Bookchin—whose tone
is "extremely confident" in the conclusions he draws—other anthropologists who take this ethnographic approach "note the paucity of the actual
data and the speculative character of the work."[9]

In truth, these critiques of Bookchin's anthropological evidence can
all be easily sustained. *The Ecology of Freedom* is clearly *not* a work of
anthropology, or indeed a work that is based primarily on anthropology
or ethnography. As such, the evidence that Bookchin does cite, whilst not
insignificant, is by no means extensive. However, whilst noting that the
lack of evidence is a problem, the notion that Bookchin presents his programmatic in his major work as "extremely confident" conclusions or facts
is patently false, and in fact it can be shown that Bookchin explicitly states
that his work is a work of speculation. In the Introduction to *The Ecology
of Freedom*, Bookchin expressly offers his "mea culpas for certain expos-
itory problems."[10] "The reader should be mindful," he warns, "that any
'fact,' firmly stated and apparently complete, is actually the result of a complex process—not a given datum that appears full-blown in a community
or society." Moreover, Bookchin notes that through his use of dialectics,

he tries to elicit possible *processes*, and "not cut and dried propositions . . . like categories in a traditional logic text."[11]

Further, we should remind ourselves of our discussion in Chapter 2, where Bookchin was explicit about the nature and intent of dialectical thought, which he saw as first and foremost a *speculative* philosophy, based on a process of reasoning out potentialities from existing facts; indeed, a way of ceaselessly contrasting the "facts" of the present "what is" with notions—derived from the "what is" of objective *potentialities*—of the "what could be." This form of reasoning is fundamentally different for Bookchin than "conventional reasoning": it is not a straightforward attempt to tabulate and classify "facts," but rather is an attempt to speculate about possible processes in natural evolution.[12] Moreover, on the materials he does use, Bookchin tells the reader that "anthropological etiquette requires that I occasionally sprinkle my remarks with the usual caveats about my use of "selective data," my proclivity for "rampant speculation," and my "normative interpretation" of disputable research materials."[13] He also concedes the same data he uses could be used to show the exact opposite: that nature and organic society was in fact competitive, aggressive, and hierarchical. Bookchin therefore claims no definitive case here, only an identification of undeniable trends—of an alternative *potentiality*—and arguably need not furnish an extensive body of facts to argue his case.

But beyond Bookchin's own defence of his anthropological evidence, it is not difficult to find in anthropology the necessary evidence to back up his claims. Although beyond the remit of the present work, even the most cursory examination of anthropological literature points to such evidence. For example, on Bookchin's central claim that the surplus was not enough to generate class society on its own, that in fact hierarchy needed to be in place for class society to emerge around the surplus—that indeed elites had to be in place to usurp the gains made on the surplus—there is much literature that bears this thesis out. As argued by Earle, the surplus alone was not enough to forge new social classes, or even "early chiefdoms." Rather, there needed to be in place "the structural preconditions of hierarchy . . . the conditions that limit a people's options and thus permit a surplus to be channeled towards a center."[14] Moreover, full-length treatments of the over-emphasis of the surplus as the forger of social classes are also evidence of Bookchin's accuracy.[15]

That population growth is not necessarily the direct result of the growing surplus—a claim inherent in Bookchin's notion of hierarchy emerging through the growth of organic society *pre*-surplus—is also an anthropological concept of some strength. According to Sussman, simply "stating that increased food production leads to an increase in population says nothing about the mechanisms involved in this increase."[16] One such mechanism is the relieving of "child-spacing pressures" that nomadic tribespeople felt. This pressure was to ensure that the birth-rate stayed low in nomadic tribes, as too many children were impossible to sustain due to the protracted dependency on the mother. Once tribes began to become sedentary—a trend that occurs with agriculture at subsistence level as well as in societies with an increasing surplus—the pressure to "space" the amount of children a mother would have was relieved, leading to population increase. See also Hassan and Sengel, and Pennington for similar claims.[17]

Elsewhere, on Bookchin's notion of the sexual division of labour as essentially complementary in organic society, as opposed to the traditional view in which the male usurped the female realm even in preliterate communities, the notion of the female being as important as the male in early horticultural society, there is also much more data than has previously been allowed. The physical exertion of horticulture and home-building (the women were to build early-Neolithic homes), coupled with the social and emotional "toil" of kinship and child rearing, were, as leading gender anthropologist Michelle Rosaldo argued, to give women "goals and strategies which were intrinsic to the process of social life . . . giving women a good deal more power than conventional theorists have assumed."[18] For a thorough discussion of the centrality of women in studies of early Sumerian society, see also Rohrlich.[19]

Again, it has to be kept in mind when looking at Bookchin's anthropology that, as noted above, Bookchin conceded the nature of his own speculative approach, of his own use of selective data, and moreover, maintained that, in fairness, "by interpreting the same material differently, one could show that organic society was egotistical, competitive, aggressive, hierarchical."[20] However, to do so, the anthropologist would have to use the same techniques that Bookchin used: would have to speculate, to draw out commonalities, to infer. Therefore, Bookchin maintains that he points to the trends and patterns of non-hierarchical social organisation in anthropology that are equally as valid as the mainstream view in anthropology that early social organisation *was* hierarchical and competitive.

Finally there is a further qualification to be made on Bookchin's anthropological evidence, and that is, that in a sense, Rudy was right: at the time Bookchin was writing *The Ecology of Freedom* (during the 1970s), there was very little evidence for the speculations he was making beyond the studies we have pointed to above (which were only to receive the attention they deserved some years after they were published, particularly those that focused on gender). However, this, for Bookchin, does not preclude the power of dialectical thought to draw out potentialities on even the most distant of facts and evidence. Moreover, Bookchin's challenge to the mainstream views of anthropology may have been less realistic in the 1980s and even the 1990s, but there is increasing evidence over recent years that goes toward proving that his attempt to redress the biases of anthropology, his dialectical challenge to the assumptions made by the mainstream, may not have been as misplaced as first thought.

One convincing argument here comes from leading anthropologist, David Graeber. In his *Fragments of Anarchist Anthropology*, Graeber—who the London School of Economics Professor Maurice Bloch has described as "the best anthropological theorist of his generation from anywhere in the world"—makes the case for a historical undervaluing of ethnographic studies and the lessons they can yield for trying to formulate notions of alternative societies to modern capitalist states.[21] Importantly, he points to biases in anthropology as a whole that have prevented much study being cast in this light—hence his notions that there are only "fragments" of an anthropology that might point to non-hierarchical, non-statist (i.e., anarchist) societies—and argues for a rethinking of this approach, for an approach that can draw out the potentialities of different ways of life.

For Graeber, much ethnographic study reveals examples of the undeniable (yet underemphasised) existence of non-statist, non-hierarchical organisations. To outline these forms and use them as possibilities, to draw conclusions for alternatives to present day statist forms is, however, to risk opprobrium about one's method and conclusions similar to those accusations against Bookchin made by Rudy and by White, noted above. As such, anthropologists have traditionally been "terrified of being accused of romanticizing the societies they study," and anthology itself "appears as a discipline terrified of its own potential."[22]

For Graeber however, this fear stems not from genuinely methodological weaknesses in the ethnographic approach, but from the biases of the university and intellectual climate of the times. In fact—and although Graeber does not share Bookchin's conclusions—ethnography is perfectly positioned for Graeber to carry approaches to social theory such as Bookchin's:

> When one carries out an ethnography, one observes what people do, and then tries to tease out the hidden symbolic, moral, or pragmatic logics that underlie their actions; one tries to get at the way people's habits and actions make sense in ways that they are not themselves completely aware of. One obvious role for a radical intellectual is to do precisely that: to look at those who are creating viable alternatives, try to figure out what might be the larger implications of what they are (already) doing, and then offer those ideas back, not as prescriptions, but as contributions, *possibilities*.[23]

As is hopefully clear, this is an almost word for word account of the way in which Bookchin used his anthropological and ethnographic materials: Bookchin tried to "figure out what might be the larger implications" of the fragments in the literature he looked at of complementary and cooperative social relations, to provide, as Bookchin admitted, one *possibility* for social organisation. Moreover, that Bookchin's evidence is sparse also points to the other conclusion of Graeber: that, due to the biases of anthropology, there was not that much more evidence of this complementarity for Bookchin to draw on at the time. This, however, should not preclude such a speculative project.

In short, then, on the notion of Bookchin's lack of evidence for his anthropological conclusions, there is as noted above, a very real sense in which the criticism stands: there *is* a paucity of evidence in Bookchin's theoretical elucidation of the rise of hierarchy. However, it is also clear that several serious qualifications need to be made, concerning: the way in which Bookchin's project is one of a speculative philosophy; the way in which he acknowledges the fact that a completely contradictory picture can be read into organic society; the fact that there was simply not that much evidence in existence when Bookchin wrote his major work; and finally, as outlined by Graeber, that such evidence may not exist historically due to the biases of the discipline of anthropology itself.

The Contradiction of the Emergence of Hierarchy

Questions of the merits of Bookchin's evidence and methodology aside, it can be argued that there is a more fundamental problem in Bookchin's historical narrative that may challenge its overall coherency, an apparent contradiction at the very base of what we have called here the "central motor" of Bookchin's project: his claim that the idea of dominating nature stemmed in the first instance from the domination of human by human in society (and not the other way around). Returning to White here, he argues that despite Bookchin's commitment to the notion of hierarchy and domination emerging *first* in organic society and then leading to the idea of dominating nature and the ultimate rise of social hierarchy, classes, and the State, that "an implicit recognition of the role that material factors played in the development of hierarchy, and even in a certain sense that the development of hierarchy is inevitable, can also be unearthed in Bookchin's work."[24] That is to say, despite Bookchin's claim that domination is a social phenomenon that develops from within society itself, White claims that Bookchin unwittingly still places domination as emerging at the intersection of society and nature. To explain, we need to return to Bookchin's discussion of the gerontocracy.

As discussed in the previous chapter, for Bookchin, more so than the sexual division of labour, the elders of organic societies are the conduits of early hierarchy. The needs of the elderly become increasingly social in the sense that the older they become, the less they contribute to the production and reproduction of society: that is, for Bookchin, as their physical and reproductive powers wane, the aged begin to create roles for themselves that are *wholly* social due to their declining positions in the biological nexus of society. As he argues, the elderly in organic society were "the most infirm, dependent, and often the most vulnerable members of the group in periods of difficulty." Moreover, the aged "had to often give up their lives in times of want that threatened the existence of a community."[25] According to Bookchin, the anthropological literature is "replete" with examples of the elders being left behind by tribes on the move in times of natural scarcity or the impinging on their lives of war or conflict.[26]

However, White points to an obvious inconsistency here: if as Bookchin claims, hierarchy emerged due to the particular pressures on the age group in precarious times for the organic society, is this not, in itself, the result of material relationship between humanity and nature rather than the purely *social* relationship that Bookchin ascribes to the emergence of hierarchy? Are not "times of want" and "periods of difficulty" which "threaten the existence of a community" produced by an interaction with a nature that dominates the elders, ultimately resulting in the elders' attempt to "dominate?"[27] Bluntly put, if this is the case, then although Bookchin claims to have reversed the traditional formula of the emergence of hierarchy stemming from an attempt to dominate nature by humanity, it appears that his own historical narrative is in fact *a reproduction of precisely this process*. That is, there is clearly a material (economic) relationship between the social and the natural world—i.e., the pressures of ageing on the aged—in Bookchin which "appears to play a decisive role in the emergence of hierarchy."[28] White concludes that as a result of this confusion concerning the causal factors of emergence of hierarchy, "Bookchin's account of historical development is perhaps not as radical a reversal of Marx and Engel's [and other post-Enlightenment social thought, it could be added] as first appears."[29]

Indeed, this is a contradiction picked up and extended by Alan Rudy. Here, Rudy asks if, as Bookchin contends, nature is "a *participatory* realm of interactive life-forms whose most outstanding attributes are fecundity, creativity, and directiveness," and that as such, organic societies are the social expression of this, operating along these same participatory processes—as denoted by "their intense solidarity internally and with the natural world"—then what are we to make of the fact that Bookchin sees the genesis of hierarchy stemming from an instance—the precariousness of the old—which seems not to represent the fecundity and creativity of the natural evolution but in fact its "stinginess" or cruelty?[30] That is to say, how, in the fecund realm of natural evolution can the elders of society find themselves in such a position as to suffer at both the hands of the natural world and the hands of their fellow human beings who are prepared to sacrifice the elders in times of material want?

Again, this seems to be a serious contradiction at the very heart of Bookchin's "central motor." As Rudy argues, Bookchin "denies that the fecund nature from which humanity evolved ever presented early human society with such forms of scarcity," yet at the same time, in his discussion on the emergence of hierarchy he unconsciously creates such a situation.[31] For Rudy, this stems from the fact that Bookchin has not simply erred in terms of pinpointing the historical emergence of hierarchy, but in fact has presented an unrealistic picture of organic society and nature in the first place, based, as noted above, on no substantial evidence. As such, this contradiction in Bookchin's notion of the emergence of hierarchy is in fact evidence that even Bookchin cannot escape the unreality of his own thesis:

> If the tenuous position the elderly feel themselves to be in during "periods of difficulty" generates . . . claims about the ability to control nature in order to control the younger members of societies, it could be argued that the social competition for unintentionally scarce resources generated the "need" within the elderly for institutionalized social domination . . . [and] Bookchin . . . cannot escape attributing domination's ideological and material roots in anything other than ecological scarcity.[32]

Even more problematically, Rudy goes on to demonstrate how this contradiction in Bookchin's view of social evolution may in fact be a direct reflection of an even more fundamental contradiction that inheres in his notion of evolution as a whole. For Bookchin, the emergence of the tensions between the elderly and the rest of the society—the elders' loss of social (re)productive power and their reaction to it—stems from the very processes of differentiation and increasing complexity that he sees as the directionality of natural and social evolution as a whole. According to Bookchin, "the violation of organic society," as represented in the emergence of nascent hierarchy within the age group, "is latent within organic society itself," as the "primal unity of the early community, both internally and with nature, *is weakened merely by the elaboration of the community's social life—its ecological differentiation.*"[33]

Although Bookchin claims that these developments do not yet represent social hierarchy as such—these "raw materials" of hierarchy would later have to be reworked into distinctly social interests—he describes these nascent developments as the "growing tensions" of organic society.[34] However, if organic society, and more widely, evolution as a whole is expressly participatory, creative, and fecund, as Bookchin claims, where does the notion of "growing tensions" fit in this natural dialectic? How can organic society be seen to be based, on the one hand, on the "internal solidarity among its members and with the natural world"—a direct reflection of nature's participatory evolution—yet on the other, begin to experience "growing tensions" through the very process of ecological differentiation?

To put the matter bluntly: if increasing differentiation and complexity are the drivers of a participatory process of evolution, as Bookchin claims, then it appears that this process also inevitably leads to organic society's "growing tensions," to competition and conflict, and *not* solely creativity and fecundity.[35] On a minimum reading, this highlights that Bookchin fails to notice the importance of competition and conflict in natural evolution that his own position suggests: these characteristics clearly exist in the very processes of natural evolution, in the growing tension of ecological differentiation as Bookchin himself describes it. As Rudy argues, it becomes apparent that Bookchin's version of evolutionary movement "is clearly weighted to lean toward preconceived, politically motivated (if admirable) notions of social freedom, participatory democracy, and personal agency."[36]

However, on a maximum reading, and most fatally for Bookchin's social history, this contradiction suggests that it is competition *instead* of mutualism, conflict *not* participation that is the ultimate driver of natural evolution. For, if ecological differentiation and increasing complexity were, by their very unfolding, to lead to the "growing tensions" of organic society, which in turn would lead to the eventual emergence of hierarchy and everything that ultimately stems therefrom, then it is "tension" that has been the main driver of historical movement. That is, it is *tension, conflict*, and *competition* that have brought forth not only these early hierarchies, but the later forms of economic strata, classes and the State. As such, Bookchin is seen here to confirm the thesis which he expressly sets out to reverse: hierarchy is seen to emerge from an attempt to control natural scarcity (by the elders) and thus creates social divisions as a result.

Indeed, if one returns to Bookchin's discussion of the emergence of hierarchy, there is certainly a lack of clarity, as although Bookchin treats at great length the "when" and the "how" of hierarchy's emergence, he fails to adequately explain the "*why*." Wherever Bookchin revisits the matter, the contradiction still prevails. On the one hand, Bookchin restates his view of the natural world: "nature is neither stingy nor intractable" he contends, but rather, "conceived as a *developmental* process . . . it is extraordinarily fecund, marked by an increasing wealth of differentiation, neural complexity, and the formation of diverse ecological niches," as evidenced by "the variety and multitude of life-forms we encounter in the fossil record and the world around us."[37] As such, early human, non-hierarchical society operated along similar lines: they were egalitarian, and the different roles of the sexes, the young and the old "were functionally complementary" to each other.[38]

Yet on the other hand, when describing the precarious status of the elderly that fosters hierarchy, Bookchin tells us that "in a world that is often harsh and insecure, a world ruled by natural necessity, the old are the most dispensable members of the community."[39] It is therefore left unclear as to how nature can be both fecund and creative yet produce "a world that is harsh and insecure, a world ruled by natural necessity." Moreover, this is the *exact* thesis that Bookchin tries to disprove: that to escape natural material insecurity, society had to try and dominate and control this scarce nature and as such had to dominate each other in the process. The only difference here is that as the traditional liberal and Marxist view place this process in society *as such*, on society as one entity, Bookchin transposes it to an individual group within society. Unfortunately, however, this does not refute the central hypothesis: that in trying to overcome the harsh realities of an insecure world, the elders tried to dominate the young.

This contradiction, therefore, does represent a serious problem for Bookchin's social theory. However, though it is clear that Bookchin fails to adequately explain his position on the *exact* relationship of scarcity to the emergence of hierarchy, two qualifications must be made. First, Bookchin does not, in fact, deny the part material want and ecological scarcity play in the natural world *and* played in organic society. Although his notion of natural evolution—as a *developmental process*—is a participatory and complementary realm, it would be foolish to suggest that these were the only characteristics. As Bookchin notes of the natural world: "That living things eat or are eaten, that they suffer pain through accidents, as prey, or in struggles for survival—all of which exposes them to selective processes that determine whether they will continue to live or disappear—is not a debatable issue in social ecology . . . however, social ecology *also* emphasize [sic] that the survival of living beings greatly depends on their ability to be supportive of one another."[40]

As with the natural world, so too with society: for Bookchin, second nature is just as much exposed to the harsher side of natural existence as they are the more creative side. As such, the factors that engendered hierarchy are for Bookchin as much material as they are subjective; they are part of the ecological differentiation that brings both cooperation and conflict, that brings stability and instability. From this inevitable process emerges the increased complexity and consciousness of life; but so too does it bring the contradiction inhered in such evolutionary change. As such, hierarchy for Bookchin is in fact a natural phenomenon: it "emerged primarily as an *immanent* development within society that slowly phased humanity from fairly egalitarian relationships into a society institutionalized around command and obedience."[41]

Therefore, contrary to traditional social thought which views nature as solely a harsh realm of necessity, Bookchin offers a *qualified* view of the natural world and early human society's relationship to it: yes, before the intellectual, technological and social developments of "civilisation," existence for humanity was much more insecure; it was undeniably life at the level of subsistence. However, this is only one part of the story, and *not* the human condition as such. Bookchin thus attempts to reformulate the more traditional, *un*qualified view of first nature as this harsh realm of necessity. Most importantly for Bookchin are the logical consequences of this unqualified conception of the natural world: such a harsh nature had to be controlled in the name of wrenching from it the sufficient means of life for the progress of humanity, and moreover, this project itself required the domination and exploitation of the majority of humanity by "a privileged, indeed supervisory class of rulers and exploiters."[42]

Thus, and as noted in the previous chapter, does social domination and exploitation appear in the traditional view as a *fait accompli* of historical progress: these characteristics become the necessary by-products of the human project to dominate the natural world. Yet for Bookchin, this view is only possible if one's starting point is this *unqualified* conception of first nature as "stingy." Indeed, this conception leads to an *ideology*, an ideology that is fixed on the domination of nature and the justified domination of human by human that this requires. Here, we come to the second qualification to be made on Bookchin's inadequately explained hierarchy thesis: it is this ideology, the idea that the domination of nature and the subsequent domination of human by human is necessary for human progress, which Bookchin attempts to dispel, and *not*, in fact, a specific claim for the absence of conflict in natural evolution. Bookchin was explicit about this in all of his writings on the subject: in every discussion of his reversal of the emergence of hierarchy and domination, he would note that it was the "notion" or the "idea" of "dominating nature" that would emerge from social domination, not the domination of nature itself.

This vital distinction in Bookchin's hierarchy thesis bears further explanation. For Bookchin, the ecological differentiation of society, as noted, is based primarily on the creative and complementary unfolding of natural evolution. However, such unfolding, such *change*, unavoidably brings uncertainty, brings tensions. Such are the manifestations of the differentiation of society that leads to the elders' creation of early, nascent hierarchies. However, although this can be explained as a material factor, indeed, as the product of the vicissitudes of nature, the elders are unaware of it: theirs is a wholly *social* reaction to their complex relationship to the natural world, a relationship more understood in organic societies through ritual, myth and magic. The result of this *material* ecological differentiation, which in and of itself brings progress and conflict, produces a *social* reaction in the elders of early organic society: the early raw materials of hierarchy emerging as a matter of survival.

However, these were not linked to a *project* to wrest the materials of life from the natural world, a project to tame the natural world, or dominate it, on behalf of society itself. Rather, this is a reaction to the natural world that is unconscious; this, as Bookchin argues, is "nature internalized, the nature of humanity itself," devoid of any notion of the need to dominate the natural world.[43] This is, in short, a product of the certainty *and* uncertainty that emerges from evolutionary change, a natural and immediate reaction to such change. For Bookchin, only later will "the attempt to dominate external nature" emerge as an idea, as an ideology, as humanity begins to develop further its social relations of antagonism, and ultimately, begin "to transfer its social antagonisms to the natural world outside."[44]

It is, therefore, the emergence of this later, *dominating nature as an ideology*, that Bookchin, through his reformulating of the emergence of hierarchy, attempts to dispel as a fundamental and fixed passage of social history. That is to say, through his focus on the emergence of the "domination of nature" solely as an *idea* that emerged from a repressive mentality that emerged in society first, he attempts to show not only the wide reaching social roots of hierarchy, but just as importantly, the invalidity of the concept of dominating nature as such. As Bookchin argues, "the domination of nature is an oxymoron that is absolutely impossible to achieve if only because all phenomena are, in a broad sense 'natural.'"[45] As such, it is impossible, conceptually, to dominate "nature." Moreover, it is impossible *materially* to dominate the natural world: as Bookchin views the movement of ecology as a whole as one of increasingly complex and differentiated interdependent relationships, to assume that it can actually *be* dominated "is worse than arrogance: it is sheer stupidity."[46] Thus the domination of nature was never a reality or realisable goal—it is solely an *idea*—and for Bookchin, this is a critical distinction: "The distinction between 'dominating nature' and *the idea* of dominating nature is not an idle one. I am not concerned exclusively with whether a given society (be it hierarchical or egalitarian) actually damages the ecocommunity in which it is located; I am also concerned with whether it ideologically identifies human progress with the idea of dominating nature. I am concerned, in effect, with a broad cultural mentality and its underlying sources—notably, the projection of the idea of social domination and control into nature."[47]

It is this "broad cultural mentality" then that Bookchin attempts to draw focus to with his hierarchy thesis. Whether it emerged from the unthinking reaction of the elders to ecological scarcity or not, is, in the final analysis, beside the point. That it emerged in society, as an *idea* is Bookchin's main contention: the ideological identification of "*human progress with the idea of dominating nature*." As we have seen, it is impossible under the Bookchin schematic for any one part of nature as a whole to dominate another, therefore it could only ever be an *ideal*. Once nature is viewed as the graded continuum of increasing complexity, of which society is both a product and part of, it can be seen, as Bookchin argues, that "'nature' can no more be 'dominated' than an electron or an atom," and

thus "what we talk about when we speak of 'the domination of nature' is
an *ideology*, not a fact."[48]

Implicitly, what this approach suggests is that other paths to progress
were possible; moreover, other paths to further progress *are* possible. The
domination of the many by the few is never a fact, never a predestined
point for humanity in its fictive battle to dominate nature: it is an *idea*,
which, although emerging immanently from the ecological differentiation
of society itself, is not the only possibility for human history. As Bookchin
argues, "history might well have followed different paths of development
that could have yielded 'destinies' quite different from those confronting
us. And if so, *it is important to ask what factors favored one constellation of
possibilities over others*."[49] This is what Bookchin does: he fixes these constel-
lations of possibilities in his analytical cross-hairs; a focus on the emergence
of the social mentality of rule, internalised by members of organic society
and later projected onto their relationship with the natural world.

It is from the internalisation of this rule in the individual and in society, the acceptance that there are in society to be both rulers and the ruled,
that the *idea* of ruling (dominating) nature emerged. Moreover, this internalisation of rule and the concurrent self-repression, latterly transmitted
to the attempt to dominate nature and ultimately the exploitation of
nature is more pressingly in need of redress than any economic project to
reverse exploitation. "This mentality," for Bookchin, "permeates our individual psyches in a cumulative form up until the present day—not merely
as capitalism but as the vast history of hierarchical society from its inception." Unless this deep rooted idea—so deeply entrenched that is seen as
the motor of human progress itself—is fully re-evaluated, then even the
most radical programme for social change will not reach the deep recesses
of the idea of domination, and as Bookchin argues, we "may eliminate
classes and exploitation," or any other such social stratum, "but we will
not be spared from the trammels of hierarchy and domination."[50]

Therefore, ultimately, Bookchin's focus in his thesis on hierarchy is *a
matter of ideology*, as opposed to the structural realities of actual domination. What is it, Bookchin asks, that has so infused human society with the
notion that it must dominate the natural world? The answer for Bookchin
lies not in the traditional notion of the natural world as a stingy realm of
necessity, which by its very harsh realities calls for the need to dominate
it, but in fact, is a much deeper problem, rooted in the deep recesses of

society and the human psyche. It is this humanity *itself* that has created the notion of domination, both of human and nature, and once this is realised, Bookchin argues, the domination of nature can be removed from the outlook of society: it loses its predetermined and *a priori* status as a product of humanity's battle with a harsh nature.

What does this do, then, for the criticism of Bookchin's contradiction in the starting point, in the age group? Again, although Bookchin himself failed to develop this fully, it was this social emergence of domination which was the important focus. In truth, it is impossible to know, *for sure*, what the many factors were that contributed to the social emergence of hierarchy, beyond conceding that they were no doubt the product of both the fecund interaction with the natural world *and* the conflict with the natural world as population began to grow and land became increasingly scarce. However, the central point for Bookchin is that the emergence of hierarchy in the reaction of the elders to their increasingly precarious position in tribal society is a social process: it is not through an under-standing of a threat to their survival stemming from the natural world, but from within their own social group. Therefore, it is the social institution-alisation of a hierarchical mentality.

Finally then, although there is confusion over how significant a role ecological scarcity played in the emergence of hierarchy in the Bookchin schematic, it does not necessarily change his overall thesis: that the *idea* of dominating nature and the necessary domination of human by human is an *ideology* that is intrinsically linked to and justified by human prog-ress and the move toward civilisation. Bookchin attempts to uncouple this notion from the history of human society by showing, irrespective of what propelled the age group to initiate control over the rest of society, that the *idea* of rule is a social creation, stemming from social changes and new social relationships that would slowly instil such a mentality of rule that domination became an accepted social mentality and consequently a material reality.

Problems of a Utopian Social History

However, even if we note the qualifications made concerning Book-chin's inadequately explained emergence of hierarchy and accept for the

moment his hierarchy thesis, does the Bookchin schema offer a satisfac-
tory explanation of the movement of social history on its own terms?
For Bookchin, as we have seen, the emergence of hierarchy and the idea
of domination ultimately leads to the vast "legacy of domination." The
emergence of this "legacy of domination" also engenders its opposite, the
"legacy of freedom." As Bookchin writes of the centrality of these two
concepts in his work, they form the "double helix" of his understanding
of historical unfolding of society and progress, a rich dialectic of varying
amounts of either legacy in relationship to each other.[51] However, does
this formula provide an accurate tool in explaining the movement of history and, just as importantly, provide a realistic base on which to form a
revolutionary politics?

According to Light and Rudy, such an approach, devoid of the materialism of the Marxist and traditional interpretations of social domination
is "hopefully utopian."[52] Based primarily on the dichotomy between the
legacy of domination and the legacy of freedom, history, for Bookchin,
"largely becomes the story of the battle between communities committed
to freedom and elites committed to domination."[53] As such, Bookchin's
project does not sufficiently investigate what Marxists call "social labour,"
which, for Light and Rudy refers to "the way in which human beings
actively organise the relations by which they (re)produce themselves
day-to-day within complex, dialectical and ambiguous historical social
structures, i.e., modes of (re)production." Moreover, these relations
"include the (re)production of ethics, culture, gender, politics, economy,
art, and geographical and ecological space."[54]

In failing to investigate this, Light and Rudy argue that there is thus
a "utopianism and insularity" to Bookchin's programme.[55] Although discussing Bookchin's social history as a whole, they take as an example the
particular transition from feudalism to capitalism as illustrative of the
simplistic nature of Bookchin's view. According to them, historical change
for Bookchin is "derived from a successful move by social elites to dominate what had been more or less organic free communities," a process
that was to reach its apogee under capitalism, wherein "even those legacies of mutual aid and cooperation that persisted or had been regenerated
since the time of the first organic societies were all but destroyed under
the nation-state and capitalism."[56] For Light and Rudy, however, this simplistic dichotomy in Bookchin is to needlessly separate and thus fail to

examine what is in fact one social process: the history of human society is a history of the production and reproduction of both domination and freedom as expressed in social interaction. For Light and Rudy, "institutionalized social relations have throughout history been composed of dialectically intertwined degrees of each relation. Neither domination nor freedom arises from society nor from nature but evolves as part of the dialectical, contextual, contingent, and largely unintended activities and consequences of human actors within environmentally and socially constrained circumstances."[57]

That is to say, that the history of human society from organic society through "civilisation" to modernity illustrates that progress has always brought forth both freedom *and* domination. It is therefore not a battle between the two, as Bookchin might have it, but a complex mix of the emergence of freedom and domination that drives historical movement; and the primary expression of this is social labour—the daily modes of social (re)production. Returning to the particular example of the transition to capitalism, Light and Rudy argue that this transition "encouraged both social homogenization and differentiation, neither of those unambiguously suffused with domination and freedom." As such, the move through historical epochs has forever been "informed by the material and social freedoms of modern society unknown to any prior epoch, as well as by the often suffocating exploitation and domination under which we live."[58]

Bookchin's version, for Light and Rudy, loses this more nuanced approach, for his focus on the two legacies means that historical change "appears as changes in the amount, or quantity of institutional relations of domination relative to mutualistic relations of freedom," rather than the social processes that bring both freedom and domination into dialectical interplay with each other and thus provide the grounds for future social change.[59] Therefore this view is not only inadequate in understanding the movement of social history thus far, but also offers a simplistic picture of the future movement to a free society: there is no viable programme that can be based on the expression of a "legacy of freedom" to counteract the legacy of domination, as Bookchin contends, for it includes no discussion of how freedom and domination are (re)produced through social interaction. The "double helix" of the legacies of freedom and domination appear removed from the social world in Bookchin, as a meta-narrative of historical change.

Again, Light and Rudy return to the transition from feudalism to capitalism to illustrate their point: for them, this final dramatic shift of society toward domination is presented by Bookchin "as a *quantitative expansion* of one set of relationships as opposed to a *qualitative transformation* to different kinds of relationships."[60] More specifically, they argue, in Bookchin's view, "the processes by which . . . feudal relations in Europe were transformed into capitalist relations are presented as the expansion of institutional political domination . . . followed by domination's further expansion into production through technological administration and machinery."[61] Arguing that because Bookchin claims that there were instances of wage-labour in pre-capitalist societies, they contend that he thus "sees only a quantitative expansion of such relations" as the basis for the move to capitalism. As such, they argue that "[t]he extraordinary power of Marxist analysis explicating the qualitatively new forces and relations associated with a mode of capitalist production is lost to Bookchin."[62]

In short then, for Light and Rudy, Bookchin ignores social labour, the qualitative changes that the new modes of (re)production under capitalism brings about, and in so doing, he fails "to investigate the political economic relations internal to capitalism, and its generation of qualitatively different (re)productive relations."[63] From this, and just as importantly, Light and Rudy argue that Bookchin provides no realistic basis for understanding how social change will be wrought in the future: unlike the Marxian approach, Bookchin has "eschewed materialist analysis of the division of social labour under capitalism" and as such it is not clear in Bookchin's work what will propel his "transclass constituency to gradualist revolutionary change."[64]

For Light and Rudy then, an objection can be raised against Bookchin's apparently non-detailed treatment of historical movement: more precisely, his lack of discussion of the *qualitative* everyday relations of social (re)production, forsaken for his meta-narrative of the interaction of the legacies of freedom and domination. Further, for Light and Rudy, this also renders Bookchin's projections for future radical change utopian, lacking the practical reality of more material approaches. That is to say, whereas Marx has the material divisions under capitalism that can be seen to push society toward revolutionary change, and provide the agent to do it in the form of the proletariat, Bookchin's programme appears devoid of such a revolutionary agent barring a class who will come to know and understand the role of his two legacies in the movement of history. That is, it seems reasonable to ask: what does Bookchin use to replace the revolutionary agent that is the proletariat and the powerful position it has in Marxist analysis? How does Bookchin replace this central motor of Marxism?

However, again, there are two significant qualifications that must be made: Bookchin's approach is in fact far more nuanced than this critique allows. In the first instance, it needs to be noted that Bookchin's project to discern a movement of history was based primarily on the need to move away from the focus on production in Marxism, from the materialism of the Marxian programme and, as such, it focuses explicitly on the subjective, *qualitative* changes that allowed the legacy of domination to take hold: it is in no sense based solely on a quantitative change in the relationship between freedom and domination, as Light and Rudy contend here. Second, to the claim that Bookchin forgoes the class analysis of Marx in the name of his historical tracing of hierarchy and domination is to seriously misrepresent him: the proletariat, the class analysis and even the dialectic of Marx are not rejected by Bookchin. Rather, they are taken forward into his own analysis, placed into the wider context of the emergence of hierarchy and domination. Indeed, both of these qualifications are mutually reinforcing, and by turning first to briefly examine Bookchin's nuanced relationship to Marx, showing that the materialism of Marx was never rejected, we begin to get a picture of that on which Bookchin built his own expressly subjective, qualitative focus.

It should be noted that from his earliest public writings on Marx, Bookchin was explicitly critical. In his infamous 1969 critique of Marxism, "Listen, Marxist!," Bookchin argues that "Marxism has ceased to be applicable to our time," but not on the basis that it is "too visionary or revolutionary," but rather, "because it is not visionary or revolutionary enough."[65] There was, for Bookchin, "a new era . . . in birth which Marxism does not adequately encompass and whose outline it only partially and one-sidedly anticipated."[66] This new era was represented by the new social movements of the late 1960s and 1970s—the ecology, the feminist, and the community movements—which for Bookchin had "demonstrably shattered the silence that socialism has left in its wake."[67]

What was important for Bookchin about these new social movements, however, was not necessarily the *particularistic* concerns of each movement—not the fight against the ecological despoilers, the sexists or the statists—but the sweeping implications that they raised as a whole. For Bookchin, the new social movements pointed to "a group of problems that reaches beyond the largely economistic conflicts of the movements of the last generation," and the reaction to these problems raised "expansive notions of freedom and an emancipatory moral sensibility, not merely [notions] of justice and material exploitation."[68] That is to say, that for Bookchin the new social movements raised *trans*-class and even *trans*-movement issues: they pointed to the concepts of hierarchy and domination which a strictly class based analysis failed to encompass, revealing hierarchy and domination as "the authentic 'social question' of human development" rather than the problems of class.[69]

However, and central to our discussion, Bookchin nowhere rejects the class analysis and the need for political action to remove classes from society. That is to say, Bookchin does not reject the materialism of Marxism, in either the focus of his theory or the political action it necessitates. As Bookchin argued in the moment of his infamous 1969 critique, although Marxism was "no longer applicable" in the form it stood in at the time, the point was "not to 'abandon' Marxism, or to annul it but to transcend it dialectically, just as Marx transcended Hegelian philosophy, Ricardian economics, and Blanquist tactics and modes of organization."[70] Therefore, although Bookchin is explicitly critical of the narrowness of the strictly material approach to social change that stemmed from Marx, he nowhere rejected Marx's analysis of class and the role it had to play in remaking society. In an interview in 1999, Bookchin would perhaps be most explicit about his (theoretical) relationship to Marx: "I must say absolutely and categorically . . . that I do not and never did intend the concept of hierarchy to *replace* the concept of class in social analysis and theory. Class society is very real, and it has existed for thousands of years in different forms. 'Asiatic' class society (in Marx's language) and slave society, feudal society and capitalist society, every one of these societies was or is a class society . . . I have never surrendered the idea that classes and class struggles exist, or that hierarchy supplants these divisions and conflicts."[71]

Rather, for Bookchin, there needed to be a *widening* of analysis that, although incorporating the class analysis and the politics that stemmed from this, would point to the "authentic social problem" of hierarchy and domination. As Bookchin notes, his was an attempt "to *enlarge* and *broaden* existing concepts of social oppression," an attempt "to indicate that hierarchies preceded the emergence of classes, indeed that hierarchy was one of the major sources of class society," an attempt to show that "social classes emerged out of hierarchies, as well as out of the division of labor, as Marx claimed."[72] Therefore, to argue as Light and Rudy do that Bookchin "eschewed materialist analysis of the division of social labour under capitalism," is to overstate Bookchin's critique and reformulation of class analysis: there is nothing in Marxism conceptually that Bookchin eschews; only the narrowness of its focus on class at the expense of a wider notion of social domination.

Moreover, on the basis of this qualification, we can turn to look at the concurrent claim from Light and Rudy—that Bookchin forgoes a qualitative interpretation of social change for an increase or decrease in the quantity of freedom or domination. Indeed, when one first encounters this objection, one is immediately struck by a question: why did Bookchin argue for this broadening of the class analysis to be based on a focus on hierarchy and domination? The answer is instructive: it was an explicit attempt, as just discussed, to avoid the narrow economisitc approach of Marxism. For Bookchin, the Marxian project "objectifies the revolutionary project" into a treatise on the economic and productive science of society "and thereby necessarily divests it of all ethical content and goals."[73] Further, in his attempt to build an objective science of society and sidestep the naiveties of a utopian approach, Marx had for Bookchin, removed all the subjectivities of the revolutionary project.

Therefore, Light and Rudy's criticism notwithstanding, Bookchin's tracing of the legacies of domination and freedom are an express attempt to understand the subjective shifts of history outside of the realm of the proletariat. It is an attempt to examine what hierarchy and domination are on *subjective* levels: not solely the economic hierarchy as experienced by the two "great warring camps" of capitalist society. As Bookchin argued, "the irreducible 'problem areas' of society lie not only in the conflict between wage labor and capital in the factory; they lie in the conflicts between age-groups and sexes within the family, hierarchical modes of instruction within the schools, the bureaucratic usurpation of power within the city, and the ethnic divisions within society. Ultimately, they stem from a hierarchical sensibility of command and obedience that begins with the family and merely reaches its most visible social form in the factory, bureaucracy and military."[74]

The wide-ranging project not only to identify these hierarchies but to work toward their dissolution would in truth mean that Bookchin detailed at length not only the material shift to hierarchy and domination, but also the *subjective* shift, and he does on a scale that encompasses the emergence of hierarchy in organic society right up to the consolidation of capitalism in society today. At every point on this scale, we find Bookchin's treatment of the quantitative and qualitative shift toward increasing domination, the material and the subjective changes. For example, as discussed in the previous chapter, the shift from early hierarchical society through to class societies was on a material level "embodied by the emergence of the city, the State, an authoritarian technics, and a highly organized market economy"—that is, in Light and Rudy's terms, on an increasing amount in the quantity of the forms of domination.[75]

However, Bookchin also stressed the importance of the subjective level of these changes, how this shift "found expression in the emergence of a repressive sensibility and body of values—in various ways of mentalizing [sic] the entire realm of experience along lines of command and obedience." This is the emergence of Bookchin's "epistemologies of rule," which stem from the personal interactions of emerging status groups in society, starting with the gerontocracy, in light of the increasing differentiation of society. Therefore, as societies began to change and grow, opening up new evolutionary pathways toward increasing complexity and consciousness, they also brought the emergence of this repressive sensibility that fostered in those being ruled "a psychic apparatus rooted in guilt and renunciation."[76]

For Bookchin, as early hierarchical society began to move increasingly toward urban life, the impact on the culture and society of both the material and subjective factors that surround the growth of the city is hard to overstate. The *material* transformation of the physical social realm away from the hearth of tribal communities to a new, larger urban centre, where different tribes and communities interacted in a new shared space, was to further develop the *subjective* formulation of this power shift. The emergence of a new social space in the city meant the emergence of a new mental space: a new shared "universalism" became apparent to the early city dweller, wherein people related to each other outside of strict tribal allegiances drawn out along family lines. This, in the Bookchin schema, is undoubtedly a positive move toward freedom: the ecological differentiation toward increasing complexity felt at the level of the subject; the nascent emergence of a universal *humanitas* that transcended the parochialism of tribal society.

However, for Bookchin, this new shared material and subjective space was also de-personalised: it became increasingly anonymous, and social practices and decisions were denuded of their personal forms, forms that Bookchin argues characterised organic society: again, the early notions of rule and organisation were removed from the hearth of the tribal world and thus became increasingly distant. In this sense, the differentiation that brought early notions of a shared humanity that crossed tribal lines also furthered the "repressive" mentality that Bookchin notes above: the early hierarchical forms had instilled the psychic apparatus that accepted rule, and for Bookchin, the dominated were ready for their own domination by an elite that, perhaps by their very distance from normal life, seemed increasingly powerful and even divine.

This same dual focus on both the material and the subjective aspects of the historical interplay between the development of both freedom and domination also runs right through Bookchin's discussion of the emergence of the State. The State, for Bookchin, "is not merely a constellation of bureaucratic and coercive institutions. It is also a State of mind, an instilled mentality for ordering reality"; the State "has a long history—not only institutionally, but also psychologically."[77] This "state of mind" developed slowly, via material changes *and* subjective changes, by quantitative developments *and* qualitative, in order that the State could take shape and gain a foot hold. For Bookchin, it has never been solely about the brute force of the State—never solely a matter of *quantity*, as Light and Rudy would have it—but of *qualitative* changes too. As Bookchin argues, "without a high degree of cooperation from even the most victimized classes of society such as chattel slaves and serfs, its [the state's] authority would eventually dissipate."[78]

Therefore, contra the critique from Light and Rudy that Bookchin dealt only with a quantitative increase in the forms of domination, in terms of the emergence of the State, Bookchin argues that "neither spontaneous nor immanent explanations of the State's origins, economic accounts of its emergence, or theories based on conquest . . . explain how societies could have leaped from a stateless condition to a State and how political society could have exploded on the world," and one might add, how capitalism consolidated these positions.[79] Rather, for Bookchin, conditions had to be in place *subjectively* that ensured that even the most victimized parts of society somehow co-operated with the State. As he argues, "the State . . . the historically complete form we find today, could have emerged only after traditional societies, customs, and sensibilities were so thoroughly reworked to accord with domination that humanity lost all sense of contact with the organic society from which it originated."[80]

Finally, even in the case of the particular example of historical transition—the move from feudalism to capitalism—that Light and Rudy use as an illustration of the naiveté of Bookchin's social history, the idea that Bookchin saw this transition, in their words, as an "expansion of institutional political domination . . . followed by domination's further expansion into production through technological administration and machinery" is refuted in Bookchin's major discussion of this transition. Bookchin deals at length with the changing sensibilities of pre-market societies that would eventually allow the emergence of capitalism.[81] Material and technological change that allowed increased domination are important for Bookchin, but again, not the only factor: "plow agriculture, grains, and the elaborations of crafts may have provided the necessary condition for the emergence of class, cities and exploitation," Bookchin wrote, "but they never provided sufficient conditions."[82] The sufficient conditions would involve the qualitative transformation of "the richly articulated social ties that past civilisations at their best elaborated and developed for thousands of years in networks of mutual aid, reciprocity, complementarity."[83]

It is clear then, that to argue that Bookchin forgoes a qualitative and subjective approach to social change and historical movement in favour of the cosmic battle between the legacy of freedom and the legacy of domination is, to say the very least, to overstate the case somewhat. It should be conceded that perhaps the prominence Bookchin has given to these two legacies in later writings and the historical studies he has structured around them do give the impression that his analysis is solely concerned with this conceptual framework. On closer inspection, however, it can be seen that these concepts fit into a larger, far more nuanced approach to social change that attempts to go beyond the materialism that often arises from approaches focused on social (re)production.

From this, it should be noted also that the separation between the legacy of domination and the legacy of freedom that Light and Rudy attribute to Bookchin, each being present to the precise amount that the other is not, is not as clearly drawn as they like to suggest. Indeed, as we saw with his discussion of the emergence of the city, the move toward hierarchical society can also be seen as a direct expression of the ecological differentiation of society itself, of the move toward increasing complexity. For Bookchin, in the "loss of innocence" that was society's move toward hierarchical forms, there also "appeared new concepts that were to have a highly equivocal effect on social development, a certain ideological armouring, a growth of intellectual powers, an increasing degree of individuality, personal autonomy, and a sense of a universal *humanitas* as distinguished from folk parochialism"—in short, the development of human consciousness and all of its associated benefits. And for Bookchin, the most "beguiling intellectual form" of this development of universal shared ideas, is "the ever-expansive meaning people give to freedom."[84]

To conclude on Bookchin's social history then, it can be argued that the three objections raised in this chapter can indeed be sustained: indeed, they are important additions to Bookchin's work; they cast important light on areas that may need further theoretical elucidation beyond Bookchin's own writings. However, it can also be argued that they do not present terminal theoretical contradictions: that is, Bookchin's anthropological evidence is, at best, patchy; his explanation of the emergence of hierarchy as a strictly social phenomenon *does* require clarification; and the pre-eminence on the meta-narrative of the battle between his double helix of the legacies of domination and freedom does need re-rooting in his wider socio-historical discussion. However, as has been shown, all three areas can be qualified, pointing to the fact that these criticisms are perhaps slightly overdrawn: the criticisms have not allowed for the subtleties of the Bookchin programme.

It is argued here that, by and large, Bookchin's social history still stands, its problems of lack of clarity and misplaced emphases notwithstanding. Moreover, as we saw with his philosophy, there is a coherence and unity in his social history: the history of his ecological dialectic has been one of differentiation from the simple to the complex; so too his history of society. In both cases, although this change, by necessity, may bring instability, conflict and contingency, the overall direction has been toward this increased complexity and ultimately in society to early and highly developed notions of freedom. This unity and coherence in Bookchin is perhaps most vividly apparent in the final step of his body of work: the practical political programme required to build upon the incipient freedom brought forth through the differentiation of nature through society and the institutionalisation of a new society in light of the history and strength of domination. It is to this political programme that the final two chapters of the present work now turn.

Chapter 6

From Anarchism to Communalism
The Politics of Bookchin

After our recovery of Bookchin's philosophy and social history from the more problematic literature that has surrounded Bookchin since 1987, after our concurrent recovery of the more robust critical literature and our use of it in putting Bookchin's work to a more thorough test, we now turn to the final part of the present work: an examination of the political programme that stems from Bookchin's qualified yet robust theoretical bases. Our contention here is that the fresh look at the theoretical foundations we have carried out thus far allows us to see a practical and coherent political programme based directly on the principles Bookchin had worked out and defended throughout the second half of the twentieth century. Most importantly, it will be suggested here that Bookchin's social programme—his *communalism*—and the theory that supports it may have a lot to offer to current trends in radical thought and practice.

However, when one turns to examine the politics of Bookchin, one is struck by a further problematic body of literature, equal in volume to his exchange with the deep ecologists but of greater magnitude in terms of acrimony, a body of literature, then, that only seemed to confirm the caricature of Bookchin as the flawed thinker. After a critique Bookchin made in 1995 of certain trends within the anarchist movement, the patterns of critique and counter-critique that characterised the exchange with the deep ecologists were repeated in full. Again here, Bookchin's motives were called into question, the exchange became increasingly personalised, and the valuable contribution and thorough critique and re-evaluation of that contribution were lost as the polemics took centre stage.

Anarchism, Social or Lifestyle

In 1995, eight years after his critique of deep ecology at Amherst, Book-chin published *Social Anarchism or Lifestyle Anarchism.*[1] In this brief essay, Bookchin pointed to those aspects of anarchism that, like deep ecology before it, had lost their focus on the *social* causes of current social and eco-logical degradation and more importantly, on the social solutions to this problem, and which thus failed to offer a serious challenge to the social order. Tracing at the outset the two "basically contradictory tendencies" in anarchism historically, the individualist anarchism of a Proudhon or a Godwin, compared to the more collectivist anarchism of a Bakunin or a Kropotkin, Bookchin argued that in the great movement of socialism from the mid-nineteenth century onwards, the individualistic arm of anarchism was always a fringe of the movement as a whole.[2]

However, toward the end of the nineteenth century, individualist anarchism had come increasingly to the fore. According to Bookchin, it was "severe repression and deadening social quiescence" that had brought about this change, as highlighted by the rise of the violence associated with "the propaganda of the deed" form of anarchism, which was borne out of desperation at the seeming impossibility of building an alternative to the status quo.[3] For Bookchin, in terms of the balance between these two tendencies of anarchism, the 1990s was very much like the 1890s: the post-cold war "reactionary social context" had tipped the balance back in favour of the individualists.[4] The failure of socialism in practice, the move away from the grand narrative of social theory to the intricacies of post-modernism, and the consolidation of capitalism as the economic system par excellence had not only quietened the social realm as such, but had reduced those bodies of thought and those movements that were set to oppose it to mere matters of *lifestyle.*

Thus, for Bookchin, did we get the emergence of "lifestyle anarchism." Foregoing any social focus, any attempt to deal with the material transfor-mation of society, this "latter day anarcho-individualism" was preoccupied with "the ego and its uniqueness," malformed by the "narcissism of the yuppie generation," and was "steadily eroding the socialistic character of the libertarian tradition."[5] For Bookchin, "ad hoc adventurism, personal bravura, an aversion to theory oddly akin to the antirational biases of postmodernism, celebrations of theoretical incoherence (pluralism), a basically apolitical and anti-organizational commitment to imagination, desire, and ecstasy, and an intensely self-oriented enchantment of everyday life, reflect the toll that social reaction has taken on Euro-American anarchism over the past two decades."[6]

Bookchin would then go on to criticise some of the texts he saw as indicative of this new lifestyle anarchism: the work of John Zerzan, Hakim Bey, L. Susan Brown, and several essays by David Watson (under the pseudonym George Bradford) in the periodical *Fifth Estate*.[7] Bookchin was characteristically forthright, and drew out from these thinkers' works the instances where individualistic tendencies prevailed at the expense of a practical political programme. Between them, Bookchin argued, these thinkers represented a tendency "to root the ills of society in 'civilization' rather than capital and hierarchy, in the 'megamachine' rather than the commodification of everyday life, and in shadowy 'simulations' rather than the very tangible tyranny of material want and exploitation."[8]

Unsurprisingly, the response to Bookchin's critique was fierce: and again, the same patterns that had so characterised the response from within deep ecology would repeat themselves in full. Bookchin's personality and motivations were everywhere called into question. In a book-length response, Bob Black would perhaps represent the furthest extreme of the responses. "I get the distinct impression," wrote Black of *Social Anarchism or Lifestyle Anarchism*, "that Bookchin, an elderly man said to be in ill-health is cashing in his chips as a prominent anarchist theorist . . . [by] demolishing all possible alternatives to his own creed."[9] Elsewhere, John Clark, under the pseudonym Max Cafard, wrote that in truth "Murray Bookchin is out to clobber the competition" and that "he has been in training for this one for decades."[10] The old notions of Bookchin as dogmatic would also emerge: for Watson, Bookchin was "The General Secretary of social ecology," who has no interest in philosophical principles and their practical manifestations and is only interested in "intellectual bullying" and "an anarchist purge."[11]

Moreover, the general tenor of the responses was further compromised by two personal disputes that Bookchin had become immersed in by the mid-1990s. Primarily a dispute with John Clark, the one-time Bookchin devotee who had edited in 1990 the collection of essays on Bookchin and dedicated to him in honour of his "magnificent contribution to ecological thought and practice" and his "continuing inspiration to us all," but also with Joel Kovel, also a former collaborator.[12] The exchanges here became increasingly strained and ad hominem. For Kovel, Bookchin was concerned not only with clobbering the opposition in anarchism, but also of waging war on Marx. "The world," Kovel informs us, "is full of bad people in the eyes of Murray Bookchin," and Bookchin is consumed with offering a critique of these people—the post-modernists, the deep ecologists, the lifestyle anarchists.[13]

Furthermore, and quite without explaining how he, like Black, has come to know the inner workings of Bookchin's mind, Kovel explains that there is an ever-present "Satan" in Bookchin's work, the slaying of which Bookchin has determined to be his role. "Let there be no mistake," Kovel contends, "that one big devil hangs over" the rest of Bookchin's opponents, and that devil is "Bookchin's bête noire, Karl Marx."[14] Much like the earlier reactions from the deep ecologists, then, Kovel enacts the same shift of focus away from the theoretical issues raised by Bookchin and on to these unknowable but inferred motivations (this time, stemming from his relationship to Marx). Continuing his ad hominem approach, Kovel informs us that Bookchin sets out not to discuss the theoretical and historical failings of Marx and Marxism, but to somehow knock Marx's work out of the way to make way for his own: "If hierarchy/domination as Bookchin understands them are to become the centerpieces of radical ecological thought, then the central contributions of Marxism—class struggle, mode of production, and the like—have to be displaced. It is an unfortunate feature of messianism [sic] that it can be worn by only one figure. Those applying for the position have to eliminate the opposition. Bookchin has to wrestle with Marx and defeat him if his own messianic ambitions are to be fulfilled."[15]

In the particular case of John Clark, his dispute with Bookchin emerged precisely at the moment that Bookchin fell from favour in the world of ecology and anarchism, and persists right up until the present day (of which more below). In 1997, ignoring Bookchin's entire body of ecological writing (a work which we have traced thus far, and, moreover, a work Clark was surely familiar with), Clark argued that "for ten years Bookchin has been obsessed with his vendetta against deep ecology." Moreover, this "vendetta" had clouded Bookchin's vision, and his critique of deep ecology in fact "consisted of hasty generalizations, ad hominem fallacies, flimsy slippery slope arguments, and outright non-sense."[16] Indeed, in this particular piece from Clark/Cafard, much like the more recent Black book, the personal slurs and name-calling are too plentiful to even begin to list, and it is left to the reader to draw their own conclusions on its quality.

Most recently, Clark has again revealed his ad hominem approach to his one-time mentor. In an ostensibly theoretical piece on Bookchin's ecological dialectic—if carried out properly, a genuinely needed avenue of investigation, as hinted at in the earlier chapters of the present work— Clark claims that instead of Bookchin's lifelong project to theorise a philosophy of nature and build a political programme thereon, stemming from a genuine attempt to create a revolutionary response to the social and ecological crises of our time, in fact, "Bookchin's concept of dialectic is implicitly an apologia for his own life and politics, and a rationalization of the failures of that life and politics."[17] The same patterns therefore that emerged in 1987 are here apparent twenty years later, as the personal informs these critics' reaction to Bookchin.

Throughout the 1990s then, following Bookchin's further critique of the movement to which he belonged, the problematic literature on Bookchin would feed upon itself, growing in both volume and acrimony. However, an important caveat must be raised here. It should be noted that in keeping with the theme of "recovery" that forms our overall thesis, there is in a sense a very real need when one turns to look at Bookchin's disputes over his political programme to undertake a process of *recovering Bookchin from himself*. That is to say, that while there is much that is accurate in his critique of lifestyle anarchism, there are significant problems that are themselves generative of the caricature of Bookchin that so swirled around him at the time.

In the first instance, the task Bookchin undertakes in *Social Anarchism or Lifestyle Anarchism* is in fact much grander in scope than the sixty pages he devotes to it. That is to say, that to offer a critique of the not inconsiderable work of Hakim Bey and John Zerzan alone in fact requires a much fuller analysis than the several quotes from each author that Bookchin uses in *Social Anarchism or Lifestyle Anarchism*. Moreover, to build a thesis that these trends are in fact indicative of the anarcho-individualism latent in Proudhon and Godwin is also not as clear cut as Bookchin makes out: it is a thesis that too would require a much more robust elucidation. Therefore, whilst the contention that Bookchin makes in *Social Anarchism or Lifestyle Anarchism* about the lack of social focus in the anarchism of the early to mid-1990s *is* broadly accurate, it is not sufficient of a fully argued case, and therefore lays itself open to the accusation that it is an unreasoned "attack." Considering the timing of the piece, following on the heels of several years of such accusations being (wrongly) levelled at Bookchin from within deep ecology, Bookchin can be seen to have been his own worst enemy here. What is more, although a case can be made that the response to *Social Anarchism or Lifestyle Anarchism* and the ongoing accusations made against Bookchin necessitated it, Bookchin also offered lengthy replies that further entrenched the acrimony.[18]

In the second instance, the nature of Bookchin's approach itself contributes to the furthering and entrenchment of his own caricature as aggressive and dogmatic. A case could quite reasonably be made that Bookchin had suffered from the previous eight years in his exchanges with the deep ecologists. The irrationality of the deep ecologists he so rightly pointed to in 1987, and their even more irrational responses, appear to have tainted his view of activists in general. Moreover, they have tainted his approach as such: in *Social Anarchism or Lifestyle Anarchism* he is at his most rancorous and yet his most unfocussed: his targets are wide and diffuse, there is no detailed discussion on which he bases his critique unlike his critique of deep ecology. Indeed, his tone has degenerated here, and whilst not the full blown attack or political manoeuvre that Black et al. claim that it was, it is more dismissive than any previous critique from Bookchin.

In *Social Anarchism or Lifestyle Anarchism*, then, Bookchin appeared to have lost *all* empathy with those he critiques, a quality he kept even at the height of the deep ecology debates.[19] This is perhaps best illustrated by returning to the underlying contradictory tendencies of anarchism that Bookchin structures *Social Anarchism or Lifestyle Anarchism* around, that of individual anarchism and collectivist anarchism. If Bookchin is correct here, that the interplay between the two is largely dependent on the scale of social repression, then it follows that the emergence of lifestyle anarchism requires a sympathetic rather than a harshly critical approach. That is, if the "reactionary social context" of the 1990s is the generative cause for the emergence of lifestyle anarchism, then are not its adherents, as misguided as they may be, victims of such repression? As such, they require a more empathetic approach than Bookchin offered here; they are in need of

guidance, not of upbraiding. As such, Bookchin can by 1995 seem uncharitable (although in fairness, by this stage it is often difficult to untangle
validity of this image from the reams of the more problematic literature).

Undoubtedly then, the caricature of Bookchin established after his
critique of the deep ecologists and the pattern of responding to him on
a personal level rather than on a theoretical level were only reinforced by
his 1995 critique of lifestyle anarchism, a dispute that would ensure the
problematic approach to Bookchin and his work would persist up until
the present. Moreover, it is a process that the brevity and harshness of
Social Anarchism or Lifestyle Anarchism only helped to contribute to. In
short, *Social Anarchism or Lifestyle Anarchism* appears in the Bookchin
canon as its weakest element. Moreover, the timing of it was terrible: hot
on the heels of several years of heated debate meant that it never had a
chance of being well received. The tone in it points to this final lack of
empathy in Bookchin, which can either be viewed as Bookchin's fault and
degeneration as a polemicist, or as partially understandable in light of the
preceding years of conflict and polemic.

However, as we have hopefully established thus far in this thesis,
there *is* more to Bookchin than these personal squabbles: there is more
philosophically and theoretically, as we found out in the previous chapters
and, as we now turn to examine, there is more *politically*. With this aim
in mind, we turn away from the specific debates Bookchin initiated with
the lifestyle anarchists and their responses as they contribute very little
to our understanding of Bookchin or his particular version of anarchism.
Instead, we turn to a critical examination of the *relevance* of Bookchin's
work today: specifically, to examine how Bookchin's political programme,
the direct expression of his philosophical and historical foundations, is
both a workable, coherent expression of his philosophical foundations
and how they both can contribute to understanding radical social change
in the present.[20]

From Anarchism to Communalism

With the important caveats made, we begin our examination of Bookchin's political programme with one final qualification: the more
problematic aspects of his 1995 critique of lifestyle anarchists should not

be overstated. That is, the brevity and perhaps even the uncharitable tone of *Social Anarchism or Lifestyle Anarchism* do not amount to the attempt to push out all other creeds except his own that so many accused him of. Nor do they suggest, as Cafard argued, that had lifestyle anarchism or deep ecology never appeared, Bookchin "would be attacking some other competing philosophy."[21] On the contrary, exactly like his exchange with the deep ecologists, the genesis of Bookchin's disagreement with lifestyle anarchism can be seen to be the result of his career-long commitment not only to an unthinking acceptance of anarchism as anti-state, anti-power and anti-authority, but also an anarchism that is *pro*-organisation, *pro*-empowerment, and *pro*-its own constant self-evaluation.[22]

Indeed, from the moment Bookchin would announce his commitment to anarchism, these characteristics are evident in his work. As discussed in Chapter 2, in his 1964 essay "Ecology and Revolutionary Thought," Bookchin would outline the "explosive implications" of the emergent science of ecology. Here, he argues that the differentiation and diversity that ecology points to in the natural world could best be given a social expression by the social theory and political practice of anarchism. As such, ecology, by its own logic, "leads directly into anarchic areas of social thought," as "an anarchist community would approximate a clearly definable ecosystem—diversified, balanced and harmonious."[23] This was a unique approach from Bookchin: at the time he was writing this, it should be remembered, anarchism was very little adhered to (or even remembered). As argued by Janet Biehl, "in the early 1960s, anarchism seemed like a historical relic. . . . Few people in Europe and North America were interested in it as an ideology," and as such, in 1962, "the historian George Woodcock pronounced anarchism all but dead, after its last flowering in Spain in 1936–39."[24]

Nevertheless, in his major political writings throughout the 1960s and 1970s, Bookchin would not only restate the case for anarchism, but would also work on his unique synthesis of anarchism and ecology: that the lessons of ecology could be made a concrete social reality through the social theory and political practice of anarchism. As a result of these works, Bookchin's contribution to the re-emergence of anarchism as a political theory and programme is hard to overstate, a point reinforced by Marshall when he argues that Bookchin is "the thinker who has most renewed anarchist thought and action since the Second World War."[25]

However, even at the very moment Bookchin began his project to reinvigorate anarchism as an ideology, he was offering the kind of qualifications that would manifest themselves in his critique of lifestyle anarchism in the 1990s. "The future of the anarchist movement," Bookchin wrote in 1964, "will depend upon its ability to apply basic libertarian principles to new historical situations." Moreover, although anarchism may provide the body of ideals most suitable for a post-Marxist, ecological, libertarian socialism, it is vital that "anarchists grasp the changing historical context in which these ideals have been applied, less they stagnate because of the persistence of old formulas in new situations."[26]

The new historical situations and the vigilance required to avoid "the persistence of old formulas in new situations" would define Bookchin's anarchism, a unique version of anarchism that led him eventually to break with anarchism altogether and call his political programme communalism (of which more below). Indeed, viewed in this long historical trajectory, *Social Anarchism or Lifestyle Anarchism* can be seen to be not a product of political manoeuvre, but rather, the product of the particular approach Bookchin took to anarchism that meant his would always be an anarchism at odds with the (re)emerging movement of anarchism as a whole, and by tracing this briefly, we can begin to pull together the precise form of Bookchin's anarchism.

As Biehl had documented well here, Bookchin's peculiar take on anarchism is evident in his earliest attempt to sketch the actual day-to-day practicalities of an anarchist programme in his 1972 essay, "Spring Offensives and Summer Vacations."[27] Referring to the largely protest-based and student-led actions of the anti-Vietnam war movement in the United States, which went on the offensive during the spring term and then dissipated as the students left for their summer vacations, Bookchin argued that a more permanent form of alternative politics be put in place, something that can not only transcend the ebb and flow of term time, but also establish a genuine daily politics that would outlive the sporadic "offensives" of mass protest and marches. The U.S. anti-war movement of the early 1970s, which had focused mainly on national demonstrations, had, for Bookchin, "*never* been a real *social* movement—*nor has it ever tried to be one* . . . the anti-war movement has been little more than a cone-like shell, shaped by a few articulate individuals and formally sustained by a few skeletal organizations. . . . After each demonstration, street action, or

confrontation, this hollow cone all but collapsed. . . . The immense numbers of people who provided the "raw materials" for rearing the cone . . .
inevitably dispersed and disappeared into the anonymity of private life."[28]

Though Bookchin nowhere dismissed the marches and protests of
the early 1970s, he describes them as "theater," and although "theater at
its best . . . reveals the inner truth of the commonplace: the state-power's
wanton brutality," it implies that the people watching the theatre "can do
nothing but witness the expiatory drama of the knowing few" who orches-
trate the theatre. However, this will never be enough for lasting change for
Bookchin, and "the hollow cone . . . must acquire a more solid geometry,"
must, for Bookchin, "be filled in by an authentic popular movement based
on the self-activity of the American people, not the theatrical eruptions of
a dedicated minority. This means that the 'war must be brought home' . . .
as a *molecular* movement, *deeply rooted in every community and neighborhood, in every block, and, if possible, literally in every home.*"[29]

According to Bookchin, this could be achieved through "popular
assemblies, and Local Action Committees, each rooted in a community,
campus, school, professional arena, and, if possible, a factory, office, and
research establishment." This should be a movement not solely to oppose
the war, but also in the long run, "to achieve a society based on self-management."[30] These popular assemblies must be decentralised, but not
beyond coordination, free to make local decisions, but also linked into
wider regional and national assemblies. Such bodies, for Bookchin, must
be completely rooted in areas in which they are located, and their appeal
"must be wide and embrace the sexes, professions, vocations, and age-
groups of the community."[31]

So far, so anarchist, one might note here: but starting in this first
outlining of his political programme, and traceable right through to his
final break with anarchism thirty years later, Bookchin would begin to
push the boundaries of anarchist thought and practice. Bookchin argues
that this local control must set itself the task of creating a "new political level," which for Bookchin meant not only "the development of the
counter-culture, changes in lifestyle and human relations" but also of "the
development of a new type of *organized politics.*"[32] Most importantly, and
uniquely, Bookchin argued that this new politics must be based on local
coalitions of non-party groups of popular assemblies, who should "act
concertedly *in choosing and presenting candidates for city councils in the*

municipalities of this country."[33] That is to say, that Bookchin *the anarchist* advocated running candidates in elections for local office.

Unsurprisingly, this was received with confusion among the anarchist community: the leading anarchist thinker of the time advocating the running for local office; the seeming acceptance by Bookchin of an adjunct of the capitalist state. Indeed, as Janet Biehl notes, in the very moment "Spring Offensives" was published, it was met with resistance: published by the Anarchos group, of which Bookchin was a member, in the periodical of the same name, the rest of the group insisted on adding an insert to qualify their position on Bookchin's call for participation in local election campaigns. Entitled "Anarchists and the Pro-Hierarchical Left," they argued against not only the "submission to the jurisdiction of the local constitutional government" that would for them stem from local electoral politics, but also warned against voting, which, "when there is no unanimity . . . becomes the tyranny of the many over the elective few."[34]

Here, then, we get to the essence of both the Bookchin political programme and the genesis of his critique of lifestyle anarchism: Bookchin did indeed call for an anarchist society, closely matched as it was to the ecological principles he discerned as the dialectical movement of natural evolution. However, this was a distinct form of anarchism, a *social* anarchism that was concerned with wresting power from the state by forming a direct political challenge to it, by in a very real sense moving *politics* away from the national centralised state and into the local community. As we examine below, Bookchin would develop these ideas into a programme of libertarian municipalism in the subsequent three decades—his programme of re-empowering the municipality through electoral politics and majoritarian voting.

It was, in fact, Bookchin's commitment to this engaged social programme coupled with the development of deep ecology, primitivism, and the general shift away from the grand narrative into personal politics from the late 1970s onwards that would generate Bookchin's call for a social anarchism to be drawn out and distinguished from lifestyle anarchism. However, after the furore of his 1995 critique, and more properly, after decades of research and activism in the field of anarchism, Bookchin, in the final theoretical piece he was to write, finally abandoned his attempt to reshape anarchism to meet "the changing historical context."[35] "Several years ago," Bookchin tells us here, "I attempted to formulate a distinction between 'social anarchism' and 'lifestyle anarchism.'"[36] However, this attempt "to retain anarchism under the name of 'social anarchism' has largely been a failure" for the Bookchin of 2002, and he now argued that "the term . . . must be replaced with Communalism, which coherently integrates and goes beyond the most viable features of the anarchist and Marxist traditions."[37]

For Bookchin, then, "communalism" now became "the overarching political category" to encompass his thinking, an umbrella term for both his libertarian municipalism and his wider philosophical base.[38] As noted, this political ideology "draws on the best of the older Left ideologies—Marxism and anarchism, more properly the libertarian socialist tradition—while offering a wider and more relevant scope for our time."[39] As such, it neither focuses on "the factory as its principle social arena or on the industrial proletariat as its main historical agent," nor "reduce the free community of the future to a fanciful medieval village."[40] Rather, its focus, as noted, is the authentic political realm of the municipality. In this final essay from Bookchin then, we see the culmination of the formulation of his distinct social programme.

How, then, do these commitments manifest themselves practically? That is to ask, what are the concrete forms we can look to that make Bookchin's philosophy and theory a living political project? To answer these questions, we need to turn to the central theoretical conception of Bookchin's politics, a theorisation of the focus of politics around which the rest of his project revolves: Bookchin's notions of *power, politics, and statecraft*, which necessitate his peculiar anarchist forms of organisation and his conception of the arena in which a genuine politics should take place.

Power, Politics, and Statecraft

For Bookchin, the key distinction in his political programme is that between politics and the state, or more precisely, between politics and the business of the state, of "statecraft." Of equal importance also, however, is Bookchin's focus on *power* and in particular, its place at the centre of a dialectical tension between these two concepts: that is, the existence of power for Bookchin is important for a revolutionary politics to the degree it either resides in the realm of the state and statecraft, or, resides in the realm of the political. It is important to note that for Bookchin, the way in which he uses "the political" purposely involves "a *redefinition* of politics, a return to the word's original Greek meaning as the management of community or the *polis* by means of direct face-to-face assemblies of the people."[41]

In his major political work, *From Urbanization to Cities: Toward a New Politics of Citizenship*, Bookchin traced at length the long history of this type of community self-management, the long history of the genuinely political. As noted in the previous chapter, the emergence of the early city in the history of humanity, forged by the material and subjective differentiation of society in the Neolithic Revolution, led, for Bookchin, to the first early notions of a universal *humanitas*. In the new emergent urban centres, a new realm began to emerge, wherein people started to relate to each other along relationships other than the blood oath or family ties. They shared the physical space and mental space of the society, and began to create a distinct *social* instinct, where rights and responsibilities began to emerge that transcended the commitments of tribal life, and to some extent, the mysticism of tribal life.

These developments produced a major shift in human consciousness—a dialectical move toward the increasing complexity and subjectivity of the human species. This process, for Bookchin, would be given its first institutional expression in the democratic experiment in Athens. Bookchin treats the development and the contours of Greek democracy (including, of course, its problems) to lengthy examination, and for our discussion, what is important here is that in the emergence of an attempt at face-to-face democracy, we get the conceptions of citizenship and its responsibilities, the notion of public service, and moreover, the very idea of politics as the business of the *polis*, the Greek city-state.[42] A precise history of Greek democracy is not our concern here; rather, its existence as an attempt at democracy and everything that we derive from it is an objective historical innovation and an important lodestone in the history of community self-management.

For Bookchin, this democratic lodestone was followed throughout history with other attempts at community self-management: the New England town meeting tradition, the Parisian sections of 1793–94, the Swiss Confederations, and the revolutionary surges of the Spanish Revolution of 1936 to name only the most prominent. This line of historic attempts at community self-management is, for Bookchin, the physical expression of the legacy of freedom: the concurrent claims for forms of freedom that forever accompany the solidification of domination in society. Crucially, these developments point, for Bookchin, to the historical existence and dialectical development of politics as originally conceived in Athens, and which persists in one form or other up to the present day, and from within these development we get the emergence of the realm of politics: "In the agora of the Greek democracies, in the forum of the Roman assemblies, the town center of the medieval commune, and the plaza of the Renaissance city, citizens could congregate. To one degree or another in this public domain a radically new arena—a political one—emerged, based on limited but often participatory forms of democracy and a new concept of civic personhood, the citizen."[43]

This new civic personhood and the conception of citizenship are vital to the Bookchin programme, and form the basis of his conception of an authentic politics. Again, after raising all the usual caveats about the problems inherent in all of these historical examples of an emergent realm of citizenship—problems of male domination, of hierarchy, of slavery—Bookchin maintains that there is something historically verifiable that points to the existence of the *ideal* of community self-management, a genuine public domain that worked on politics in one form from its instigation by the Greeks. It should be noted here that nowhere does Bookchin call for a *return* to idealised notions on these political entities of any of his historical examples, but solely for a restatement of the concepts and principles which can guide the creation of a new politics of the future.

However, for Bookchin, the meaning of this conception of politics as originally conceived has been lost to the present, to both the citizen and the radical. Politics today has come to mean the business of the state. Politics is used to refer today "to the domain of professional legislatures, military, and bureaucrats," and not the original "Hellenic notion of politics as a public activity, the domain of authentic citizenship."[44] Historically, the centralisation of power in societies meant the domain of authentic citizenship that emerged in the early city and in its later institutional expressions was usurped by the emergence of a "professional politics" based on the centres of power, and eventually, the state. Politics became the realm of the politician, the bureaucrat, the political party, the pollster, the political editor, the national press: all of these figures that orbit around the state, which had usurped the original political realm.

This focus on the usurpation of the genuinely political realm by the state is vital to understanding Bookchin's political programme, as the usurpation of the political realm is first and foremost a usurpation of *power*. As noted, for Bookchin, power exists insofar as it is controlled either by the authentic realm of the citizen, the genuinely political, or the state. "The state and the practice of statecraft have no authentic basis in community life," according to Bookchin, and as such, any power that the state has, has had to be wrested from the authentic political realm.[45] That is to say, that the growth of the state is almost completely predicated on the reduction of its polar opposite, the political realm: the state, in fact, can only exist if politics as originally conceived is removed from its sphere of influence. As Bookchin argues, history shows that the state "is not only the repository of agents and institutions that have made a mockery of politics," but that it is also a process that has "degraded the individual as a public being, as a citizen who plays a participatory role in the operations of his or her community."[46]

The state, therefore, "parasitizes the community . . . draining the community of its material and spiritual resources . . . steadily divesting it of its power, indeed of its legitimate right, to shape its own destiny."[47] Again, this focus on the power struggle between the authentic realm of the citizen and the state, between politics and statecraft, is central to Bookchin's practical programme, for, if the state has grown to the extent that it has divested the political realm of power, then the recovery and re-empowerment of the political realm—the re-empowerment of local, directly democratic controlled communities—is the only way to resist the state and to build a new society. There is no other way to reverse the social and ecological crises of our time, for Bookchin, other than addressing the notion of state power and the creation of alternative forms which will take this power back from the state and into the local community.

For Bookchin, however, because of the historical confusion of politics and statecraft, the radical movements of the past have "repeatedly mistaken statecraft for politics" and failed to understand that "the two are not only radically different, but exist in radical tension—in fact, opposition—to each other."[48] That is to say, the movements of the past have not successfully dealt with *politics* in its original Hellenic sense, nor dealt with the state as a set of apparatus and social relations that are set *specifically* to the task of facilitating the domination and exploitation of *politics*, of citizens in full control of their own locality. As such, they hold confused notions of power and its role in revolution and the creation of a free society. For the Marxists, the seizure of the power of the state, mistaken as the political, became the goal: the working class need take control of this repressive entity and wield it in their own interests. For the anarchists, on the other hand, power was seen as the sole repository of the state, and they thus condemned any institutional form of power, no matter how radical.

According to Bookchin, both views mistakenly conflate both politics and the state, and thus the notion of power is denied a full analysis: on the one hand, political power and its apparatus need to be seized; on the other hand, it needs to be rejected wholesale. However, for Bookchin, this is to misunderstand the tension that exists between politics and the state and their fight over the reins of power. For Bookchin, power can never exist in solely one realm; can never be fought for in the institutional framework of the state. Moreover, nor can it be uncoupled from an institutional framework as such: one such framework must be built to incorporate power, but it has to be built in direct opposition to the state. The refusal to institutionalise power in opposition to the state is ultimately no challenge to the state whatsoever. As Bookchin argues, "power that is not retained by the people is power that is given over to the state. Conversely, whatever power the people gain is power that must be taken away from the state. *There can be no institutional vacuum where power exists: it is either invested in the people or invested in the state.*"[49]

It is in this sense that Bookchin argues that, in contrast to the radical programmes of the past, communalism is "above all . . . *engaged with the problem of power.*"[50] Power, for Bookchin, cannot be read solely as state power, to be rejected out of hand: it "must be conceived of as real, indeed, solid and tangible, not only spiritual and psychological. To ignore the fact that power is a muscular fact of life is to drift from the visionary into the ethereal."[51] As Bookchin explains,

> power itself is not something whose elimination is possible. Hierarchy, domination, and classes can and should be eliminated, as should the use of power to force people to act against their will. But the *liberatory* use of power, the empowerment of the disempowered, is indispensable for creating a society based on self-management and the need for social responsibility—in short, *free institutions.* It seems

inconceivable that people could have a free society, both as social and personal beings, without claiming power, institutionalizing it for common and rationally guided ends, and intervening in the natural world to meet rational needs.[52]

The Minimum Programme: Local Electoral Politics

It is to the institutionalisation of power—this liberatory use of power to create free institutions—to remove it from the realm of the state and place it in the authentic realm of the citizen—the directly democratic municipality—that Bookchin directs his political programme. In essence, this commitment to the institutionalisation of power in the municipality leads him to perhaps the most controversial tenet of his whole approach: Bookchin argues that in this process of political empowerment "adherents of Communalism mobilize themselves to *electorally* engage in a potentially important center of power—the municipal council—and try to compel it to create legislatively potent neighborhood assemblies."[53]

Again here, as he first suggested in "Spring Offensives" in 1972, we see Bookchin's unique call for electoral politics at the municipal level. However, as our discussion of Bookchin's key distinction between politics and statecraft and the realms in which they take place has shown, the call is not as problematic as it first seems: the municipal is not simply the local arm of the state for Bookchin, but is rather conceptualized "as the developmental arena of mind and discourse," and, "potentially at least, as a transformative development *beyond* organic evolution into the domain of *social* evolution."[54] That is, the local, municipal level is, for Bookchin, the continuation of the material and subjective shifts toward notions of a universal *humanitas* that began when human kind first began to move to cities and shed the parochialism of the past. Or rather, it is the *recovery* of this shift, from their perverted current form under the state.

At the outset of the next chapter, we will turn to questions of the validity of Bookchin's conception of the municipality, but suffice to say here, Bookchin does not accept the municipality as it *currently* stands. "Quite to the contrary," Bookchin notes, "the modern municipality is infused with many statist features and often functions as an agent of the bourgeois nation-state."[55] However, Bookchin's call for electoral engagement at the municipal level "resolutely seeks to eliminate statist municipal structures and replace them with the institutions of a libertarian polity."⁵⁶ The ultimate goal therefore is the radical restructuring of the municipal to accord with its *potentiality*, that is, to accord with the liberatory potential it has as the civic arena where humanity has historically transcended its early tribal animism and, in the future, can further develop its rational consciousness.

In fact, Bookchin's entire analysis in his major political work is based on the contention that the early promise of the city has, through the increasing centralisation and gigantism of the state, been lost to a process of urbanisation. The urban sprawl we call cities today, for Bookchin, stopped being cities centuries ago: the great leap forward in consciousness that was early citification, given its greatest institutional expression the Greek experiment with democracy, was forgone as the urban centre was increasingly given over to distant rule. Nowhere are this distant rule and the disempowerment it brings more vividly on display than in the major cities of the world today. Therefore, Bookchin does concede that "the problem of restoring municipal assemblies seems formidable."⁵⁷

However, Bookchin argues that the task seems overly foreboding only if municipalism "is cast in strictly structural and spatial terms." Under these terms, it is indeed impossible for people to even be aware of the possibilities of self-management and community control, or to even be aware of what marks the boundaries of their community: if currently existing local municipal structures stretch only to state and city level, then even the politics that citizens can get involved in seems distant and impersonal. Bookchin notes therefore that it is obvious that places like "New York City and London have no way of 'assembling' if they try to emulate ancient Athens." However, the fundamental tenet, for Bookchin, that still runs through these urbanisations is that they are also made up of neighbourhoods, "of smaller communities that have a certain measure of identity, whether defined by a shared cultural heritage, economic interests, a commonality of social views, or even an aesthetic tradition such as Greenwich Village in New York or Camden Town in London."⁵⁸

Bookchin thinks that it is at the level of these neighbourhoods— even at the level of blocks in places like New York—where the process of municipalisation should happen. And although these neighbourhoods *in their present incarnation*, actually require a central coordination by "experts and their aides"—essentially, by statist forms—they are still in fact "*potentially* open to political and, in time, physical decentralization."[59] This distinction between *political* decentralisation and *physical* decentralisation is important: this is where the running for local office emerges, for, as noted above, Bookchin's process of municipalisation is built explicitly on the notion of taking power from the state, and this is the very first step. The citizen of a neighbourhood of New York or London who wants to be empowered has two options: first, they can enter the realm of statecraft, of official politics, and run for local and national office.

Or second, they can initiate and institutionalise their own empowerment: they can form a local communalist group in their neighbourhood; draw up a platform of principles to which they are committed, of aims and goals. They can educate themselves through reading groups, meetings, and local campaigns. Then, and only then, do they turn to local structures, infused as they currently are with statist structures and mind-sets, and attempt to take a hold of them with their own set of principles in place. As Bookchin argues, in the present climate (the U.S. of the 1990s), a libertarian municipalist project "will more likely lose electoral races today rather than win even slight successes," and furthermore that modest success "might take years." However, "in a very real sense," this is to be welcomed, and the educational processes involved in local electoral activity will be substantial, as communalists enter the public sphere, expose their ideas to public rigour, and interact with many more people in their communities.[60]

In this sense, the act of municipalising even the smallest units of a large city can be seen as part of the larger continuum of reclaiming the city, and as part of the larger recovery of the empowered citizen, of the politically engaged. Here, the process is as important as the endpoint: for Bookchin, means and ends here "meet in a rational unity."[61] Even though a project to recover the municipality is initially likely to fail, there is a dual transformation at work: first, there is a transformation in the citizen's conception of future physical decentralisation and the notion of a new citizenship: the very notion of libertarian municipalities is posited in the campaign to try and attain local office. The process of local electoral engagement therefore produces "a *changing and formative perspective*" in those involved and those exposed to the campaign: a new concept of politics and citizenship emerges that raises the idea of transformation, both politically and spatially, ethically as well as physically.[62]

Second, the members of local neighbourhood groups and nascent assemblies and their push for local office are themselves transformed by the process itself. They are educated as to the possibilities for a future society, as just noted, but also as to their own roles therein, their own responsibilities and creative potential in an actively self-run community. Even though that vision remains a distant proposition in the early stages of creating a libertarian municipalist society, the participant in the project cannot help but be exposed to the characteristics required of an active citizenry. "No one who participates in a struggle for social restructuring," argues Bookchin, "emerges from that struggle with the prejudices, habits, and sensibilities with which he or she entered it."[63] Rather, the participants in a communalist project "are transformed by education and experience into active citizens." Moreover, as the means and ends here continues to conflate, the dual aspect of this type of social transformation is mutually reinforcing and continuous, as in the continuing education of the participant as an active citizen, "the issue of humanly scaled cities can hardly be avoided as the 'next step' toward a stable and viable form of city life."[64]

In addition to both the development of the vision of a future society and the active citizen, the long process of trying to attain local office even where it fails, for Bookchin, is a matter of community empowerment, for even if they fail to gain recognised political and legal power, they still accrue a moral power. As Bookchin explains, the nascent assemblies and growing community groups may have "no legal power," but they "can exercise enormous moral power." "A popular assembly that sternly voices its views on many issues," Bookchin continues, "can cause considerable disquiet among local authorities and generate a widespread public reaction in its favour over a large region, indeed even on a national scale.[65]

The above steps, faltering in many ways at first, are for Bookchin a vital part of the radical remaking of society and a central part of his overall political programme. However, for Bookchin, rather than being an endpoint, the attainment of local office, they are solely the initial steps, the "minimum programme" of communalism, and they are the initial steps for Bookchin in attempting to establish "new rules of engagement between the people and capital."[66] They would start from local meetings and reading groups, as noted. They would direct their action toward immediate local issues, such as "adequate park space or transportation" and other such issues that would "aim to satisfy the most elemental needs of the masses, to improve their access to the resources that make daily life tolerable."[67]

The Maximum Programme: The Building of a Dual Power

All of these activities, though not in themselves revolutionary, are part of the slow process noted above of transforming not only the municipality but also the individual into an active citizen. However, according to Bookchin, this minimum programme does not render communalism a reformist programme, wherein a communalist *society* "can be legislated into existence."[68] Rather, these initial steps are part of the process as a whole, the "transitional programme in which each new demand provides the springboard for escalating demands that leads toward more radical and eventually revolutionary demands."[69] Here, the "maximum programme" of communalism comes into view, whose ultimate aim is the full institutionalisation of these early forms of community self-management.

Ultimately, for Bookchin, these developments would eventually lead to electoral success at the municipal level, and once office was actually attained, the new power of the office, rooted in the community organisation, would be used "to legislate *popular assemblies* into existence"—not the new society, it should be noted, just its institutional starting point—as the newly active citizens start to envision and create "lasting organizations and institutions that can play a socially transformative role in the real world."[70] This maximum programme then, for Bookchin, "seeks to radically restructure cities' governing institutions into popular democratic assemblies based on neighborhoods, towns, and villages. In these popular assemblies, citizens—including the middle classes as well as the working classes—deal with community affairs on a face-to-face basis, making policy decisions in a direct democracy, and giving reality to the ideal of a humanistic, rational society."[71]

This, for Bookchin, is the institutionalisation of power back into the community and away from the state that can offer a real programme of "changing the relationship between people and capital." But more than this, it changes the relationship of the people to each other. The creation of these assemblies "seeks to not only alter the political life of society but also its economic life."[72] In terms of economic reconstruction, then again, the municipality is central: the aim, Bookchin argues, is "not to

nationalize the economy or retain private ownership of the means of production but to *municipalize* the economy." To do this, the assemblies "seek
to integrate the means of production into the existential life of the municipality, such that every productive enterprise falls under the purview of
the local assembly."[73]

In so doing, Bookchin says, the assembly takes decisions of production and the economy in general based on the interests of the community
as a whole. Not only does this posit the axiomatic fact that the community, gathered in local assemblies, is best equipped to know what its own
interests are but it also means that the strict separation between life and
work is overcome, as people make economic decisions not solely based on
self-interest, and removed from all other facets of their lives, but with all
aspects of community life in mind, both work and leisure, play and production. Most importantly, for Bookchin, this would mean that "workers
of different occupations would take their seats in popular assemblies not
as *workers*—printers, plumbers, foundry workers, and the like, with special occupational interests to advance—but as *citizens*, whose overriding
concern should be the *general interest* of the society in which they live."[74]

Here we see the practical manifestation of Bookchin's theoretical
widening of social theory that we discussed in the previous chapter: the
move away from a strictly economic analysis in Bookchin to cover all
facets of life and all forms of hierarchy is matched here in his political
structures. In identifying the *citizen* as his revolutionary agent, Bookchin
opens up the idea that the revolution has to take place in every facet of
life. For this to happen, the citizen "should be freed of their particularistic identity as workers, specialists, and individuals concerned primarily
with their own particularistic interests," and see that the control they have
often sought in the past in the economic realm can be extended to mean
a creative control over their lives as a whole.[75] The citizen, as a fully active
member of the community, can begin to see that full citizenship is a much
fuller expression than their own economic betterment. Involvement in
the newly reinvigorated municipal life, for Bookchin, will in this sense
"become a school for the formation of citizens," through which this new
perspective is created, and the assemblies would "function not only as
permanent decision-making institutions but as arenas for *educating* the
people in handling complex civic and regional affairs."[76]

However, even now, the emergence of these assemblies does not automatically mean that a communalist society has been legislated into existence. Perhaps the most important final step in the maximum programme is that these municipalities must confederate. That is to say, that these new, directly democratic communities should *never* be conceptualised, for Bookchin, as self-sufficient. The notion of a community's self-sufficiency is regressive: the power of the state could never be opposed by myriad individual and unconnected municipalities; indeed, the state could happily exist with these under its orbit. For Bookchin, therefore, "localism should never be interpreted to mean parochialism; nor should decentralisation ever be interpreted to mean that smallness is a virtue in itself."[77] That is, the reinvigorated municipal assemblies should never be conceived as the end-point of social change: rather a large confederation of assemblies, a commune of communes, is the vital final part of the programme that makes the building of a viable alternative institutional structure—a dual power in society—that can oppose the nation-state a real possibility.

To be clear here: the municipal assemblies are the key organisational unit in Bookchin's political programme. It is they that seek "to delegitimate and depose the statist organs that currently control their villages, towns, or cities and thereafter act as the real engines in the exercise of power"; it is they too that are the vital new school of citizenship.[78] However, it is only once they "methodically confederate into municipal leagues" that they begin to "challenge the role of the nation-state and, through popular assemblies and confederal councils, try to acquire control over economic and political life."[79] It is important to remember that, as discussed above, the notion of power and where it resides is central to Bookchin's programme: power can be attained by the people in a libertarian society only insofar as it can be taken from the state. Therefore, ultimately, this can be achieved not via decentralised, directly democratic municipalities that remain interested solely in their own sufficiency, but in a confederation of these municipalities, "a network of administrative councils whose members or delegates are elected from popular face-to-face democratic assemblies."[80] It is this confederation of democratic, libertarian municipalities—this commune of communes—that emerges as a *dual power* in society, "in flat opposition to the centralised nation-state."[81]

Finally here, in defining the relationship between the local, municipal level, and the confederal level, Bookchin inserts an important distinction:

that between *policy making* and *administration*. For Bookchin, policy is *only* ever made in the assembly, in the face-to-face decision making that will determine how a society will be run. The confederal level is, as such purely an *administrative* realm, a coordinating body to implement the policy decided in the assemblies, their function thus "a purely administrative and practical one, not a policy-making one."[82] We return to the validity and the practicalities of this distinction in Chapter 7.

It is argued here then that the political programme outlined above is Bookchin at his most utopian—and yet most practical. His is a programme that calls for the complete remaking of society, yet does so through concrete organisation and realist interpretations of power. Moreover, based on our discussion throughout the present work, it is argued that this political programme can be seen as the direct expression of the dualism that runs through Bookchin's work as a whole: that of the existence of both the unfolding, creative potentiality of natural and social evolution culminating in increased complexity, consciousness and ultimately freedom, and the forms of hierarchy and domination that lie in opposition to it and prevent its unfolding.

The political forms and institutions Bookchin tries to create embody a reaction to both of these things: the directly democratic assemblies, as we have seen, are the creative and formative school in which the potentiality of the fully rounded citizen—of the ultimate expression of nature rendered self-conscious—is hopefully allowed to flourish. Simultaneously, however, these forms are also there to ensure the power of the present day capitalist sate—the ultimate embodiment of the legacy of domination—is diminished, as power is taken by the confederated communities. This dual focus on both utopianism and practicality, on the creation of the forms of freedom yet with a constant watch on the forms of social domination imparts a uniqueness to the Bookchin programme that perhaps explains some of the difficulties he would have with the movements to which he belonged.

That is to say, the uniqueness of Bookchin's theoretical and political programme has rendered it, from its inception, a prickly beast: it has always transgressed the boundaries of disciplines and movements; it would always provoke argument and disagreement: the anarchist who calls for elections, for example. Of course, there are problems with Bookchin's political programme, as we now turn to examine in Chapter 7. However, these are not problems that stem from his desire to dominate the anarchist movement, from his desire to "clobber the opposition," from his attempt to remove any other political movement but his own—or even from the uncharitable tone of his critique—that we noted at the outset. As hopefully the above and the subsequent discussion make clear, these problems stem from a commitment to make a utopian politics *practical* in confronting the unparalleled power of the advanced state.

Chapter 7

Reassessing Bookchin's Political Project

With our outline of Bookchin's political programme in place, in the present chapter we turn to put Bookchin's politics to the test in the same way we did with his philosophy and his social history. Here, again, we find significant questions asked of Bookchin, questions that once they are removed from the more problematic literature, allow us to shed light on Bookchin's framework, allow us to sharpen our picture of it, and indeed, allow us to acknowledge the problems therein. Indeed, whether one is critical or appreciative of Bookchin's work, these searching and necessary questions of his practical political programme, built on the back of the questions we have asked of his philosophy and his social history (and all removed from the literature that has marred both Bookchin and his critics since 1987) finally complete our recovery of Bookchin's project as a whole, and allow us to discern an accurate picture of the actualities of that programme.

Across the more robust critiques of Bookchin's political programme then, there can be seen to be two broad principle objections, and around these we will frame our full examination of his political project. The first objection concerns the conceptual basis of Bookchin's communalism: the validity of Bookchin's concepts of the city, the municipality, the citizen, and the people. The second objection concerns the actual organisation and the practicalities of communalist political activity: primarily, concerns around the institutional framework of confederalism. We turn to this second, more substantial problem in due course, but we begin with an examination of the problems of the conceptual base of Bookchin's political project. After examining both these objections we then turn to our responses to them.

Problems of the Conceptual Base of Communalism

Perhaps the most obvious problem concerning the concepts on which Bookchin constructs his political programme is the creative, central role he ascribes to the municipality. As noted in the previous chapter, the municipality for Bookchin is "the authentic unit of political life," whether taken as a whole or in the various subdivisions of the neighbourhood.[1] Furthermore, the municipality is "not only the basis for a free society; it is the irreducible ground for genuine individuality as well." The significance of the municipality is therefore greater than exerting a strictly political control over decision making in a community, as in addition to this, the municipality also, "constitutes the discursive arena in which people can intellectually and emotionally confront one another, indeed, experience one another through dialogue, body language, personal intimacy, and face-to-face modes of expression in the course of making collective decisions . . . the all-important process of *communizing*, the ongoing intercourse of many levels of life."[2]

Succinctly put, the municipality is *the* central political unit in Bookchin's transformative political project. It is from the municipality that everything else stems: the municipality "is the living cell that forms the basic unit of political life . . . from which everything—such as citizenship, interdependence, confederation, and freedom—emerges." For Bookchin, "there is no way to piece together any politics unless we begin with its most elementary forms: the villages, towns, neighborhoods, and cities in which people live on the most intimate level of political interdependence beyond private life."[3]

However, questions can be quite reasonably asked here about exactly how realistic a vision of the municipal level this is from Bookchin. As argued by John Clark in one of his more sober pieces on Bookchin, "it is far from clear . . . why the municipality should be considered the fundamental social reality" as Bookchin claims it is.[4] Clark argues that Bookchin's specific focus on the municipality as the realm beyond personal life in which social and political needs can be met is to reduce "the importance of the dialectic between the personal dimension and a variety of institutional spheres in the shaping of the self" in society at large.[5] That is to say, that there are many different realms of social experience through which the individual is formed, and for Clark, "it is not true that the individual deals in a somehow more "direct" way with the municipality than with other institutions." As such, Bookchin's insistence on the primacy of the municipal realm as the grounds for socialisation is "remarkably superficial." As Clark continues, "Millions of individuals in modern society deal more directly with the mass media, by way of their television sets, radios, newspapers, and magazines, until they go to work and deal with bosses, coworkers, and technologies, after which they return to the domestic hearth and further bombardment by the mass media. The municipality remains a vague background to this more direct experience."[6]

David Watson also raises a similar objection to the primacy Bookchin ascribes to the municipality. For many people, according to Watson, "the municipality is now nothing but a sterile, checkered moonscape of subdivisions, malls, industrial complexes and offices, filled with remote government bureaucracies."[7] Watson takes the criticism further: not only has Bookchin erred in presenting an idealised image of the municipality that bears no resemblance to reality, but in his emphasis on the municipal as the realm in which a general social interest can emerge and counter the particularistic interests of class and professional differences—a fundamental part of his entire political programme, as noted in the previous chapter—he has also overlooked the fact that, in reality, it is "the workplace [that] provides the last remnant of community."[8] As such, Bookchin's call for a generalised citizen who shares the same economic interests as everyone else in the assembly, through which they make collective economic decisions, is not only an "optimism [that] knows no limits" in light of the existing reality, but actually denigrates the tiny slither of community left that is the workplace.[9]

Indeed, this apparent idealisation of the municipality on Bookchin's part is also apparent throughout his historical treatment of civic life. Although Bookchin always qualifies his descriptions of the historical examples of the legacy of freedom as represented by civic experiments down the ages—most notably, in his discussions of the Athenian polis—the combined force of these lengthy treatments and his elevating of the municipal realm mean that, although qualified, his view of the city-state is overwhelmingly positive. However, as Black argues, this focus contradicts Bookchin's claim to be opposing the power of the state by the radicalisation of the city. "A city-state is not an anti-state," according to Black; moreover, historically speaking, the city "is where the state originated," and the various examples of free city-states that Bookchin invokes, actually "startlingly anticipated the modern police-state."[10] As Watson also attests to here, despite the transformative role in the development of human consciousness and progress that Bookchin ascribes to the early city, it is important to remember that "the city as polis created not only politics, but *the police*."[11]

Furthermore, if our critics above are correct, and Bookchin's central political unit—the municipality—can be seen to be problematic, then so too can its proposed constituent parts: the notion of the citizen. According to Clark, Bookchin's elevation of the citizen, the individual participants of the municipality, to the role of revolutionary agent—Bookchin's attempt to transcend the particularism of the worker in the Marxian analysis— actually falls back into the same logic it is trying to overcome. For Clark, citizenship can never be the generalised concept that Bookchin claims it is. "The fact is," Clark argues, "that [citizenship] indicates membership in a nation-state and subdivisions of nation-states, including states that are in no way authentically democratic or participatory." No matter how much Bookchin claims that the citizen can be the liberatory experience in his version of a "new politics," "the vast majority of actually living people (who are expected to be the participants in the libertarian municipalist system) conceive of citizenship primarily in relation to the state, not the municipality."[12]

Thus does Bookchin's political programme appear to be in a double-bind with the state: Bookchin appeals to the individual through a concept of citizenship that has only ever been tied to the notion of statehood and its subdivisions, whilst at the same time, appealing to the collective with the very forms that brought that state into being: the people acting together in the *polis*. Therefore, although an avowed attempt by Bookchin to create the constituent parts of his version of a radical politics based on a general interest, using only the tools of the state, he serves only to replicate the forms of statecraft he attempts to oppose. For a thorough widening of the elements of a radical politics, concepts much wider than these traditional concepts would be required. Moreover, in a very real sense, our discussion of the uniqueness of Bookchin's attempt to wed a utopian project to a practical political plan may perhaps suggest that these problems stem from a compromise between the particular and the universal that Bookchin makes right at the heart of his theorisation of a political framework (a point to which we return below).

Returning to Clark for the present, he argues that the concept of "personhood," rather than citizenship, could provide the basis for a truly general interest. Whilst "civic virtue requires diverse obligations to one's fellow citizens," according to Clark, it goes no further. Personhood, in contrast, encompasses the fact that "respect, love and compassion are feelings appropriately directed at all *persons*."[13] Furthermore, Clark argues that "the political significance of our role as members of the earth community can hardly be overemphasized," and requires that "we think of ourselves not only as citizens of a town, city, or neighborhood, but also as citizens of our ecosystem, of our bioregion, of our georegion, and of the earth itself."[14] Of course, Bookchin had, by the mid-1990s, precluded himself from such a wide-ranging conception of the revolutionary individual and the collectives they would form: as Clark argues, Bookchin could not accept personhood or membership of the earth community as his critique of deep ecology had shown.

Taken together then, these criticisms suggest that Bookchin's focus on the municipal realm and his notion of citizenship and the new general interest it would generate are not only flawed but that they offer an even more problematic revolutionary praxis than the earlier models they attempt to replace. As discussed in Chapter 6, for Bookchin, the assemblies of the directly democratic municipality will be the place where "workers of different occupations would take their seats in popular assemblies not as workers ... but as *citizens*, whose overriding concern should be the *general interest* of the society in which they live."[15] For Clark, however, although the citizen's "workerism" may be overcome in such assemblies, they would still be *particularistically* wedded to their community: a citizen's commitment to their own community, "certainly would ... conflict with the needs of other communities and regions," as there would "always no doubt be communities that have an abundance of certain natural goods," while there would exist "other communities entirely lacking these goods."[16] Furthermore, "it is quite possible for a municipality to put its own interest above that of other communities, or that of the larger community of nature. The concept of 'citizen of a municipality' does not in itself imply identification with 'a general public interest.'"[17]

Clark concedes that in Bookchin's "ideal system"—in his "maximum program"—the focus on confederation is his attempt to manage these differences nationally, and ultimately, to manage them globally. However, for Clark, this future vision of a free society requires a much wider conceptual base, such as the notion of personhood—"a broadened horizon of citizenship," in which each person "would see a fundamental dimension of his or her political being (or citizenship) as membership in the human community and, indeed, in the entire earth community."[18] Although conceding that Bookchin does hold this long-range view, his programme is compromised by the narrowness of his central concepts—the citizen, the municipality—in which he roots it according to Clark. As such, there is "a strong tension in Bookchin's thought between his desire for universalism and his commitment to particularism," a tension that "rigidifies into contradiction." Ultimately, Clark argues that in fact, "Bookchin's 'citizenship' is a regression from the universality of membership in the working class, whatever serious limitations that concept may have had. While one's privileged being qua worker consisted of membership in a *universal* class, one's being qua citizen (for Bookchin) consists of being a member of a *particular* group: the class of citizens of a given municipality."[19]

Problems of Political Practice

Moving away from the *conceptual* critiques of Bookchin's politics to the critique of his *practicalities*, perhaps the most glaring issue on an initial reading of Bookchin's political programme—our second key area of concern in this chapter is his calling for the running for local, municipal office: his appeal to electoral activity. From an anarchist perspective, this is indeed problematic: it is to become involved in the structures of the state and as such appears as reformist to the anarchist movement as social democracy did to the Marxists at the end of the nineteenth century. As Black notes, "It has to be said . . . Bookchin is not an anarchist . . . he is not an anarchist because he believes in government."[20] But more problematically, this apparent "belief in government" can be most vividly seen in the structures of confederation that Bookchin calls for. As argued by Robert

Graham, these confederal structures lead to Bookchin's endorsement of "various forms of legal government and political authority," and as such Bookchin has "reintroduced hierarchy and domination into [his] vision of a free society."[21]

According to Graham, hierarchy and domination begin to re-emerge in Bookchin's politics from the moment he posits the assembly as the democratic realm of unmediated, face-to-face, community self-management. Though Bookchin identifies these political relationships as the way of challenging the distant power of hierarchical elites, he fails to see, for Graham, that they lead directly back to the same phenomenon. As we shall see, this hierarchy is most acutely expressed in the growing power of the confederation that Bookchin's programme allows for, but it starts with Bookchin's commitment to majoritarian voting in the assembly. For Graham, the problem with a commitment to majoritarian voting is that "whenever there is a lack of unanimity on a policy decision . . . a hierarchical relationship will arise," because when "factions develop, as they invariably do, the very real possibility arises that some people will find themselves in the minority on many issues."[22]

Graham says that this minority faction, unable to garner sufficient support for their own ideas, "will find their votes ineffective" and may even withdraw from or rebel against an assembly "due to their lack of real decision making power." As such, that majority may find *themselves* in the position of having to "enforce their decisions against a recalcitrant minority," meaning that the majority "will hold political authority over the minority." For Graham, unless a minority can overturn a decision with which it disagrees, "it remains subject to the decision, and the authority, of the majority."[23] Indeed, Graham argues that the nature of this majoritarian approach means that these patterns become entrenched: the majority becomes stabilised as a source of political authority, and perhaps resented, calling forth more people to vote against the majority. Thus does the existence of minorities become more commonplace, and thus does the political authority of the state in the need to rule against them. In this perpetual circle, the commitment to electoral equality begets the need for more rule, and thus "hierarchical relationships will be created and recreated with every vote."[24]

As such, this introduction of political authority at the very base of direct face-to-face democracy becomes—through a commitment to majoritarianism—more pronounced and problematic the more removed it is from that basic; and Bookchin's programme encourages such a removal. As discussed in Chapter 6, Bookchin calls for "a network of administrative councils" in various sectors of society to implement the policy which has been decided at the assembly level. To try and combat this removal, Bookchin introduces the key distinction in communalism between policy making (the realm of the directly democratic assemblies) and administration (the coordinated implementation at the confederal level of the policies decided in the assemblies).

However, this distinction between policy and administration is not as clear cut as Bookchin suggests. As Graham argues, the fact is that the various administrative bodies "will have the authority and power to implement and enforce the power adopted by the assembly, and the individual members and groups in the community will have an obligation to comply with these policies," whether they voted for them or not. Thus, for Graham, these "authority and power relations" between the administrative bodies and the people, and especially those in the minority, "are a kind of hierarchical relationship, even if the alleged legitimacy of the authority and power exercised by these administrative bodies is based on policy making functions being reserved to the community assemblies."[25]

Finally, this development of hierarchy and authority—indeed, the recreation of forms of statecraft—is given its full expression at the confederal level, wherein Bookchin's ultimate transgression of his commitment to face-to-face democracy is complete. As Graham explains, if on a matter of confederal interest there is disagreement about a policy between two or more assemblies, under the Bookchin schema there will be a referendum.[26] If in this referendum a majority of citizens within one particular assembly were to vote *against* the policy, yet the confederation as a whole votes *for*, the individual assembly majority would still be bound by the policy. Therefore, the very principle of local, community self-management in the assembly, so central to Bookchin's political programme as "the living cell" from which his entire schema emerges, is foregone in the name of the confederal majority. The direct decision making that is the heart of the communalist project is foregone, as a majority in an assembly who had voted *against* a policy will be forced to accept it through a distant, non-direct relationship with the confederal level. As such, for Graham, this is the slow reproduction of "a system of majority rule based on indirect and mediated relationships."[27]

Perhaps most problematically for Bookchin, and despite his distinction between policy (made by the assembly) and administration (carried out by the confederation), the capacity for policy *enforcement* at the confederal level is explicitly provided for in his work. As Bookchin wrote in 2002, the individual components of a confederation, "functioning in a democratic manner through citizens" assemblies may withdraw *only* with the approval of the confederation *as a whole*."[28] Elsewhere, he argues that should "particular communities or neighborhoods—a minority grouping of them—choose to go their own way to a point where human rights are violated or where ecological mayhem is permitted, the majority in a local or regional confederation has every right to prevent such malfeasances through its confederal council."[29]

Clearly then, and leaving aside the difficult question of what forms would be used in the prevention of an individual assembly's malfeasances, this is surely a case of policy being decided at the confederal level at the cost of the local. But to restate, Bookchin is unequivocal about policy decisions being taken in any place other than the assemblies: we cannot "omit the distinction between policy making and administration" from our notion of confederalism, he writes, "for once policy making slips from the hands of the people, it is devoured by its delegates, who quickly become bureaucrats."[30] Yet the action taken by a confederation to censure, to "prevent the malfeasances" of wayward assemblies, must be seen as actions on *policy*: they are the majority making a decision to bring in line a minority. Moreover, as Clark argues, the decisions taken as to when an assembly was breaching human rights or creating ecological mayhem can encompass many different activities, and if "the majority of communities acting confederally through a council acts coercively to deal with such basic issues, then certain state-like functions would emerge at the confederal level."[31]

As Graham notes further, these state-like functions, the policy making and enforcing role of the confederation, will more than likely only increase under Bookchin's schema, because of Bookchin's commitment to assemblies only being allowed to leave with the support of a confederal majority. Not only will this mean growth, as more assemblies join than leave, but it is likely that the nature of political practice in a confederal organisation that may contain units that want to leave but that cannot, can only become more conflicting, and thus generating more dissenting minorities and therefore more need for the coordination of such diverse viewpoints by the confederal level. Therefore, for Graham, the "policy making role of the assemblies will simply evaporate as the confederation assumes authority over more and more policy matters."[32]

As such, the face-to-face democratic basis of the entire Bookchin programme is increasingly lost. The "living cell" which is to form the creative, artistic realm of the citizen, is subsumed by the re-emergence of a level of policy making once removed in the form of the confederation, policy "made by people with whom they have no direct relationships at all." Graham concludes that:

> People in individual assemblies will not be able to debate policy directly with people in other assemblies. They will not be able to assess their motives or character or confront them when they engage in manipulative, demagogic behavior. They can debate policy issues directly with members of their own assembly, but when that assembly as a result of those deliberations endorses a policy rejected by the majority of the confederation, those deliberations will be ineffective. Instead of being educated into active citizenship, moral probity and self-empowerment, members of an assembly that find itself repeatedly in the minority on confederation-wide policy issues will learn that their voices do not count.[33]

From the above critical questions on Bookchin's political programme, it seems that there are problems in the way his practical changes, designed to overcome hierarchy and domination may in fact replicate them in different forms. However, in order to assess these problems, we need to return to Bookchin's work briefly to show that, in a sense, Bookchin had partly provided for the problems raised here in his programme as a whole. That is to say, that these *are* the possible problems of Bookchin's programme: there is the very real possibility that social power will yet again be usurped by a controlling, dominating elite or individual. However, it can be argued that Bookchin built his programme *specifically* with these problems in mind: that is, his programme is an express attempt to try and transcend the contradiction between particularism and universalism and to prevent the emergence of distant rule and hierarchy. To argue this, we offer two responses to the critiques of Bookchin's politics discussed above: one general, one specific.

The General Response

As we have seen, the direct democracy of the assemblies is hoped, for Bookchin, to be the school in which a new way not only of ordering the world is fostered but also a new way of responding to the social problems of hierarchy and domination. True, there are no guarantees for Bookchin that his project will work, and on this point he was explicit: communalism is a *process* for Bookchin, and the process is just as important as the end point. As Bookchin concedes, any of the myriad problems that can be raised against his political programme may be true, but, "alas, all social and economic change is filled with risk . . . we 'might' lose! We 'might' be suppressed! We 'might' have to rise in a futile insurrection!" But crucially for Bookchin "then again, we 'might' not!"[34]

The process of striving for municipal confederalism is, therefore, explicitly about *raising the possibility* of a new politics of institutionalised community control: there is nothing set in stone other than the ideal of a communalist society. For Bookchin, the sweeping changes required for this "do not occur in a social vacuum," and as such, the process of making these changes—that is, the political programme of communalism—does "not guarantee that a decentralized municipality, even if it is structurally democratic, will necessarily be humane, rational, and ecological in dealing with public affairs." "But when," Bookchin maintains, "have basic social changes ever been without risk?"[35] Bookchin argued further that in the attempt to move toward a communalist society, "many misjudgements will be made, many failures will occur, many retreats will be necessary, and many years will pass when there will seem to be no positive response" to a communalist project.[36]

That Bookchin never claimed that his vision of a future rational society is guaranteed, that, indeed, he was explicit about the very opposite, is not merely a matter of semantics: it goes to the very heart of the uniqueness of Bookchin's *processual* approach. To criticise Bookchin for the possible future problems of his project is, of course, to raise valid objections, valid warnings about potential future pitfalls. These issues should be examined by adherents of the communalist approach, should be worked upon and integrated into an approach that holds the potential problems of the programme at the forefront of its thought and action. However, to dismiss the Bookchin programme as a whole as "fatally compromised" because of possible future irrationalities, as Graham does above, is to misunderstand the way in which his programme is formulated as a *process*, in which, as already noted, there is "a rigorous and ethical concordance . . . of means and ends."[37]

Simply put, the future rational society for Bookchin is never a given. Rather, the vision of this society, the *maximum programme* of communalism, is seen solely as a *potentiality*. At the same time, however—and this is what has made Bookchin's programme unique *and* the source of much confusion—there is a practical *minimum programme*, real changes in the way communities are run, that can be enacted today (discussed in Chapter 6). The crucial roles these actions play—from the convening of communalist reading groups to the running for local office—is that they begin to open up the image of the *potentiality* of the maximum programme: the full, direct democratic control to communities that have long lost sight of it. Indeed, it is in this minimum programme that the concepts of the new society are introduced to the political realm. This process is the school for the "new politics" Bookchin calls for, it is the process through which the participants learn of community self-management, of politics as originally conceived, of citizenship and its responsibilities and rewards: in short, through which *power* is reformulated and re-institutionalised as the province of the people.

Moreover, it is *only* in this process that the new concepts of the future society can be actively formulated, both in the sense that the directly democratic practices it fosters are the building blocks of such a future vision, but also in the sense that it is the only realistic way in which power can be wrested from the state. As discussed, for Bookchin, to accept the state as a legitimate target to take control of can only beget more of the state; conversely, to withdraw from the state is to offer no challenge at all. It is only in a direct, democratic confrontation with the state that power can be given a liberatory form in free institutions. Furthermore, given the vast capacities of the state in terms of its armamentarium, it is, for Bookchin, only through a rational, moral claim that stems from a genuinely democratic process that the state can be challenged: though Bookchin provides for citizen's militias and armed vigilance in his programme, the only way the state power can be realistically challenged is *politically*, in the classical sense of the word.

Again, all of these concepts and ideas are to be raised in the *means* of Bookchin's minimum programme, and, it is hoped, will open up new pathways and ideas, new possibilities and insight that will inform and strengthen a community's notion of the *ends*. These new pathways and insights will, it is hoped, inform a community as to how to deal with the possible pitfalls like those raised by Graham and Clark noted above. As Bookchin argues, "in a society that was radically veering toward a decentralistic, participatory democracy, guided by communalistic and ecological principles, it is only reasonable to suppose that people would not choose . . . irresponsible social dispensation."[38] Again, the supposition is important: the future rational society is not inevitable, not guaranteed, but the practical implementation today of means concordant with the end vision makes it an increasingly realistic possibility. It is in this "very *fight* for a municipal confederation," Bookchin argues, that there lies the possibility of "achieving a new ethos of citizenship and community."[39]

In this sense, then, it can be argued that Bookchin's political programme is expressly built on two separate factors. First, it is a statement of the ideals of a future ecologically and socially rational society and a concurrent suggestion of the *possible* institutional forms this would take. Second, in light of the current irrational society, and of the formidable obstacles that the project to create such a society would face, it is a statement of the initial steps in creating *not* the future society itself, but rather the *possibility* of it, to create an awareness of it, an awareness of all of the concepts on which it rests—the municipality, the citizen, the free institutionalisation of power. In short, it is to begin the process of creating "new rules of engagement between the people and capital."[40]

Taken together, these two factors mean for Bookchin that it is impossible "to provide a *detailed* institutional and economic map of what a future society should or must look like." Rather, the detailed working out *now* of the full problems or possibilities that might face the future ecological society and then to make a decision about its efficacy, *in the present*, is to deny the process intrinsic to the Bookchin programme. Indeed, to do so would be "to foist a preconceived grid of ideas on *a future that must create itself* without being overloaded with blueprints and schemes . . . rather than a rational use of lessons of the past and present in remaking society. To offer—or to demand—a detailed recipe to resolve every problem that every decentralized human community will face is to deny the future any creativity."[41]

The Specific Response

More specifically, in terms of both Clark's and Graham's objections to majoritarian voting on the basis that it inevitably reinvents hierarchy and rule, then Bookchin was even more explicit in his awareness of the possible pitfalls of the majoritarian approach; indeed, these pitfalls can be seen to be integral parts of his overall conception of citizenship. For Bookchin, in a genuinely democratic community, the majority does not "rule" a minority, or maintain any illegitimate authority over it: the differing interests of a society based on face-to-face democracy, differentiated along the various issues up for debate, stem from a process that "not only permitted but *fostered* the fullest degree of dissent . . . the fullest expression of all views."[42] Furthermore, once the decisions were made and the votes were taken at the end of this process, "the minority who opposed a majority decision would have every opportunity to dissent, to work to reverse through unimpaired discussion and advocacy."[43]

More fundamentally, to deny the engendering of majorities and minorities in decision making in the name of consensus or any variation thereof is, for Bookchin, to silence "that most vital aspect of all dialogue, *dissensus.*"[44] Bookchin explains: "In majority decision making, dissent plays a creative role, valuable in itself as an ongoing democratic phenomenon. Even after a minority temporarily accedes to the majority decision, the minority can dissent from the decision on which they have been defeated, and work to overturn it. They are free to openly and persistently articulate reasoned and potentially persuasive disagreements. The dissent may be ongoing, and a passionate dialogue may persist."[45]

For Bookchin, any other system of voting based on consensus or consensus-like approaches "honors no minorities but mutes them. . . . It stifles the dialectic of ideas that thrives on opposition, confrontation, and yes, decisions with which everyone need not agree and should not agree, lest society become an ideological cemetery."[46] Even the mode of consensus voting that Graham points to which allows consensus to be foregone and a majority to rule but, crucially, allows the dissenting minority not to be bound by the decision, is not enough under the Bookchin programme: this too circumvents the democratic exchange of ideas, and foregoes the development of the individual's political skills in persuasion and debate, in the mediation of power: in short, it lessens the experience of political activity that is vital in the schooling of citizenship.[47]

Indeed, this brings us full circle in the present chapter, back to the opening criticisms of Bookchin's central political concepts that provided the arena for the schooling of citizenship. As discussed, for Watson, the municipality is a "checkered moonscape of subdivisions, malls, industrial complexes and offices, filled with remote government bureaucracies."[48] For Clark, the municipality is a "vague background" in most people's lives, containing no radical or even creative content. Moreover, for Clark, the concept of citizen is reactionary, a concept forever associated with "nation-states and subdivisions of nations states."[49] Therefore, the concepts that Bookchin builds his programme on are abstractions, bearing no resemblance to the radical, transformative concepts he describes them as.

However, when one reads these critiques, one is tempted to answer: *precisely*. That is to say, the currently existing state of the municipality and its citizens is *precisely* why Bookchin builds his political programme upon them: his entire political work, like his philosophical work, is structured around the contradiction between the current existing state of political forms and their liberatory *potentialities*. Simply put, the recovery of the concepts of the municipality and the citizen, the schooling required to make the processes of genuine politics that emerges from them a living reality, is all built *explicitly* on the denuded, hollowed out, exploited state of the citizen and the municipality. Exactly as Bookchin's ecological principles are based on the fact that they are being transgressed in the present anti-ecological society, so too are his political principles being transgressed in the present anti-*social* society.

It is argued, therefore, that to criticise Bookchin for the current deracinated state of the political arena, which his entire political programme is a project to rebuild, is to criticise him for an unawareness of a reality from which his work has undoubtedly stemmed. To be clear, Bookchin is under no illusions about the condition of the advanced capitalist society

in which he lived at the end of the twentieth century and what it meant to
be a citizen therein: as much as any other thinker, Bookchin detailed the
extent of the social crisis that beset society in the present. One can look
at any of his expressly political works to find examples of the extent of
his treatment of the currently existing background of political life, but we
take one illustrative example here. Bookchin wrote in 1986 of the condition of the citizen in relation to the state in the present:

> The nation-state makes us less human. It towers over us, cajoles us,
> disempowers us, bilks us of our substance, humiliates us—and often
> kills us in its imperialist adventures. To be a citizen of the nation-
> state is an abstraction which removes us from our lived space to a
> realm of myth, clothed in the superstition of a "uniqueness" that sets
> us apart, as a national entity, from the rest of humanity—indeed,
> from our very species. In reality, we are the nation-state's victims,
> not its constituents—not only physically and psychologically, but
> also ideologically.[50]

It is in light therefore of the extent of the victimhood of the citizen at
the hand of that state that Bookchin builds his programme in the municipal: this is the realm that can be re-empowered to challenge the citizen's
reduction to an abstraction under the nation-state. Of course, Bookchin
concedes that no one can argue "that society *as it exists* and cities *as they
are structured today* can *suddenly* be transformed into a directly democratic
and rational society," but minimum steps can be taken, steps to "expand
local freedom at the expense of state power . . . by example, by education,
and by entering the public sphere . . . where ideas can be raised among
ordinary people that open the possibility of a lived practice."[51] Therefore,
contra both Clark and Watson, rather than an idealisation of the municipal and the citizen, Bookchin's treatment of them is based on the explicit
knowledge of their defilement under the state.

Moreover, the recovery of these concepts is the ultimate goal, but
even in their deracinated state, they still exist as a tendency. Therefore,
Bookchin is not appealing to abstracted concepts, but to a realm that,
although seemingly in the background in the present, still persists in
spite of the onslaught of the state. "The municipality is close at hand," for
Bookchin: though we may not see it, it is "existential, and ever present in

our lives. The nation-state is remote, largely the product of ideology, and almost ethereal." In our everyday lives, when not dealing with the abstraction of the state, and whether we are aware of it or not, for Bookchin, we deal primarily not only with our "personal world which we call our 'homes,' but also a village, town, neighbourhood, or city that is the real locus of our lives as social or political beings."⁵² It is this realm, from which we are so removed psychologically but still rooted in geographically, to which, Bookchin argues, "we must repair if we are to be truly human."⁵³

To repair to this realm fully is, as noted, the maximum programme for Bookchin, and it is when (and only when) this *process* is complete that the concepts of citizenship and the municipality acquire their full emancipatory forms. That is, as they exist today they are far from liberatory. Indeed, they are only made so, for Bookchin, by the process of physically reforming them through the project of communalism. And, as illustrative of the radical transformation required, of the huge gulf between the municipality and the citizen as they exist today and the finished forms they need to become, Bookchin explains what the full extent of the schooling of the citizen in a new politics must entail:

> The development of citizenship must become an art, not merely an education, and a creative art in the aesthetic sense that appeals to the deeply human desire for self-expression in a meaningful political community. It must be a personal art in which every citizen is fully aware of the fact that his or her community entrusts its destiny to his or her moral probity and rationality. If the ideological authority of state power and statecraft today rests on the assumption that the "citizen" is an incompetent being, the municipalist conception of citizenship rests on precisely the opposite.⁵⁴

To return to the critique of Bookchin's commitment to majoritarian voting then, we can see that to forgo it in the name of consensus at the face-to-face level, would reduce the political and aesthetic schooling of the citizen: dissensus and debate are vital parts of this schooling for Bookchin, as noted. The factionalism that emerges from the commitment to the majority principle is vital to fostering the discussion of ideas. It is in this process that the individual and the community as a whole are educated in the ways and means of managing their own community. To raise objections to the principle as a whole on the basis that it *could* lead to undemocratic or demagogic future practices is in fact to deny the efficacy of the programme itself. It could indeed lead to these practices, but Bookchin's utopian vision of the development of citizenship is predicated on forms that, as much as is possible in the present, would prevent this from happening.

If Bookchin can be thus seen to provide a convincing argument for a commitment to the majoritarian principle at the level of direct, face-to-face decision making, what of the wider criticism of Graham, and of Clark, that this commitment is inevitably transgressed by Bookchin's commitment to the enforcement power of the confederal level? As discussed, Graham points out that, even if consensus was achieved in an assembly, the commitment to majoritarianism at the confederal level could result in this particular assembly being outvoted on issues it had accepted at the face-to-face level. Moreover, this assembly would have to accept the vote, as secession from the confederation is only permitted should the confederation as a whole permit it. Further, any actions taken by individual assemblies deemed to be in breach of human rights or eco-logical principles by the confederation as a whole—even if these actions had been determined by the practices of direct democracy—the individual assembly can expect censure from the rest of the confederal body.

All of this was, for Graham, to deny the very principles on which Bookchin builds his programme—community self-management in directly democratic assemblies—and to reinvent the practices of distant, non-direct decision making, and ultimately the hierarchy that this entails. However, for Bookchin, the same principle of citizenship that applies at the assembly level should also apply at the confederal: the democratic process of reaching decisions, of the generation of minority and majority positions therein, and the respecting of both the existence and rights of both—simply put, the acceptance and respect of the fact that not every-one can always get what they want at all times—is in itself democratic practice. Again, in the slow implementation of these practices, it is to be assumed that the answers to the problems of exactly how problems such as those raised by Graham will be resolved will become more apparent as the process develops. However, as a basic principle, majoritarian voting must apply at the confederal level in the hope that it will engender the demo-cratic principles discussed so far.

If this results in minorities being subject to the will of the general interest of the region as a whole, then for Bookchin, this general interest, as represented by the majority of the confederation, is the *policy* decision. Though this may indeed have to be enforced by the confederation, this still represents the implementation and administration of a policy that has been decided upon by the majority of people of a region in a directly democratic way. The existence of dissenting assemblies does not disprove this fact. Nor do dissenting minorities challenge the notion of the confederal level as based on the rational, fully informed, democratic processes of the *majority* of the assemblies, as based on the interests of the region as a whole worked out rationally in their own political practices in the assemblies. For Bookchin then, the majoritarian principle at the confederal level, "is not a denial of democracy but the assertion of a shared agreement by all to recognize civil rights and maintain the ecological integrity of a region. These rights and needs are not asserted so much by a confederal council as by the majority of the popular assemblies conceived as one large community that expresses its wishes through its confederal deputies. Thus policy making still remains local, but its administration is vested in the confederal network *as a whole*."[55]

In fact, an excellent clarification of how Bookchin viewed the maintenance of the policy-making power of the assembly at the confederal level is offered by Janet Biehl.[56] Dealing specifically with the example Bookchin raises of an assembly that may be transgressing the agreed social and ecological principles of a confederation, and of the confederation taking action to bring the community back in line with those principles, Biehl maintains that the confederal action "would be purely administrative and coordinative, executing the policies that the municipalities have adopted." To show exactly how this coercive action remains purely administrative, Biehl returns to the notion of the confederal referendum. That is, for the confederal level to take action against any assembly, it would first have to be determined by the majority of the assemblies in a confederal "vote on whether [the wayward] community may persist in its noxious practice."[57]

This vote would be first carried out separately in each municipality, the results and the full details of the vote of each municipality would then be carried by the delegate of each to the confederal council and aggregated and counted *as a whole* in order to determine the full vote as spread out through the confederation. Thus, in such matters as the coercive action of the confederal level, the region as a whole must determine, through referenda, "the assertion of a shared agreement by the majority of citizens within the confederation that the ecological integrity of a region or human rights must be maintained." As such, assembly supremacy would be maintained within the confederation, for it "would not be the confederal council that made this decision, but the cumulative majority of all the citizens in all the assemblies, conceived in the aggregate as one large community that expressed its wishes through the confederation."[58]

This notion of confederal level referenda to determine the sensitive matter of coercing wayward assemblies into adhering to agreed social and ecological principles by the confederation also casts light on how the general day-to-day decision making is still based on the supremacy of the assembly. That is to say that, theoretically, on all the day-to-day decisions taken in the assemblies that would require administration and coordination at the confederal level, a confederal-wide tally could be taken that, exactly like the referendum, would show the entire region that in their daily practices, not only were they dealing with each other, but they were part of the wider region too. Every decision taken at the confederal level, via the mandated delegates of each assembly, could thus be seen to be the aggregate of the decisions reached in the rational and creative political realm of the municipalities.

Of course, to carry out such tallying would in all probability be too impractical in the running of most societies today, but the point still stands: the confederal level, through commitment and vigilance, should be conceived of and constructed as the collective expression of the decisions reached in the directly democratic practices of the individual municipalities. To be, as undoubtedly everyone will be at different times and junctures, either in the minority or the majority, is to be in a democracy for Bookchin. The very experience of being so, of experiencing the nuances of such positions, of the subtleties of consciousness and sensibility required of knowing that one could quite easily be in a majority at the local level but in a minority at the confederal, is all a part of the process of becoming aware of what it means to be a citizen of a genuine political realm.

Having revisited Bookchin's political work, and clarified the notion of the *process* of his political programme, a factor that perhaps has been underplayed in the critiques of his programme, it should be conceded again here that the objections raised *are*, taken individually, sustainable as the possible pitfalls of his programme. But as discussed above, not only are they possibilities, their existence as possibilities form one of the main reasons why Bookchin constructed his programme in the particular way he did: only through the reinvigoration of the political realm, and the empowerment of the people generally that this brings, can the people's *disempowerment* be checked, reversed, and continually monitored. It is this central aim that Bookchin hopes the process as a whole will enable, from the initial, minimum steps of simply introducing the ideas of community self-management through to example and practice, to the slow development of the vision of the fully rational society and the achievement of that end. That this crucial Bookchin principle has been underplayed stems in part from the problematic body of literature that has surrounded Bookchin since 1987, the critiques and counter-critiques and the caricature they engendered. Hopefully, the present work has proven that there is more to Bookchin than this caricature.

Conclusion

At the age of seventy-eight, Bookchin was asked in an interview how he had managed to remain a revolutionary for so long. "Capitalism devours us," he responded. "At the molecular level of everyday life, it changes us for the worse, and it compels people to make extremely unsavory rationalizations for why they believe things they know—or at least they once knew—are false and for doing things that are trivializing and dehumanizing." Bookchin concluded that he had remained a revolutionary into his old age because "I do not care to come to terms with an irrational society that corrodes all that is valuable in humanity, that eats away at all that is beautiful and noble in the human condition."[1] This opposition to the irrationalities of society under capitalism, as hopefully has become clear throughout the present work, is the essence of the Bookchin project as a whole: it is the building of a theoretical corpus to address the underlying causes of the ecological and social destructiveness of capitalism and, perhaps most importantly, to build a practical political programme thereon.

Indeed, when assessing Bookchin's work, this underlying commitment must be taken into account. There is no separation in Bookchin between theoretical and philosophical commitments and the political practices they necessitate. There is a very real attempt to achieve a unity of ideals and practice throughout Bookchin's work. As a result, in line with the questions we have asked of Bookchin's work throughout the preceding chapters—questions regarding his methodology, his conceptual basis, and his use of evidence—there is a further, important question to ask: does Bookchin achieve the creation of a coherent revolutionary *praxis*? That is to ask, does Bookchin manage to provide a coherent project that can offer a genuine opposition to the irrationalities of capitalism?

From our discussions of Bookchin's philosophical bases, our discussion of his social history, and our discussions of his political programme—and the attendant objections we raised in all three areas—the present work has argued that Bookchin does indeed provide such a project. Of course, there are significant and important problems with this project, as discussed. But it is argued that there is nothing that undermines his project as a whole, there is no terminal contradiction that renders the project obsolete. On the contrary, the objections we have raised to the Bookchin theoretic are in fact useful to Bookchin and social ecology: once exposed to a full analysis these objections can help to qualify his project, help to point to the areas of his work that are perhaps under-examined or inadequately explained. The task now is to develop this theoretic further.

Moreover, as we have also examined throughout, it is this process of critically re-examining the Bookchin theoretic that has been partially obscured because of the emergence of the more problematic literature on Bookchin. As outlined in Chapter 1, this stemmed from the extraordinary response to Bookchin's 1987 critique of deep ecology, where, clearly, the focus quickly slipped from the issues Bookchin raised and his wider philosophy and onto Bookchin *himself* and his personal motivations. This way of approaching Bookchin was, as discussed in Chapter 6, cemented in 1995 after Bookchin's critique of "lifestyle anarchism." Here, and as noted, partly because of Bookchin's own degeneration as a polemicist after seven years of acrimonious exchanges with the deep ecologists, the focus on Bookchin became even more personal, as the reams of critique and counter critique attest to.

It was from this body of literature that the caricature of Bookchin as dogmatic, as out to attack, would emerge. By returning specifically to a full examination of Bookchin's 1987 critique—*the* generative cause of this literature—we have pointed to the fact that rather than ill-founded or ill-conceived, this critique was an important and timely warning against the dangers of ill-thought-out responses to the ecological crisis. Moreover, the notions that Bookchin was concerned with anything other than the issues he raised in 1987—that he was launching a turf war, a strictly political manoeuvre—are dispelled in our discussion of the way in which this

critique can be seen to be the direct expression of his fundamental philosophical and theoretical foundations. Also here, we suggest that a full
awareness of Bookchin's exchange with the deep ecologists may help the
ecology movements of the present to avoid the dangers of an unthinking
approach to the ecological crisis of today.

Here, in fact, we return to the underlying essence of Bookchin's
approach, noted above. If it was to the irrationalities of capitalism that
Bookchin was opposed in the first instance, then, it was the irrationalities
of the movements set to oppose capitalism that concerned him in the second instance. Bookchin's uncompromising criticism of capitalism, of the
ecological and social irrationalities it engenders, was matched exactly by
the uncompromising critique of the movements to which he belonged.
Bookchin feared no censure, no fall-out from such critiques. In the age
of advanced capitalism, he argued, wherein the values of capitalism had
come to represent society as such, this constant vigilance of the values and
principle of the radical oppositional thought is more needed than ever.
Moreover, "coherence" was Bookchin's favourite word, as he told us in the
introduction to *The Ecology of Freedom*, and a movement to oppose the
irrational society *par excellence* should be explicitly committed to a coherence of ideals and practice. In his own project, this coherence is seen in his
lifelong theoretical elucidation of the philosophy of social ecology and its
attendant political programme.

As we have argued here, it is from these basic principles of the uncompromising critique of not only capitalism but of the movements set to
oppose it, and the commitment to a coherence of theoretical foundations
and political practice, that his critiques of the ecologists and the anarchists would stem—and not from the ill-founded motivations that form
the bedrock of the Bookchin caricature. Moreover, with this acknowledgment in place, as noted above, the task now is to apply the theory and
practice of Bookchin to the present. Here, perhaps more so than any time
during Bookchin's life, we find that his work has a resonance in present
day resistance to capitalist society: none more so that in the theories and
practices of the alter-globalisation movement, from the theory of thinkers
like Hardt and Negri, and John Holloway, to the practice of movements
like the Zapatistas, and, more recently, El Movimiento 15-M in Spain.[2]
Across all of these developments, we see a clear reflection of some of
the key Bookchin principles: his appeal to grand historical narrative, his

primary political focus on the particular and the general, and his notion of getting from here to there.

Again, this is beyond what the present work has tried to do, but it posits the notion here that there can be seen to be a series of intersections between the work of Bookchin and present-day anti-capitalist theory and practice. The task for future work is to examine further these intersections, for it is on the points where Bookchin's work meets present-day thought and practice where we can find two things: first, that Bookchin's work can be clarified and strengthened by examining the wealth of experience of the alter-globalisation movement have now left us to analysis, showing perhaps an accuracy in Bookchin that it is now much easier to gauge; and second, that the detailed theoretical and practical programme that Bookchin developed through the second half of the twentieth century can prove very useful indeed to current movements in search of ideas and practices to challenge the social and ecological crises of the present day.

It is hoped that the present work will prove a contribution to such a task. It is hoped that, through our examination of Bookchin's philosophy, the insights he provided can be tested as a possible contribution to responding to the ecological crisis. It is hoped that, through our examination of Bookchin's social history, there may emerge worthwhile insights will may prove a useful contribution to responding to deeply entrenched problems of social hierarchy and domination. It is hoped further that our examination of the eminently practical political project of Bookchin will prove useful in contributing to a way of visualising and realising social change in a globalised world. Finally, it is hoped that this coherent and important body of work can be revisited as a whole, with fresh eyes, devoid of the controversy and caricature, and examined on its own terms. Because of the misrepresentations of the past, we owe it to Bookchin to offer a full reassessment of his work; for the insights it contains for formulating a response to the ecological crisis, we owe such a reassessment to ourselves.

Notes

Introduction

1. Murray Bookchin, *The Ecology of Freedom: The Emergence and Dissolution of Hierarchy*, 2nd ed. (Montreal: Black Rose Books, 1991).
2. Murray Bookchin [under the pseudonym Lewis Herber], "The Problem of Chemicals in Food," *Contemporary Issues* 3, No. 12 (June–August, 1952): 206–41.
3. Murray Bookchin, "Listen, Marxist!," *Anarchos* (May, 1969), 5.
4. Damian F. White, "Hierarchy, Domination, Nature: Considering Bookchin's Critical Social Theory," *Organization & Environment* (2003), 35.
5. Murray Bookchin, "Listen, Marxist!," *Anarchos*, 3–30; Murray Bookchin, "Marxism as Bourgeois Sociology," in Murray Bookchin, *Toward an Ecological Society* (Montreal: Black Rose Books, 1980), 195–210; Murray Bookchin, "Post Scarcity Anarchism," in Murray Bookchin, *Post-Scarcity Anarchism*, 2nd ed. (Oakland: AK Press, 2004), 5–35; Murray Bookchin, *Ecology and Revolutionary Thought*, 2nd ed. (New York: Times Change Press, 1970); Murray Bookchin, "Spontaneity and Organisation," in Murray Bookchin, *Toward an Ecological Society*, 251–74.
6. Bookchin, *Post-Scarcity Anarchism*, 2nd ed.; Bookchin, *Toward an Ecological Society*, 251–74.
7. Pat Murtagh, "Hierarchy and Freedom," *The Ecologist* 13, No. 1 (1983): 45, 46, emphasis in original.
8. Robin Clark, "Earth Deserves a Better Fate," *New Scientist* (November 16, 1982): 754.
9. Murray Bookchin, *The Modern Crisis* (Philadelphia: New Society Publishers, 1986); Republished as Murray Bookchin, *From Urbanization to Cities: Toward a New Politics of Citizenship*, 2nd ed. (New York: Cassell, 1995); Alwyn Jones, "Towards a Moral Economy," *The Ecologist* 18, Nos 2/3 (1988): 107.

10. John Clark (ed.), *Renewing the Earth: The Promise of Social Ecology: A Celebration of the Work of Murray Bookchin* (London: Green Print, 1990).

11. Clark, *Renewing the Earth*, 3.

12. White, "Hierarchy, Domination, Nature," 35.

13. Stuart Best, "Murray Bookchin's Theory of Social Ecology: An Appraisal of the Ecology of Freedom," *Organization & Environment* 11, No. 3 (1998): 334, 335.

14. Peter Marshall, *Demanding the Impossible: A History of Anarchism* (London: Fontana, 1992), 602.

15. Colin Ward, "The Bookchin Prescription," *Anarchist Studies* 5, No. 2 (October, 1997): 170.

16. Joel Kovel, "Negating Bookchin," in Andrew Light, ed., *Social Ecology After Bookchin* (New York: Guilford, 1998), 34, 38; David Watson, *Beyond Bookchin: Preface for a Future Social Ecology* (Detroit: Black and Red, 1996), 9; John Clark, "Municipal Dreams: A Social Ecological Critique of Bookchin's Politics," in Andrew Light (ed.), *Social Ecology After Bookchin*, 156.

17. Max Cafard [pseudonym of John Clark], "Bookchin Agonistes: How Murray Bookchin's Attempts to Re-Enchant Humanity Became a Pugilistic Bacchanal," *Fifth Estate* 32, No. 1 (1997): 20–23.

18. Bob Black, *Anarchy after Leftism: A Farewell to the Anarchism That Was* (Columbia: CAL Press, 1997), 13.

19. Black, *Anarchy after Letfism*; Watson, *Beyond Bookchin*; Light, *Social Ecology after Bookchin*.

20. For contemporary examples of this kind of approach to Bookchin, see: Chuck Morse, *Being a Bookchinite* (available at: https://theanarchistlibrary .org/library/chuck-morse-being-a-bookchinite) and Bob Black, *Nightmares of Reason* (available at: https://theanarchistlibrary.org/library/bob-black-nightmares-of-reason). For a response to Morse's caricature of Bookchin, see: Andy Price, "Communalism or Caricature: Patterns of Bookchin Critique," *Anarchist Studies* 16, No. 1 (2008): 76–82; Andy Price, "Closing Down the Debate or Just Getting Started? On Personal Recollection and Theoretical Insight," *Communalism* 15 (2008).

21. Kovel, "Negating Bookchin," 27.

22. See, for example, Bookchin's essays in *Toward an Ecological Society*.

23. Arne Naess, "The Shallow and the Deep, Long-Range Ecology Movement: A Summary," *Inquiry* 16 (1973): 95–100.

24. Bill Devall and George Sessions, *Deep Ecology: Living as if Nature Mattered* (Utah: Gibson Smith, 1985).

25. Devall and Sessions, *Deep Ecology*, 68–73.

26. Murray Bookchin, "Toward a Philosophy of Nature: The Bases for an Ecological Ethics," in Michael Tobias (ed.), *Deep Ecology* (San Diego: Avant Books, 1984), 213–39. Bookchin's early affinity with deep ecology should not, however, be overstated: Bookchin from the very beginning would have a problem with deep ecology's view of the "population problem," as

expressed in their fourth platform principle: "4. The flourishing of human life and cultures is compatible with a substantial decrease of the human population. The flourishing of non-human life requires such a decrease," (Devall and Sessions, *Deep Ecology*, 70). This is a point to which we return in Chapter 2.

27. Janet Biehl, email to the author, October 11, 2007.
28. See Edward Abbey, *The Monkey Wrench Gang* (London: Penguin, 2004).
29. Devall and Sessions, *Deep Ecology*.
30. Dave Foreman, in Bill Devall, "A Spanner in the Woods: Dave Foreman talks with Simply Living," *Simply Living* 2, No. 12 (1987): 2–4.
31. See for example Bookchin's articles from Amherst and immediately afterwards: Murray Bookchin, "Social Ecology versus Deep Ecology: A Challenge for the Ecology Movement," *Green Perspectives*, Nos. 4–5 (Summer 1987): 1–23; Murray Bookchin, "Yes!—Whither Earth First!?," *Green Perspectives* 10 (September 1988): 1–7.
32. Bookchin, "Social Ecology versus Deep Ecology," 3.
33. Ibid., 4–5.
34. Ibid., 3.
35. Ibid., 4.
36. Walter Schwartz, "Anatomy of an Eco-anarchist," *The Guardian*, May 15, 1992, 25.
37. Murray Bookchin and Dave Foreman, *Defending the Earth: A Debate Between Murray Bookchin and Dave Foreman* (Montreal: Black Rose Books, 1991).
38. It should be noted here that all of the literature—positive and negative—that surrounds Bookchin's ecology, place the emergence of the critical literature at the same point—at Amherst, 1987. That is, before this one event, there was very little critical literature of Bookchin. Therefore, Bookchin's address plays a central role in the contested nature of his reputation today, and will be examined in full detail below.
39. Murray Bookchin, *Social Anarchism or Lifestyle Anarchism: An Unbridgeable Chasm*.
40. See Max Stirner, *The Ego and its Own* (London: Jonathon Cape, 1971).
41. Bookchin, *Social Anarchism or Lifestyle Anarchism*, 8.
42. Ibid., 9.
43. See Black, *Anarchy after Leftism*, and Watson, *Beyond Bookchin*.
44. See: Murray Bookchin, "The Crisis in the Ecology Movement," *Green Perspectives* 6. (May 1988): 1–6; Murray Bookchin, "The Population Myth I," *Green Perspectives* 8 (July 1988): 1–6; and Bookchin, "Yes!—Whither Earth First!?," 1–7.
45. R. W. Flowers, "Of Old Wine in New Bottles: Taking up Bookchin's challenge," *Earth First!* (November 1, 1987): 19; Black, *Anarchy after Leftism*, 13.
46. Biehl notes here that this is a fact reflected in Bookchin's personal correspondence: "At one point I was going through his personal correspondence,

sorting it by year. Up until 1987, the piles of letters coming in—saying 'How can I help'?, 'Come speak at my college'—were high. After June 1987, such letters almost disappeared." (Janet Biehl, email to the author, October 11, 2007).

47. Cafard, "Bookchin Agonistes," 20–23. The author of this pugilistic analogy, Max Cafard, it should be noted, is in fact the pseudonym of John Clark, the one-time devotee of Bookchin who less than a decade earlier had collated the anthology of essays dedicated to Bookchin's "magnificent contribution to ecological thought and practice." It is interesting to note that this one writer plays a significant part in the creation of the Bookchin caricature, as both Clark and Cafard, and is perhaps more personal in his approach to Bookchin than most other critics. Indeed, the personal nature of his critical approach to Bookchin is matched only by his seemingly uncritical devotion to Bookchin during their years of collaboration (see Clark, *Renewing the Earth*).

48. On Bookchin's break with anarchism see: Murray Bookchin, *Social Ecology and Communalism*, edited by Eirik Eiglad (Oakland: AK Press, 2007); Janet Biehl, "Bookchin Breaks with Anarchism," *Communalism* 12 (October 2007): 1–20.

49. White, "Hierarchy, Domination, Nature," 35. Indeed, this is a project that White has since extended, with the recent publication of *Bookchin: A Critical Appraisal* (London: Pluto, 2008), a welcome sign that there is a growing realisation, as White himself puts it, that "the tale of Murray Bookchin is one worth telling, and one worth engaging with" (p. 4). White admirably *attempts* to move away from the problematic critical literature in his latest work (as he did in his earlier work) and does indeed open the possibility of an objective approach to Bookchin that permits an engagement with his ideas previously obscured by the caricature. However, his approach differs fundamentally from the present work in two key ways. First, White rejects Bookchin's project *taken as a whole*, his "grand narrative" of natural and social evolution and the political practice it necessitates, and bar an acknowledgement of Bookchin's visionary writings (for White, mainly pre-1982) and his undoubted influence on "environmentalism," there is no attempt to apply Bookchin's political project to the present. However, as will be argued herein, this is the entire point of Bookchin's social ecology: it is an attempt to formulate, theoretically and practically, a way of radically remaking society. To forego the overarching radical intent of Bookchin is, in many ways, to offer an appraisal as misplaced as the critiques that led to the caricature from which White intends to move away. Second, and compounding the problem just outlined, whilst White *does attempt* this move away from the more problematic literature, in failing to deal with it directly, he cannot escape it. In almost every discussion of Bookchin's key principles, White is drawn back into discussions that in truth have no place in a scholarly appraisal of Bookchin. The present work is *explicitly* set to circumvent this problem: in the opening section, we deal with

the problematic literature on Bookchin and its roots extensively, precisely so we can critically discount it and give his work the full reassessment it deserves untainted by the caricature engendered by the more problematic literature of the last two decades.

50. See, respectively: Michael Hardt and Antonio Negri, *Empire* (New York: Harvard University Press, 2000); Michael Hardt and Antonio Negri, *Multitude* (London: Penguin Books, 2005); John Holloway, *Change the World Without Taking Power: The Meaning of Revolution Today* (London: Pluto Press, 2002); John Holloway, *Crack Capitalism* (London: Pluto Press, 2010). For background info on both the Zapatistas and 15-M, see: Subcomandante Marcos, *La Otra Campana: The Other Campaign* (San Fransisco: City Lights, 2005); Andy Price, "From Arab Spring to Spanish Summer," *ZNet*, 22 May 2011.

51. David Harvey, *The Enigma of Capital and the Crisis of Capital* (London: Profile Books, 2010).

Chapter 1: The Genesis of the Bookchin Caricature

1. Naess, "The Shallow and the Deep," 95.
2. Ibid., 96, emphasis added.
3. Ibid., 96.
4. Arne Naess, "Identification as a Source of Deep Ecological Attitudes," in M. Tobias, ed., *Deep Ecology* (San Marcos: Avant, 1984), 268, emphasis added.
5. Ibid., 268, emphasis added.
6. Ibid., 267–68.
7. Warwick Fox, "Deep Ecology: A New Philosophy of Our Time?" *The Ecologist* 14, Nos. 5–6 (1984): 194.
8. Ibid., 194, emphasis added.
9. Ibid., 194.
10. Bill Devall and George Sessions, *Deep Ecology*.
11. Ibid., 66.
12. Ibid., 67.
13. Ibid., 67.
14. Ibid., 67.
15. Ibid., 68.
16. Ibid., 67.
17. Ibid., 69.
18. Ibid., 70.
19. Ibid., 70, emphasis in original.
20. Ibid., 70.
21. Ibid., 73.
22. Ibid., 71.
23. Ibid., 70, emphasis added.
24. Ibid., 71, 72.

25. And still reads, it should be added, as Earth First! still does exist.

26. Dave Foreman, "Around the Campfire," *Earth First!* (June 21, 1987): 2.

27. Devall, "A Spanner in the Woods," 4.

28. Ibid., 2.

29. Ibid., 4.

30. Ibid., 4.

31. Ibid., 4.

32. Ibid., 4, emphasis added.

33. Ibid., 4, emphasis added.

34. Edward Abbey, "Letter to the editor," *The Bloomsbury Review* (April–May 1986), 43.

35. Edward Abbey, *One Life at a Time, Please* (New York: Henry Holt and Company, 1988), 43, emphasis added.

36. Ibid., 43, emphasis in original.

37. Ibid., 44.

38. Ibid., 44. To fully appreciate the links between Abbey and Earth First!, it is worth noting here that in an *Earth First!* article titled "Is Sanctuary the Answer?," Foreman would explicitly endorse Abbey's problematic position on immigration. Telling the reader that he feared that "good-hearted liberal solutions [to the problems of Latin America] only perpetuate the evils that they seek to overcome," he argues that immigration into the U.S. from Latin America should be halted immediately. "The would-be immigrants would go back to unfortunate and, in some cases, bloody fates," Foreman continues, but in the long run, not only would this would build anger and pressure in their own countries and (in an unspecified time scale) eventually lead them to a revolution of their own social conditions, but also it would stop the "unruly" immigrants from tainting the social conditions of the United States. Re-stating the unquestionably brutal "let them sort out their own problems" approach outlined by Abbey, Foreman concludes that "in the long run, the most humane solution is the one advanced by Edward Abbey: send every illegal alien home with a rifle and a thousand rounds." See Dave Foreman, "Is Sanctuary the Answer?," *Earth First!* (November 1, 1987): 21–22.

39. Miss Ann Thropy [pseudonym for Christopher Manes], "Population and AIDS," *Earth First!* (May 1, 1987): 32.

40. Ibid., 32.

41. Ibid., 32, emphasis in original.

42. Ibid., 32, emphasis in original.

43. Ibid., 32.

44. Bookchin, "Social Ecology versus Deep Ecology," 3, 4.

45. Ibid., 3.

46. Ibid., 4–5.

47. Foreman was in fact still editor of *Earth First!* at this point.

48. The Editors, "'Dangerous' Tendencies in Earth First!," *Earth First!* (November 1987), 17.

49. Flowers, "Of Old Wine," 18.
50. Ibid., 19.
51. Ibid., 19.
52. Flowers, "Of Old Wine," 19.
53. Ibid., 19.
54. Chim Blea, "Why the Venom?," *Earth First!* (November 1987), 19.
55. Ibid., 19.
56. Ibid., 19.
57. Ibid., 19.
58. Ibid., 19.
59. Dave Foreman, "Whither Earth First!?," *Earth First!* (November 1987), 20.
60. Ibid., 20.
61. Ibid., 20.
62. Bill Devall, "Deep Ecology and its Critics," *Trumpeter* 5, No. 2 (Spring 1988): 55.
63. Ibid., 55.
64. Ibid., 55.
65. Ibid., 55, emphasis added.
66. Warwick Fox, *Toward a Transpersonal Ecology: Developing New Foundations for Environmentalism* (Boston: Shambhala Publications, 1990), 37.
67. Devall, "Deep Ecology and its Critics," 55.
68. There was a curious pattern to the deep ecology responses to Bookchin's critique: the appeal to cordial exchange whilst proposing philosophical positions that offer quite the opposite. To be explicit in the publication of statements about letting the victims of famine in Africa starve and then to ask for restraint in people who responded to this belies the unthinking nature of deep ecology. It is almost as if those who take up the positions of deep ecology simply refuse to see them through to their logical conclusions. When others do, and point out the serious problems therein, there is a shockwave through deep ecology. The cordial/un-cordial nature of Bookchin's critique and a judgment as to its significance is a matter we return to at the outset of Chapter 2.
69. Ibid., 55.
70. Ibid., 55, emphasis added.
71. Ibid., 57. Indeed, Devall takes this notion of the deep ecologists being "less interested in political economy" even further to include the entire Western philosophical tradition on the list of things deep ecologists are less interested in. "Deep ecology theorists," he argues on p. 57, "tend to see the whole path of Western philosophy (except for a few mavericks such as Spinoza) as leading to a dead end." As noted, and as will be fully examined below, this is one of the two central planks of Bookchin's criticism: the discounting of the thinking and writing of the human cannon which in part explains both the emergence of humanity from nature and also attempts to explain where

things went wrong in terms of its current destructive relationship with the rest of the natural world.

72. Ibid., 58, 59.
73. Ibid., 58–59.
74. Ibid., 59.
75. Ibid., 59.
76. George Sessions, "Radical Environmentalism in the 90s," *Wild Earth* (Fall 1992): 66.
77. It is a further contradiction in the deep ecology response to Bookchin that the academic deep ecologists often attempt to distance themselves from the comments in *Earth First!* that sparked the debate—as Sessions does here with the term "casual remarks"—yet at the same time take up wholesale the terminology employed first in the pages of *Earth First!*—like "turf war" and "attack"; ibid., 66, emphasis added.
78. Ibid., 66.
79. Ibid., 68.
80. Bookchin, *Ecology and Revolutionary Thought*, 6.

Chapter 2: The Ecology of Bookchin

1. Blea, "Why the Venom?," 19; Fox, "Deep Ecology," 37; Flowers, "Of Old Wine," 18.
2. Bookchin, "Social Ecology versus Deep Ecology," 2.
3. Ibid., 3.
4. Ibid., 5.
5. Ibid., 14.
6. Schwartz, "Anatomy of an Eco-anarchist," 25, emphasis added.
7. Bookchin and Foreman, *Defending the Earth*, 99.
8. Bookchin, "Yes!—Whither Earth First!?," 1.
9. Miss Ann Thropy, "Aids and Population," 19.
10. Ibid., 123, emphasis is original.
11. Ibid., 123.
12. Foreman, "Yes!—Whither Earth First!?" 20.
13. Miss Ann Thropy, "Aids and Population," 19.
14. Devall, "Deep Ecology and its Critics," 59.
15. Sessions, "Radical Environmentalism," 68; Flowers, "Of Old Wine," 19.
16. Bookchin, "The Problem of Chemicals in Food," 210.
17. Ibid., 210.
18. Lewis Herber (pseudonym of Murray Bookchin), *Our Synthetic Environment* (New York: Alfred A. Knopf, 1962), 26–27.
19. Clearly based on a reading of the emerging science of ecology, Bookchin would offer an early social discussion of global warming, and was inaccurate only in his time-scale. "Since the Industrial Revolution," Bookchin explained in 1964, "the overall atmospheric mass of carbon dioxide has

increased by 13% over earlier, more stable, levels. It could be argued on very sound theoretical grounds that this mounting blanket of carbon dioxide, by intercepting heat radiated from the earth into outer space, leads to rising atmospheric temperatures, to a more violent circulation of air, to more destructive storm patterns, and eventually, it will lead to a melting of the polar ice caps (possibly in two or three centuries), rising sea levels, and the inundation of vast land areas." See Bookchin, *Ecology and Revolutionary Thought*, 8.

20. Bookchin, *Ecology and Revolutionary Thought*, 6, emphasis added.
21. Ibid., 7, emphasis in original.
22. Ibid., 17.
23. Ibid., 23.
24. Ibid., 6.
25. Bookchin, "Spontaneity and Organisation," 271, emphases added.
26. Ibid., 271.
27. Bookchin, "Social Ecology versus Deep Ecology," 2.
28. Ibid., 3.
29. Fox, "Deep Ecology," 194.
30. Devall and Sessions, *Deep Ecology*, 67.
31. Bookchin, "Social Ecology versus Deep Ecology," 11.
32. Ibid., 9.
33. Ibid., 11.
34. Ibid., 9.
35. Ibid., 13, emphasis added.
36. Ibid., 9.
37. Ibid., 9.
38. Ibid., 9, emphasis in original.
39. Ibid., 9.
40. Ibid., 10.
41. Murray Bookchin, "Thinking Ecologically: A Dialectical Approach," *Our Generation*, No. 18, Spring/Summer (1987), 21.
42. Ibid., 21.
43. Ibid., 22.
44. Ibid., 21, emphasis in original.
45. Bookchin, "Freedom and Necessity in Nature: A Problem in Ecological Ethics," *Alternatives* 13, No. 4 (November 1986): 31.
46. Bookchin, "Thinking Ecologically," 24, emphasis in original.
47. Ibid., 24, emphasis in original.
48. Ibid., 14, emphasis in original.
49. Ibid., 15.
50. Murray Bookchin, *The Modern Crisis*, 56, emphasis in original.
51. Ibid., 57.
52. Bookchin, *passim*.
53. Ibid., 57, emphasis in original.

54. Murray Bookchin, "Rethinking Ethics, Nature, and Society," in *The Modern Crisis*, 25.
55. Ibid., 26.
56. Ibid., 26.
57. Ibid., 58–59.
58. Ibid., 57, first emphasis in original, second added.
59. Ibid., 58.
60. Ibid., 11, emphasis added.
61. Bookchin, "Thinking Ecologically," 29.
62. Ibid., 29, emphasis in original.
63. Ibid., 30.
64. Ibid., 31.
65. Bookchin, *The Modern Crisis*, 11.
66. Bookchin, "Thinking Ecologically," 31, emphasis added.
67. Ibid., 31.
68. Ibid., 31.
69. Ibid., 31–32.
70. Ibid., 25, emphasis in original.
71. Ibid., 26.
72. Ibid., 35.
73. Ibid., 11.
74. Ibid., 11.
75. Ibid., 26.
76. Ibid., 11.
77. Ibid., 11–12, emphasis added.
78. Ibid., 12, emphasis in original.
79. Murray Bookchin, "Freedom and Necessity in Nature," 36, emphasis added.
80. Bookchin, *The Modern Crisis*, 13.
81. Ibid., 10. fn 1, emphasis in original.
82. Bookchin, "Thinking Ecologically," 35–36.
83. Bookchin, *The Ecology of Freedom*, 315.
84. Bookchin, "Thinking Ecologically," 36, emphases added.
85. Ibid., 32, emphasis added.

Chapter 3: Reassessing Bookchin's Philosophy of Nature

1. Bookchin, *The Ecology of Freedom*, 364.
2. Bookchin, "Thinking Ecologically," 31, emphasis added.
3. Robyn Eckersley, "Divining Evolution and Respecting Evolution: The Ecological Ethics of Murray Bookchin," *Environmental Ethics* 11 (1989): 99–116.
4. Eckersley, "Divining Evolution," 109.
5. Ibid., 109.
6. Ibid., 109.

7. Bookchin, "Thinking Ecologically," 14–15.
8. Ibid., 17, emphasis in original.
9. Ibid., 30.
10. G.A. Albrecht, "Ethics and Directionality in Nature" in Andrew Light (ed.), *Social Ecology After Bookchin* (New York: Guilford, 1998), 97.
11. Murray Bookchin, *Remaking Society: Pathways to a Green Future* (Boston: South End Press, 1990), 36, emphasis in original.
12. Ibid., 37.
13. Eckersley, "Divining Evolution," 109.
14. Bookchin, *The Modern Crisis*, 10, fn. 1, emphasis in original.
15. Eckersley, "Divining Evolution," 107, emphasis in original.
16. Ibid., 83.
17. Don Alexander, "On Murray Bookchin's Philosophy of Social Ecology," *Capitalism, Nature, Socialism* 9, No. 33 (1998): 126.
18. Ibid., 130.
19. Bookchin, *The Modern Crisis*, 13; see, for example: Bookchin, *The Ecology of Freedom*, 31; Murray Bookchin, *The Philosophy of Social Ecology: Essays on Dialectical Naturalism* (Montreal: Black Rose Books, 1996), 18; ibid., 18.
20. Ibid., 18.
21. Ibid., 13, emphasis added.
22. Bookchin, *Remaking Society*, 35.
23. Murray Bookchin, *Free Cities: Communalism and the Left*, edited by Eirik Eiglad (unpublished manuscript; Taminent Library: New York, 2008), 68.
24. Albrecht, "Ethics in Nature," 96, emphasis added.
25. Ibid., 100.
26. Ibid., 101.
27. Ibid., 101.
28. Ibid., 101.
29. Ibid., 102.
30. Ibid., 102, emphasis added.
31. Ibid., 105, 110.
32. Eckersley, "Divining Evolution," 106.
33. Ibid., 107.
34. John Clark, "Domesticating the Dialectic: A Critique of Bookchin's Neo-Aristotelian Metaphysics," *Capitalism, Nature, Socialism* 19, No. 1 (2008): 82–97.
35. Bookchin, *The Philosophy of Social Ecology*, 23–24.
36. Clark, "Domesticating the Dialectic," 90.
37. Ibid., 90.
38. Janet Biehl, "Reply to John Clark's 'Domesticating the Dialectic,'" *Capitalism, Nature, Socialism* 20, No. 1 (2009): 122.
39. Ibid., 122.
40. Ibid., 124, emphasis in original.
41. Bookchin, *Social Ecology and Communalism*, 116, emphasis added.

42. Enrique Leff, "Murray Bookchin and the End of Dialectical Naturalism," *Capitalism, Nature, Socialism* 9, No. 4 (December 1998): 67.
43. Ibid., 68.
44. Ibid., 68.
45. Ibid., 69.
46. Ibid., 71.
47. Ibid., 70.
48. Ibid., 71.
49. Ibid., 93.
50. Bookchin, *The Philosophy of Social Ecology.*
51. Murray Bookchin, *Free Cities*, 68.
52. Bookchin, "Thinking Ecologically," 32.
53. Eckersley, "Divining Evolution," 99, emphasis in original.
54. Ibid., 102.
55. Ibid., 110.
56. Ibid., 110–11.
57. Ibid., 111.
58. Ibid., 111.
59. Ibid., 111–12.
60. Ibid., 112–13.
61. Ibid., 114, emphases in original.
62. Ibid., 114, emphases in original.
63. Ibid., 115, emphases in original.
64. Alexander, "On Bookchin's Philosophy," 126.
65. Ibid., 126–7.
66. Ibid., 127.
67. Bookchin, *Social Ecology and Communalism*, 29, emphasis added.
68. Bookchin and Foreman, 128.
69. Bookchin, *The Ecology of Freedom*, 315.
70. Ibid., xxxiv.
71. Ibid., xxxii.
72. Ibid., xxxii–iii, emphasis in original.
73. Ibid., xxxiii, emphasis added.
74. Bookchin and Foreman, *Defending the Earth*, 128.
75. Fox, "Deep Ecology," 194.
76. Eckersley, "Divining Evolution," 114, emphasis in original.
77. Ibid., 115.
78. Alexander, "On Bookchin's Philosophy," 127.
79. Harold Fromm, "Ecology and Ideology," *The Hudson Review* xlv, No. 1 (Spring 1992): 28, emphasis in original.
80. Bookchin, *The Ecology of Freedom*, xxvi, emphasis in original.
81. Eckersley, "Divining Evolution," 116.
82. Fromm, "Ecology and Ideology," 30.

Chapter 4: On Hierarchy and Domination

1.   Bookchin, "Toward a Philosophy of Nature," 229.
2.   Bookchin, *Social Ecology and Communalism*, 29, emphasis added.
3.   Bookchin, *The Modern Crisis*, 11.
4.   Bookchin, "Thinking Ecologically," 32.
5.   Ibid, 32, emphasis added.
6.   Ibid., 32, emphasis added.
7.   Ibid., 33, emphasis in original.
8.   Devall and Sessions, *Deep Ecology*, 67.
9.   Bookchin, "Toward a Philosophy of Nature," 234.
10. Bookchin, "Social Ecology versus Deep Ecology," 3.
11. Ibid., 3.
12. Ibid., 4.
13. Ibid., 4.
14. Ibid., 10.
15. Bookchin and Foreman, *Defending the Earth*, 30–31.
16. Ibid., 31.
17. Bookchin, "Social Ecology versus Deep Ecology," 10.
18. Ibid., 10, emphasis added.
19. Ibid., 10, emphasis added.
20. Sessions, "Radical Environmentalism," 66.
21. Bookchin, "Ecology and Revolutionary Thought," 10, emphasis in original.
22. Murray Bookchin, "The Power to Destroy, the Power to Create," in Murray Bookchin, *Ecology and Revolutionary Thought* (New York: Times Change Press, 1970), 51.
23. Ibid., 49, emphases in original.
24. Ibid., 49.
25. Ibid., 49–50.
26. Ibid., 51.
27. Bookchin, "Social Ecology versus Deep Ecology," 17, emphasis in original.
28. Ibid., 17–18.
29. Ibid., 3.
30. Bookchin, "Thinking Ecologically," 33, emphasis added.
31. Bookchin, *The Ecology of Freedom*, 63.
32. Ibid., 63.
33. Ibid., 63.
34. Ibid., 63–64.
35. Ibid., 64.
36. Ibid., 64.
37. Ibid., 65.
38. Ibid., 65.
39. Ibid., 65.
40. Ibid., 65–66.

41. Ibid., 66.
42. Ibid., 66.
43. Ibid., 66, first emphasis added, subsequent in original.
44. Ibid., 86–87, emphases in original.
45. Ibid., 44.
46. Ibid., 47.
47. Ibid., 48, emphasis added.
48. Ibid., 72–73.
49. Ibid., 74.
50. Ibid., 72.
51. Ibid., 74.
52. Ibid., 78.
53. Ibid., 77.
54. Ibid., 79–80.
55. Ibid., xxii.
56. Ibid., xxii.
57. Ibid., 29, 30.
58. Ibid., 80.
59. Ibid., 81.
60. Ibid., 81, emphasis in original.
61. Ibid., 81.
62. Ibid., 81.
63. Ibid., 81.
64. Ibid., 88.
65. Ibid., 89.
66. Ibid., 89.
67. Ibid., 89.
68. Ibid., 43.

Chapter 5: Reassessing Bookchin's Social History

1. Bookchin, *The Ecology of Freedom*, xxii.
2. Bookchin, *The Modern Crisis*, 67.
3. Ibid., 14.
4. White, "Hierarchy, Domination, Nature," 43.
5. Bookchin, *The Ecology of Freedom*, 44.
6. Alan P. Rudy, "Ecology and Anthropology in the Work of Murray Bookchin: Problems of Theory and Evidence," in Andrew Light (ed.), *Social Ecology After Bookchin*, 278.
7. Ibid., 280.
8. White, "Hierarchy, Domination, Nature," 45.
9. Rudy, "Ecology and Anthropology," 280.
10. Bookchin, *The Ecology of Freedom*, 13.
11. Ibid., 12.

12. Bookchin, "Thinking Ecologically," 31.
13. Bookchin, *The Ecology of Freedom*, 56.
14. T. Earle, "The Evolution of Chiefdoms," *Current Anthropology* 30, No. 1 (1989): 86–87.
15. See, for example, R. L. Pennington, "Causes of Early Human Population Growth," *American Journal of Physical Anthropology* 99, No. 2 (1996): 259–74; J. D. Walla and M. Przeworski, "When Did the Human Population Size Start Increasing?" *Genetics* 155 (2000): 1865–74.
16. R. W. Sussman, "Addendum: Child Transport, Family Size, and Increase in Human Population During the Neolithic," *Current Anthropology* 13, No. 2. (1972): 258.
17. F. A. Hassan, and R. A. Sengel, "On Mechanisms of Population Growth During the Neolithic (in Discussion and Criticism)," *Current Anthropology* 14, No. 5 (1973): 535–42; Pennington, "Causes of Early Human Population Growth."
18. Michelle Rosaldo, "Women, Culture and Society: A Theoretical Overview," in Michelle Rosaldo and L. Lamphere (eds.), *Women, Culture and Society* (Stanford: Stanford University Press, 1974), 11.
19. R. Rohrlich, "State Formation in Sumer and the Subjugation of Women," *Feminist Studies* 6, No. 1 (1980): 76–102.
20. Bookchin, *The Ecology of Freedom*, 56.
21. David Graeber, *Fragments of an Anarchist Anthropology* (Boston: Prickly Paradigm Press, 2004). Graeber was, in 2005, refused an extension of his contract at Yale, the year after the publication of his *Fragments*. Widely thought to be a reaction to both the critical nature of *Fragments*—in its damning of anthropology as a discipline "terrified of its own potential"— and to Graeber's claim of the prevalence of anarchist forms in anthropological and ethnographic literature, this technical dismissal of Graeber by Yale was protested by an international campaign. Here, anthropology departments from around the world would write letters of protest to Yale and decry the dismissal of an anthropologist with a "remarkable reputation in the world of anthropology" (Sussex), whose work is "at the forefront of anthropological work internationally" (Manchester), making him "a major new voice in cultural anthropology" (Chicago), and as Maurice Bloch describes him above (despite the fact that Graeber was a fierce critic of Bloch's own work), the dismissal of "the best anthropological theorist of his generation from anywhere in the world." Graeber's leading status, then, in the world of anthropology (the problems at Yale aside) make his work important in our discussion of Bookchin's anthropology.
22. Graeber, *Fragments*, 75, 79.
23. Ibid., 11–12, emphasis added.
24. White, "Hierarchy and Freedom," 44.
25. Bookchin, *Remaking Society*, 53.
26. Bookchin, *The Ecology of Freedom*, 81.

27. White, "Ecology and Freedom," 44.
28. Ibid., 44.
29. Ibid., 45.
30. Rudy, "Ecology and Anthropology," 278; Bookchin, *The Modern Crisis*, 55, emphasis in original; Bookchin, *The Ecology of Freedom*, 44.
31. Rudy, "Ecology and Anthropology," 278.
32. Ibid., 279–80.
33. Bookchin, *The Ecology of Freedom*, 80, emphasis added.
34. Ibid., 80.
35. Rudy, "Ecology and Anthropology," 288.
36. Ibid., 290.
37. Bookchin, *The Ecology of Freedom*, xxvii–viii.
38. Ibid., xxiv.
39. Ibid., 81.
40. Ibid., xxviii, emphasis in original.
41. Ibid., xxiv, emphasis in original.
42. Ibid., xxvii.
43. Ibid., 82.
44. Ibid., 82.
45. Murray Bookchin, "Recovering Evolution: A Reply to Eckersley and Fox," *Environmental Ethics* 12 (Fall 1990).
46. Bookchin, *Ecology of Freedom*, 25.
47. Bookchin, "Recovering Evolution: A Reply to Eckersley and Fox," emphasis added.
48. Murray Bookchin, "Reply to John Moore," *Social Anarchism* 20 (1995), emphasis in original.
49. Bookchin, *The Ecology of Freedom*, 66, emphasis added.
50. Ibid., 8.
51. Bookchin, "Reply to More."
52. Andrew Light and Alan P. Rudy, "Social Ecology and Social Labour: Consideration and Critique of Murray Bookchin," *Capitalism, Socialism, Nature* 6, No. 2 (1995): 103.
53. Ibid., 81.
54. Ibid., 90.
55. Ibid., 90.
56. Ibid., 91.
57. Ibid., 91.
58. Ibid., 91.
59. Ibid., 92.
60. Ibid., 92, emphasis added.
61. Ibid., 92.
62. Ibid., 92. fn. 83.
63. Ibid., 94.
64. Ibid., 98.

65. Bookchin, "Listen, Marxist!," 5.
66. Ibid., 5.
67. Ibid., 14.
68. Bookchin, *Toward an Ecological Society*, 13.
69. Ibid., 29.
70. Bookchin, "Listen Marxist," 5.
71. Murray Bookchin, *Anarchism, Marxism and the Future of the Left: Interviews and Essays, 1993–1998* (Oakland: AK Press, 2001), 271, emphasis in original.
72. Ibid., 271, emphases in original.
73. Bookchin, *Toward and Ecological Society*, 197.
74. Ibid., 29.
75. Bookchin, *The Ecology of Freedom*, 89.
76. Ibid., 89.
77. Ibid., 94.
78. Ibid., 95.
79. Ibid., 95.
80. Ibid., 95.
81. See in particular his two major works, *The Ecology of Freedom* and *From Urbanization to Cities*.
82. Ibid., 96
83. Bookchin, *The Modern Crisis*, 30.
84. Bookchin, *The Ecology of Freedom*, 140–41.

Chapter 6: From Anarchism to Communalism

1. Murray Bookchin, *Social Anarchism or Lifestyle Anarchism: An Unbridgeable Chasm*.
2. Ibid., 5.
3. Ibid., 8.
4. Ibid., 8.
5. Ibid., 9.
6. Ibid., 5.
7. John Zerzan, *Future Primitive and Other Essays* (New York: Autonomedia, 1994); Hakim Bey, *T.A.Z: The Temporary Autonomous Zone, Ontological Anarchy, Poetic Terrorism* (New York: Autonomedia, 1991); L. Susan Brown, *The Politics of Individualism: Liberalism, Liberal Feminism and Anarchism* (Montreal: Black Rose Books, 1993); George Bradford, "Civilization in Bulk," *Fifth Estate* (Spring 1991): 12.
8. Bookchin, *Social Anarchism or Lifestyle Anarchism*, 2.
9. Black, *Anarchy After Leftism*, 13. It should be noted here that Black continues to this day in the vein we find here. Indeed, in 2010, he posted online a book-length manuscript, *Nightmares of Reason*, which is a treatment of what he sees as the largely personal failings of Bookchin. This manuscript is so highly personalised—almost psychotic in its attacks on Bookchin—that in

my opinion it cannot be treated as a serious text on Bookchin, and should be omitted from serious analysis of social ecology.

10. Cafard, "Bookchin Agonistes."

11. Watson, *Beyond Bookchin*, 17, 192.

12. Clark, *Renewing the Earth*, 3.

13. Kovel, "Negating Bookchin," 37.

14. Ibid., 37.

15. Ibid., 38.

16. Cafard, "Bookchin Agonistes."

17. Clark, "Domesticating the Dialectic," 82.

18. See: Murray Bookchin, "Comments on the International Social Ecology Network Gathering and the 'Deep Social Ecology' of John Clark," *Democracy and Nature* 3, No. 3 (1997): 154–97; Murray Bookchin, "Whither Anarchism? A reply to recent Anarchist Critics" in Murray Bookchin, *Anarchism, Marxism and the Future of the Left*, 160–259; Murray Bookchin, "Turning Up The Stones: A Reply To John Clark's 13 October Message," originally posted on the listserv Research on Anarchism (available at http://dwardmac.pitzer.edu/Anarchist_Archives/bookchin/turning.html).

19. It is interesting indeed to compare the Bookchin of 1987 with the Bookchin of a decade later. For example, at Amherst, he opens his critique by explaining to the audience that he "loves" everyone present, that he has no intention to attack, to be aggressive. Indeed, in the article he would publish of his critique, he refers to the "well-meaning people" in the ecology movement. However, by the time of the anarchy debates, this tone had largely disappeared. Again, a case can be made here for Bookchin being affected by several years of acrimony. However—and although inexcusable the instances of overt polemics—amongst the harsh tones of the later Bookchin, there was still a clear political critique underpinning his work.

20. It is noted here that, in keeping with the rest of the work so far, those critiques (or even any parts of individual critiques) from the anarchist debates that were more robust, that helped shed light on any possible problems in Bookchin's work will of course be taken into account.

21. Cafard, "Bookchin Agonistes."

22. Indeed, even in the heat of the debate, not everyone saw Bookchin's *Social Anarchism or Lifestyle Anarchism* as wholly problematic. As Martin commented at the height of the furore, it was still important to look past the problems of tone and focus on the issues raised, and as such, in an attempt to get past the notions of people engaged in attacks, Martin suggested that "we can better appreciate what is happening here if we remember that we are witnessing an open and fruitful exchange, not a conflict." Thomas S. Martin, "Bookchin, Biehl, Brown: An Unbridgeable Chasm?" *Anarchist Studies* 6, No. 1 (1998):43.

23. Bookchin, *Ecology and Revolutionary Thought*, 6, 26–27.

24. Biehl, "Bookchin Breaks," 3.

25. Marshall, *Demanding the Impossible*, 602.
26. Bookchin, *Ecology and Revolutionary Thought*, 29.
27. Biehl, "Bookchin Breaks," 1–20.
28. Murray Bookchin, "Spring Offensives & Summer Vacations," *Anarchos* 4 (1972): 56, emphases in original.
29. Ibid., 56.
30. Ibid., 56.
31. Ibid., 57.
32. Ibid., 57, emphasis in original.
33. Ibid., 58, emphasis added.
34. Biehl, "Bookchin Breaks," 7.
35. Murray Bookchin, "The Communalist Project"—written in 2002, it was republished and is used here in Murray Bookchin, *Social Ecology and Communalism*.
36. Ibid., 97, fn 7.
37. Ibid., 108–9, fn. 17.
38. Ibid., 97.
39. Ibid., 97–98.
40. Ibid., 99.
41. Bookchin, *From Urbanization to Cities*, 260, emphases in original.
42. Ibid., 41–86.
43. Bookchin, *Social Ecology and Communalism*, 60.
44. Bookchin, *From Urbanization to Cities*, 129.
45. Ibid., 202.
46. Ibid., 203.
47. Ibid., 203.
48. Bookchin, *Social Ecology and Communalism*, 93.
49. Bookchin, *From Urbanization to Cities*, 242, emphasis added.
50. Bookchin, *Social Ecology and Communalism*, 109.
51. Bookchin, *From Urbanization to Cities*, 242–43.
52. Ibid., 183, emphases in original.
53. Bookchin, *Social Ecology and Communalism*, 109, emphasis added.
54. Ibid., 99, emphases in original.
55. Ibid., 100.
56. Ibid., 101.
57. Bookchin, *From Urbanization to Cities*, 223.
58. Ibid., 223.
59. Ibid., 223, emphasis added.
60. Ibid., 229.
61. Ibid., 261.
62. Ibid., 223, emphasis in original.
63. Ibid., 264.
64. Ibid., 223.
65. Ibid., 230.

66. Bookchin, *Social Ecology and Communalism*, 114, 115.
67. Ibid., 114.
68. Ibid., 115.
69. Ibid., 114.
70. Ibid., 115.
71. Ibid., 101.
72. Ibid., 102.
73. Ibid., 102; 102–3.
74. Ibid., 103-4, emphases in original.
75. Ibid., 104.
76. Ibid., 104, emphasis in original.
77. Bookchin, *From Urbanization to Cities*, 237.
78. Bookchin, *Social Ecology and Communalism*, 101.
79. Ibid., 109.
80. Bookchin, *From Urbanization to Cities*, 252–53.
81. Ibid., 10, emphasis in original.
82. Ibid., 252–3.

Chapter 7: Reassessing Bookchin's Political Project

1. Bookchin, *From Urbanization to Cities*, 222.
2. Ibid., 226.
3. Ibid., 241.
4. Clark, "Municipal Dreams," 152.
5. Ibid., 152–53.
6. Ibid., 153.
7. Watson, *Beyond Bookchin*, 179.
8. Ibid., 179.
9. Ibid., 181.
10. Black, *Anarchy after Leftism*, 79–78.
11. Watson, *Beyond Bookchin*, 172, emphasis in original.
12. Clark, "Municipal Dreams," 146.
13. Ibid., 145, emphasis added.
14. Ibid., 146.
15. Bookchin, *Social Ecology and Communalism*, 103–4, emphases in original.
16. Clark, "Municipal Dreams," 148.
17. Ibid., 171.
18. Ibid., 148.
19. Ibid., 148, emphasis in original. Although beyond the remit of the present work, it is clear that the "tension" found in Bookchin's political programme between the particular and the general is a clear precursor to one of the main theoretical trends to have emerged in the theory and practice of the alter-globalisation movement of the last decade or so. Suffice to note here that the key thinkers and practical experiments of the movement

appear to have collectively embraced this tension as a positive, as perhaps one of their greatest strengths. The near-universal leitmotif of alter-globalisation—"think globally, act locally"—is testament to the centrality of this concept. And though these trends of anticapitalism had begun to emerge at the time Clark was writing, it appears he was unaware of them, and his critique must be revisited in light of such developments.

20. Black, *Anarchy After Leftism*, 76.
21. Robert Graham, "Reinventing Hierarchy: The Political Theory of Social Ecology," *Anarchist Studies* 12, No. 4 (2004): 16.
22. Ibid., 19.
23. Ibid., 19, 21.
24. Ibid., 19.
25. Ibid., 19.
26. Janet Biehl explains this well in Janet Biehl, *Libertarian Municpalism: The Politics of Social Ecology* (Montreal: Black Rose, 1998), a text we return to below.
27. Ibid., 32.
28. Bookchin, *Social Ecology and Communalism*, 98, fn. 8, emphases in original.
29. Bookchin, *From Urbanization to Cities*, 263.
30. Ibid., 254.
31. Clark, "Municipal Dreams," 177.
32. Graham, "Reinventing Hierarchy," 32.
33. Ibid., 32–33.
34. Murray Bookchin, "Comments on the International Social Ecology Network Gathering and the 'Deep Social Ecology' of John Clark," 186.
35. Bookchin, *From Urbanization to Cities*, 262.
36. Bookchin, "Whither Anarchism," 159.
37. Bookchin, "Comments."
38. Bookchin, *From Urbanization to Cities*, 249.
39. Ibid., 267–8, emphasis in original.
40. Bookchin, *Social Ecology and Communalism*, 114, 115.
41. Bookchin, *From Urbanization to Cities*, 228, emphasis added.
42. Bookchin, *Anarchism, Marxism, and the Future of the Left*, 147, emphasis added.
43. Ibid., 147.
44. Ibid., 148, emphasis in original.
45. Ibid., 149.
46. Ibid., 194.
47. Graham, "Reinventing Hierarchy," 21–22.
48. Watson, *Beyond Bookchin*, 179.
49. Clark, "Municipal Dreams," 153, 146.
50. Bookchin, *The Modern Crisis*, 44.
51. Bookchin, "Comments," emphasis in original.
52. Bookchin, *The Modern Crisis*, 43.

53. Ibid., 44.
54. Bookchin, *From Urbanization to Cities*, 232.
55. Ibid., 263, emphasis in original.
56. Biehl, *Libertarian Municipalism*, 101–8.
57. Ibid., 108.
58. Ibid., 108.

Conclusion

1. Bookchin, *Anarchism, Marxism, and the Future of the Left*, 346.
2. See, respectively: Michael Hardt and Antonio Negri, *Multitude*; John Holloway, *Change the World Without Taking Power*; John Holloway, *Crack Capitalism*; Marcos, *Shadows of Tender Fury: The Letters and Communiqués of Subcomandante Marcos and The Zapatista Army of National Liberation* (New York: Monthly Review, 1995); for more info on developments in Spain, see ZNet, Spain Content (available at zcommunications.org). For a general survey of different practices within alter-globalisation, see: Notes from Nowhere (eds.), *We Are Everywhere: The Irresistible Rise of Global Anti-Capitalism* (London: Verso, 2003); Paul Kingsnorth, *One No, Many Yeses: A Journey to the Heart of the Global Resistance Movement* (London: Free Press, 2003); Derek Wall, *Babylon and Beyond: The Economics of Anti-Capitalist, Anti-Globalist, and Radical Green Movements* (London: Pluto, 2005); Tom Mertes, *A Movement of Movements: Is Another World Really Possible?* (London: Verso, 2004); Naomi Klein, *Fences and Windows: Despatches from the Front Lines of the Globalisation Debate* (London: Flamingo, 2002).

Index

Leff, Enrique, 79–82
"lifestyle anarchism," 10, 150–60 passim
"Listen, Marxist!," (Bookchin), 141
local assemblies. *See* popular assemblies (municipal assemblies)

M

majoritarianism. *See* voting (majority rule)
Manes, Christopher, 28–29, 30
Marshall, Peter, 4, 156
Martin, Thomas S., 218n22
Marx, Karl, 2–3, 4, 58, 140–43 passim, 152
Marxism, 1–2, 4, 52, 140–43 passim, 152, 164
mass extinction of species, 75, 76
"maximum programme," 169–72, 186
means and ends, 84, 89, 167, 168, 186, 187
"minimum programme," 165–69
The Modern Crisis (Bookchin), 3
monkeywrenching, 8, 26, 27–28
municipal assemblies. *See* popular assemblies (municipal assemblies)
municipalities and municipalism, 165–71 passim, 176–80 passim, 185, 189–91 passim
mutualism, 53, 56, 61, 67, 131; Eckersley, 72, 83, 85; human mutual aid, 101, 138, 139, 146

N

Naess, Arne, 6–7, 8, 21–24 passim, 32, 37, 100

National Gathering of American Greens, Amherst College, 1987, 7, 19–20, 31
nation-states, 165, 171, 178, 189, 190, 191
natural dialectics. *See* dialectical naturalism
natural evolution. *See* evolution
natural scarcity. *See* scarcity
nature. *See* first nature (nonhuman realm); second nature (human realm)
nature-humanity dualism/antagonism, 53, 59, 62, 89; human domination of nature, 105, 107, 108, 116, 119, 128–37 passim. *See also* first nature (nonhuman realm); second nature (human realm)
Nazism (Germany), 8
neighbourhoods, 165–69 passim, 176, 183
Neolithic Revolution, 106, 109–10, 113, 121, 122, 125, 161

O

old people. *See* elders
Our Synthetic Environment (Bookchin), 45
overpopulation, 25, 28, 29, 38, 48, 52, 98–103 passim

P

patriocentricity, 111
personhood, civic, 162, 179, 180
politics and statecraft, 160–67 passim, 178, 191
popular assemblies (municipal assemblies), 169–72, 179, 182, 183, 185, 192, 193

population, human. *See* human
population
Post-Scarcity Anarchism (Bookchin), 2
potentiality of life-forms, 60, 67,
72–77 passim, 81, 83, 86, 97
"The Problem of Chemicals in
Food" (Bookchin), 45

R
*Renewing the Earth: The Promise of
Social Ecology* (Clark), 3
*The Rise of Urbanization and the
Decline of Citizenship* (Book-
chin), 3
Rosaldo, Michelle, 125
Rudy, Alan, 122–30 passim, 138–46
passim

S
scarcity, 105–10 passim, 129–37 passim. *See also* "stingy" nature
second nature (human realm),
51, 53, 57, 61, 67, 83–91 passim,
96–97, 104, 133; hierarchy and,
111. *See also* human stewardship
of nature/Earth
self-reflexivity (self-awareness),
57–62 passim, 67, 97, 104
Sessions, George, 32, 35, 38, 39,
100–101; *Deep Ecology*, 6,
22–24
sexual division of labour, 123, 125
shamans and warrior-chiefs, 113,
120
"social anarchism," 10, 159–60
*Social Anarchism or Lifestyle Anar-
chism: An Unbridgeable Chasm*
(Bookchin), 10, 150–57 passim,
218n22

social class. *See* class
"Social Ecology versus Deep Ecology" (Bookchin), 7, 8, 19
social evolution, 50–54 passim,
66, 67, 78, 79, 115, 130, 165, 172;
"highly aberrant form," 104,
108, 113, 121; White, 204n49.
See also second nature (human
realm)
social history, 12–18 passim, 72,
95–98 passim, 101–48 passim
speciation rate, 76
species, "high" and "lower." *See*
"higher" and "lower" species
species mass extinction. *See* mass
extinction of species
"Spring Offensives and Summer
Vacations" (Bookchin), 157–58,
159, 165
state, 144–46, 162–65 passim, 181,
186–87; emergence of, 114, 120,
128, 131, 144, 145. *See also* city-
states; nation-states; politics
and statecraft
stewardship of nature/Earth. *See*
human stewardship of nature/
Earth
"stingy" nature, 59, 105–9 passim,
114–16 passim, 129, 134, 136. *See
also* scarcity
surplus (agriculture, etc.), 105–10
passim, 114, 115, 121, 124, 125
Sussman, Robert W., 125

T
technology, 45, 50, 52, 105–8
passim, 140, 146; authoritarian, 140, 144; Eckersley, 84;
"ecotechnologies," 97; Leff, 80;
Neolithic, 113

AK PRESS is small, in terms of staff and resources, but we also manage to be one of the world's most productive anarchist publishing houses. We publish close to twenty books every year, and distribute thousands of other titles published by like-minded independent presses and projects from around the globe. We're entirely worker run and democratically managed. We operate without a corporate structure—no boss, no managers, no bullshit.

The **FRIENDS OF AK PRESS** program is a way you can directly contribute to the continued existence of AK Press, and ensure that we're able to keep publishing books like this one! Friends pay $25 a month directly into our publishing account ($30 for Canada, $35 for international), and receive a copy of every book AK Press publishes for the duration of their membership! Friends also receive a discount on anything they order from our website or buy at a table: 50% on AK titles, and 30% on everything else. We have a Friends of AK ebook program as well: $15 a month gets you an electronic copy of every book we publish for the duration of your membership. *You can even sponsor a very discounted membership for someone in prison.*

Email **friendsofak@akpress.org** for more info, or visit the website: **https://www.akpress.org/friends.html**.

There are always great book projects in the works—so sign up now to become a Friend of AK Press, and let the presses roll!